Pro Visual C++ 2005 for Developers: Featuring C++/CLI

Dean C. Wills

Apress®

Pro Visual C++ 2005 for Developers: Featuring C++/CLI

Copyright © 2006 by Dean C. Wills

ISBN-13: 978-1-59059-608-1

ISBN-10: 1-59059-608-0

Printed and bound in the United States of America 9 8 7 6 5 4 3 2 1

Lead Editor: Ewan Buckingham
Technical Reviewer: Alvin Chardón
Editorial Board: Steve Anglin, Ewan Buckingham, Gary Cornell, Jason Gilmore, Jonathan Gennick, Jonathan Hassell, James Huddleston, Chris Mills, Matthew Moodie, Dominic Shakeshaft, Jim Sumser, Keir Thomas, Matt Wade
Project Manager: Elizabeth Seymour
Copy Edit Manager: Nicole Flores
Copy Editor: Heather Lang
Assistant Production Director: Kari Brooks-Copony
Senior Production Editor: Laura Cheu
Compositor: Dina Quan and Kinetic Publishing Services, LLC
Proofreader: Elizabeth Berry
Indexer: Brenda Miller
Cover Designer: Kurt Krames
Manufacturing Director: Tom Debolski

Distributed to the book trade worldwide by Springer-Verlag New York, Inc., 233 Spring Street, 6th Floor, New York, NY 10013. Phone 1-800-SPRINGER, fax 201-348-4505, e-mail orders-ny@springer-sbm.com, or visit http://www.springeronline.com.

For information on translations, please contact Apress directly at 2560 Ninth Street, Suite 219, Berkeley, CA 94710. Phone 510-549-5930, fax 510-549-5939, e-mail info@apress.com, or visit http://www.apress.com.

The source code for this book is available to readers at http://www.apress.com in the Source Code/Download section.

For Ariel and Anna

Contents at a Glance

PART 1 ■■■ Fast Track to C++/CLI

PART 2 ■■■ Details

PART 3 ■■■ Advanced Concepts

Contents

PART 1 ■ ■ ■ Fast Track to C++/CLI

PART 2 ■■■ Details

PART 3 ■ ■ ■ Advanced Concepts

Foreword

C++/CLI was originally envisioned as a high-level assembler for the .NET runtime, much like C is often considered a high-level assembler for native code generation. That original vision even included the ability to directly mix in IL with C++ code, mostly eliminating the need for the IL assembler ilasm.

As the design of C++/CLI evolved, this vision was scaled back. We, the Microsoft C++ team, still wanted C++/CLI to be a systems programming language for .NET, but we decided that exposing the full capabilities of the CLR to other languages wasn't a good idea. After all, language interoperability is a significant factor in the success of .NET.

We knew C++ programmers would expect powerful features unavailable in other languages, like C#, so we decided exposing common C++ constructs in a familiar manner when using C++/CLI was critical. For example, the RAII idiom frequently used in ISO standard C++ programs needed to work in a similar syntactic manner when using a reference type. Likewise, programmers expected templates to work seamlessly with reference types, value types, and interfaces.

We were a bit surprised that programmers found C++/CLI's predecessor Managed C++ unacceptably ugly. We thought new keywords should have leading double underscores, because that was the way to add such extensions while conforming to standard C++. Early in the C++/CLI design process, we looked for ways to make the language look nice and still contain strictly conforming extensions. While contextual and whitespace keywords are a little unconventional (and a bit of a pain to implement), they certainly make C++/CLI look much nicer and give it that first-class feel we were looking for.

In the end, I think we found the right balance between C++ power and familiarity and a clean syntax to enable access to the .NET runtime. Hopefully, you'll enjoy using C++/CLI as much as we enjoyed creating it. After working with Dean on the Visual C++ compiler front end, I know you'll find his insights and explanations valuable as you learn, and eventually master, C++/CLI.

Jason Shirk
Software Development Engineer
Visual C++ Front End
Microsoft Corporation

About the Author

DEAN C. WILLS is a freelance programmer with over 20 years' experience in system programming areas such as BIOS, assembly language, C, and C++. He is the owner of Sandpaper Software and has worked for companies like Compucorp, Cyrix, National Semiconductor, and Virtio. He was a developer on the Visual C++ front end during the Visual Studio 2005 ship cycle.

About the Technical Reviewer

 **ALVIN CHARDÓN** grew up in Ponce, Puerto Rico with a passion for academic competitions, computers, and basketball. He obtained bachelor degrees in computer engineering and electrical engineering at the University of Puerto Rico, Mayagüez Campus (UPRM), where he was valedictorian.

Already in love with C++, Alvin first encountered .NET in 2001 during Microsoft internship. Since 2002, he's been a Microsoft employee. He's been a member of the Visual Studio and Visual C++ teams as a software design engineer and occasionally plays the role of program manager or software developer. Alvin has also worked in the front end of Microsoft's C++ compiler, assisted in the design and testing of C++/CLI, and helped develop the future road maps for the IntelliSense and Browsing technologies. He now works on the Visual C++ IDE team, where he contributes to the development of new testing methodologies, including compiler-abstract syntax-tree–based test generation and engine-level UI testing. Alvin has published on MSDN and has been featured in publications ranging from the newspaper *El Nuevo Día* and *.Code* magazine in Latin America to www.microsoft.com in the United States.

Alvin is still part of the Visual C++ family and loves coming to the office every day. When he is not thinking C++, he likes to read, write stories, go dancing, play a good game of chess or basketball, and occasionally bungee jump or paraglide from a cliff.

Acknowledgments

A work of this magnitude is always greater than the sum of its parts, and I feel likely to carry on in this fashion by forgetting to acknowledge half of the people who were vital to its production.

Perhaps it's best to play it safe and thank groups rather than individuals. That said, let me categorically thank my family and friends, the Microsoft Visual C++ team, and everyone at Apress.

Those of you who deserve special mention, please feel free to add your own names here:

1.

2.

3.

4.

5.

Preface

I reined my horse to the precipitous brink of a black and lurid tarn that lay in unruffled lustre by the dwelling, and gazed down—but with a shudder even more thrilling than before . . .

—Edgar Allan Poe, "The Fall of the House of Usher"

Why C++?

Shall I begin this book by confessing that many a harried day and restless night have I pondered this exact question? Though that might be a bit melodramatic, stating the exact opposite (that I've never even considered it) would be an outright lie. Luckily, the answer is clear. No other high-level language offers you the same degree of control over the system. In C++, you can specify exactly what you want to occur, make the difficult design choices along the way, and customize general-purpose algorithms to fit your application. For this reason, C++ is the first choice for operating system writers, game developers, and for that matter, writers of large systems and high-performance applications everywhere. It simply allows you to do whatever you want to do.

However, sometimes what you really want to do is not worry about all the things you could do and just get down to producing a simple, modular, secure application. Enter C#, followed by Visual C++ 2005 and C++/CLI. C# is a language designed with a .NET mind in a C++ body. It strips out many of the complexities of C++, but it limits what you are able to do at the same time. C++/CLI aspires to harness the power of the .NET Framework and managed code without sacrificing any of the power of C++.

What's in a Name?

C++/CLI is a bit of a misnomer. It is a set of extensions that allow C++ to expose the power of the Common Language Infrastructure (CLI). Really, it portends the future of C++. There is no reason that C++/CLI features, such as events and properties, could not be a part of standard C++.

In reality, the CLI is just an abstraction of a different target platform, like Win32. Just because C++/CLI targets a different platform and supports features endemic to that platform, like generics, doesn't mean that it's a different language. It's still C++.

Mix It Up a Bit

One of the most powerful features of Visual C++ 2005 is the ability to create mixed-platform code effortlessly. You can begin in native C++, switch to C++/CLI, call C#, and unwind back to native C++ with ease. I'll cover this in detail in Chapter 19.

The Flow of Progress

If C++/CLI were an animal, that animal would have to be a salmon, because migrating from C# to C++ seems a lot like swimming upstream. Just remember that when salmon swim upstream, they are revisiting their roots, and that's what we're doing with C++/CLI. There are still many compelling reasons to choose C#, but there are as many to choose C++. Now, programmers have more freedom than ever in selecting the language that is best suited to developing their applications.

Obtaining Updates for This Book

I think being human is a good thing. Acknowledging that to err is human, of course, gives any author a unique feeling of inadequacy that can only be earned by struggling for months to get something exactly right and blowing it in the end. Since it would be presumptuous to expect this book to be the one that came out perfect on the first pass, instead, let me pledge to continue to strive to get it right. Any errata, as well as contact information for reporting errors, will be published on the Apress web site. If you would like to contact me directly, you can e-mail me at dean@sandpapersoftware.com.

Introduction

. . . for as ten millions of circles can never make a square, so the united voice of myriads cannot lend the smallest foundation to falsehood.

—Oliver Goldsmith

Apology

This is a book built on a presumption, and that presumption is about you. It presumes that you have C# experience and that you know your way around the .NET Framework.

Well, I apologize up front. In law school, I learned that a presumption may be no more than an assumption that becomes the foundation of a faulty argument. In this case, we might be building our foundation on quicksand.

In this Introduction, I will attempt to fortify your knowledge a bit, with the aim of shortening the distance between the average reader and the expert, so that all will profit from the remainder.

The .NET Framework

The .NET Framework is often touted as being merely Microsoft's answer to Java, but that's far too cynical a summary. The reality is that the inadequacies of Java and Win32 opened up business opportunities for something big to happen, and .NET was it.

With .NET, Microsoft turned software design upside down. The .NET Framework is built on open standards in the software industry and answers growing user concerns over interoperability, reliability, and security. It is built on Unicode, XML, HTTP, SOAP, and others, and it does not mandate C++ as a single, correct language choice. The file formats are all public and standardized, and there are now several .NET-compatible languages.

The Common Language Infrastructure

The Common Language Infrastructure (CLI) is a standard that describes the execution engine and file formats of .NET. All .NET implementations follow this standard, although they may implement the various elements in different ways on different platforms.

The .NET Framework on Windows is made up of an execution model, called the Common Language Runtime (CLR), and a set of libraries that implement the various features of .NET. Since the CLR complies with the CLI, it is said to be CLI-compliant. In fact, the CLI was written in tandem with the development of the CLR, selecting a core subset that would be portable without sacrificing the essence of the CLR.

The CLR has elements that go beyond the specifics of the standard. For example, the standard specifies that the Virtual Execution System (VES) be able to execute Common Intermediate Language (CIL) instructions, but it does not mandate how. The implementation must determine whether CIL instructions are translated to native code at load time or at runtime. Future hardware architectures may even run CIL natively. Microsoft's implementation in the CLR uses a special compiler called a just-in-time (JIT) compiler, which translates the CIL to native code during execution only as needed. This is a CLR optimization that is not specified by the CLI standard.

The CLR is the Microsoft Windows implementation of the execution engine, but .NET was not designed to run exclusively on Windows. Several non-Windows implementations exist, and they run on the Mac, Unix, and Linux operating systems. These include Mono, Rotor, and Portable .NET, and they run under FreeBSD and Mac OS X.

Elements of the CLI

The CLI standard defines the various components that make up the CLI, as well as the CIL and the comprehensive data format called metadata. The primary components follow:

- The VES, which executes code. There are provisions within the CLI for executing both CLI-compliant code, called *managed code*, as well as code compiled by existing compilers, called *unmanaged* or *native code*. Managed code that has been translated to a particular host is called *managed native code*.

- The CTS, which defines the types available to a CLI-compliant language.

- The CLS, which defines language interoperability rules for items that are exported from an assembly. It does not apply to internal implementation within an assembly. It affects a subset of the CTS types as well as methods that pertain to these types.

- Assemblies, which are units of deployment for one or more modules. Applications themselves are not defined by the standard, but the VES defines how to isolate applications running in the same operating system process using application domains. In C++/CLI, variables may be per application domain or per process. We will revisit this in Chapter 20.

- Modules, which are building blocks of the assemblies.

- Metadata, which contain the descriptions of the types, methods, and attributes contained within the module, as well as a manifest, which describes how the module is deployed. Attributes (see Chapter 20) are user-definable types that can extend CLI-compliant languages. The manifest includes versioning information for the module and solves the age-old Windows problem of DLL hell. Modules also support reflection, which is the process of discovering information about a module, and the types contained therein, by examining the metadata.

- Portable Executable (PE) File Format.

- The CIL, which is the managed instruction set. The Microsoft Windows CLR implementation of the CIL is called Microsoft Intermediate Language (MSIL).

- Exceptions and exception handling, which are given special mention in Chapters 12 and 20.

Standard Libraries

The CLI defines a standard set of libraries to provide the CLI types and runtime mechanisms. The libraries are fairly self-explanatory and include the following:

- Runtime Infrastructure Library

- Base Class Library

- Network Library

- Reflection Library

- XML Library

- Extended Numerics Library

- Extended Array Library

The CTS

The CTS defines various types and accessors. A quick overview of the principal elements follows, and we will revisit these in context later in this book.

Type Classes

The CTS supports two basic kinds of data types—value types and reference types—each of which has advantages and disadvantages. Since they each have a long list of characteristics and instructions to say how they can and cannot be used, it is difficult to describe them succinctly beyond saying that value types meet all of the listed requirements for classification as a value type. Introducing them according to the way they are intended to be used is more accurate.

Value Types

A *value type* is a data type that typically contains a small amount of data. It is passed between methods by value, by copying all of the data. Built-in types including int and float are value types. Value types are typically allocated on the stack or statically initialized memory, which is not particular to an instance. Value types may contain other value types. A C# struct or enum is a value type. Value types are covered in Chapter 6.

Reference Types

A *reference type* is a data type that typically contains a large amount of data. It is passed between methods by reference, by copying just a handle to the data. System.Object is a reference type. Reference types are typically allocated on the managed heap. Reference types may contain either value types or reference types and may also extend other reference types. A C# class or string is a reference type. Reference types are the houses; value types are the boards and nails. Reference types are covered in Chapter 6.

Boxing and Unboxing

Most .NET methods accept reference types as parameters. Value types may be converted to a managed-heap–based reference type object by a process known as *boxing*. The reverse of this process, extracting the core value type from the interior of a boxed object, is called *unboxing*. In general, boxing is done implicitly, but unboxing must be done explicitly because of information loss. Boxing and unboxing are covered in Chapter 6.

Properties

Types contain fields that are instances of reference or value types. *Properties* are methods to get and/or set data that mimic a field. Although properties do not perform as well as direct data access, they allow controlled and independent access to the act of reading or writing data objects. Properties are covered in Chapter 10.

Interfaces

An *interface* is an abstract type that is intended to represent a contract between the class designer and the class consumer. Interfaces are similar to C++ abstract base classes with pure virtual functions. Unlike reference types, they support multiple inheritance, so a single class or interface may be made up of several interfaces. Interfaces are covered in Chapter 6.

C#

C# is a CLI-compliant language. This means that it produces metadata in the correct file formats. C# primarily uses CTS types, and the types are manipulated using CIL instructions.

Managed C++

Managed C++ was an evolutionary step in the development of C++/CLI. It is still supported by Microsoft Visual C++ 2005 using the `/clr:oldSyntax` command-line option. I am not going to cover it in this book.

Why? Some beautiful quotes from fellow authors follow to answer that:

> When I joined Microsoft back in the winter of 2001, it was on the condition that they accept the fact that I considered their new product, Managed Extensions for C++, an abomination.

—Stan Lippmann

> I'd rather have my teeth drilled than work with managed C++.

—Jesse Liberty

Personally, I don't think the managed extensions for C++ are as bad as all that. (Note to self: Send Jesse a copy of this book. He's earned it for that quote.) They just have the feel of extensions rather than a language, which makes them somewhat counterintuitive. C++/CLI is a true extension of C++, a language within a language, which looks at .NET differently. For example, the managed extensions for C++ deal with reference types using a literal pointer to an item on the managed heap (R __gc *r), where C++/CLI introduces the concept of a handle to a type (R^r). In addition to being cleaner, it's also more intuitive when migrating from C# and mixing native and managed code.

C++/CLI

C++/CLI, or C++ for the CLI, is also a CLI-compliant language. At the same time, its capabilities go far beyond that. You can write CLI-compliant code, or you can write code that executes natively on platforms lacking .NET. The choice is yours.

The Common Language Runtime

The CLR is the Microsoft Windows implementation of the CLI. It is CLI-compliant, and it has a host of features that go beyond the CLI, including the following:

- **Security**: The CLR allows you to add a digital signature to your assemblies using the strong name (SN) utility. Strong-named assemblies may be added to the global assembly cache (GAC).

- **JIT Complier**: As introduced previously, the JIT compiler converts CIL into managed native code for host execution. Compiling the CIL is significantly faster than interpreting it, and JIT compilation reduces latency by compiling as needed rather than at load time.

A Note About the C++ Compiler

The C++ compiler has several compilation options, as it is able to produce managed code, native code, or a combination of the two. I will go over the implications of the various options in Chapter 9. Here's a preview to tide you over until then:

- /clr:safe: Produces an IL-only verifiable output file and is used with managed types and managed code only.

- /clr:pure: Produces an IL-only output file (no native executable code) and is used with managed and native types and managed code only.

- /clr: Produces a mix of native and IL. Managed and native types and managed code and native code are allowed.

- <default>: No option specified. The program compiles for native execution.

Summary

When I started programming, you needed to know how to use octal, punched cards, and teletype machines; a personal computer was a fancy programmable calculator; and raw intelligence and esoteric knowledge were the elements of power.

The Wild West of computer programming is gone. Today the game is different. Everyone is just a surfer on a wave of changing technology, and the ability to find, consume, and classify information quickly is far more important than the ability to memorize it.

.NET, C#, and C++/CLI are all examples of this difference. Hopefully, this text will help you gain the information you need to catch and hold this wave until the next one comes along.

PART 1

■■■

Fast Track to C++/CLI

CHAPTER 1

■ ■ ■

Hello, World

Consistency is the last refuge of the unimaginative.

—Oscar Wilde

Since time immemorial, which pretty much dates back to the release of the Kernighan and Richie book on C, there has been a tradition of opening a book on C or its descendants with a short example of how easy it is to display "Hello, World". This book is no exception. Let's examine the C# and C++ versions of "Hello, World" side by side (see Table 1-1).

Table 1-1. *"Hello, World" in C# and C++*

C#	C++
`using System;`	`using namespace System;`

```
C#                                          C++

using System;                               using namespace System;

class HelloWorld
{
    static void Main()                      void main()
    {                                       {
        Console.WriteLine("Hello, World");      Console::WriteLine("Hello, World");
    }                                       }
}
```

As you can see in Table 1-1, the languages are clearly different. On the other hand, C# and C++ are like French and Italian; although the C++ syntax may appear foreign, the meaning is clear.

Here are some things to notice:

- In C#, `Main()` is always a method of a class. In C++/CLI (Common Language Infrastructure), `main()` is not a class method; it is a global function. It's easy—just remember that global functions have no class.

- In the same way that you have a unique static member function named `Main()` in any C# program, you have a unique global function named `main()` in any C++ program. It is possible to get around this requirement in C# and have multiple `Main()` methods by embedding them in different classes. You can then tell the compiler using the `/main:<type>` option which class contains the startup method. This trick does not work in standard C++ since `main()` must be a global function and any versions of `main()` would have the same signature and clash in the global namespace.

- C++ uses :: (colon-colon) to separate namespaces and class names and a dot (.) to access class members; C# uses a dot for everything. C++ expects you to be more specific about what you're doing.

- The C++/CLI using statement requires the additional keyword namespace.

■Note In Microsoft Visual C++, the entry point can be any function as long as it follows the valid list of signatures. It can be a global function or a member function. You do this by specifying the /entry:<function_name> linker option. Standard C++ requires a unique global function named main with an integer return value and an optional argument list. See Section 3.61 of the C++ standard, ISO/IEC 14882:2003(E). A PDF version of this standard can be downloaded from http://webstore.ansi.org for a small fee.

Starting the Visual Studio 2005 Console

I bet you're just itching to give this a try. "Real programmers" use the command line, so let's start there. We're now going to construct a console application.

Go to the Start menu, and navigate to the Visual Studio 2005 command prompt, as shown in Figure 1-1.

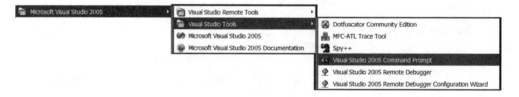

Figure 1-1. *Select the Visual Studio 2005 command prompt.*

This spawns a new command prompt with the environment variables set to work with Visual Studio 2005. All of the Visual Studio compilers may be run from the command line, including Visual C++, Visual C#, and Visual Basic.

Retrieving the Source Files

Either pop up notepad.exe (surely your favorite editor) or fetch the source from the Source Code section of the Apress website. Go to www.apress.com, and search for this book using the ISBN, 1-59059-608-0.

Executing HelloCpp.cpp

Navigate to the sample directory for this chapter, and go to the HelloWorld subdirectory. Here is HelloCpp.cpp:

```
using namespace System;
void main()
{
    Console::WriteLine("Hello, World");
}
```

Enter the following command:

```
cl /nologo /clr HelloCpp.cpp
```

This command directs the C++ compiler to compile this file targeting the Common Language Runtime (CLR) and creates a C++/CLI (Common Language Infrastructure) executable. The executable is a managed assembly that contains metadata and Common Intermediate Language (CIL), just like C# executables. CIL is also known as MSIL on the CLR.

Let's execute this example. First, type

```
HelloCpp
```

Next, press Enter. You should see the following:

```
Hello, World
```

and that's a good thing.

A Quick Tour of the Visual C++ IDE

In this section, we go over the steps for making an elementary C++/CLI project using the Visual Studio 2005 C++ Integrated Development Environment (IDE). This is very similar to creating a C# project.

1. Load Visual Studio 2005.

2. From the File menu, select New Project. My system is set up with Visual C++ as the default language, so my New Project dialog box looks like the one shown in Figure 1-2.

3. Navigate to the CLR project types under Visual C++.

4. Select CLR Console Application under "Visual Studio installed templates".

5. Enter the name **HelloWorld** in the Name text box.

6. Click OK.

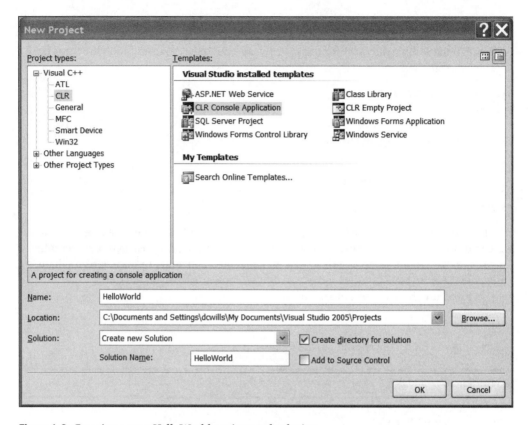

Figure 1-2. *Creating a new HelloWorld project and solution*

By default, Visual Studio 2005 creates new projects in My Documents\Visual Studio 2005\Projects. Feel free to change the directory and place the project elsewhere if you like. Click OK.

Understanding Projects and Solutions

The Visual C++ CLR Console Application Wizard creates a new project called HelloWorld in a solution also called HelloWorld. What is the difference between the project and the solution?

The basic paradigm used in Visual Studio is that you create a solution, which is your main application. This solution can consist of several projects, which are class libraries or executables. Each project is language specific, though it is also possible to mix languages within a single project using custom build rules.

In our case, we want a single Visual C++ project that will generate a single executable named HelloWorld.exe, so our solution has a single project. By default, the project is created in a subdirectory, but we can change this behavior by deselecting "Create directory for solution". Later in this book, we'll have more sophisticated solutions that depend on several projects.

Now you should see two tiled windows: the Solution Explorer and the editor window containing HelloWorld.cpp. It appears that Visual C++ 2005 has gone to all of the trouble of writing the program for us; now isn't that nice?

Understanding the Differences

There are a few differences between our basic HelloCpp application and the HelloWorld application created by the Visual Studio C++ CLR Console Application Wizard, shown in Figure 1-3. The most obvious difference is that the wizard created several additional supporting files.

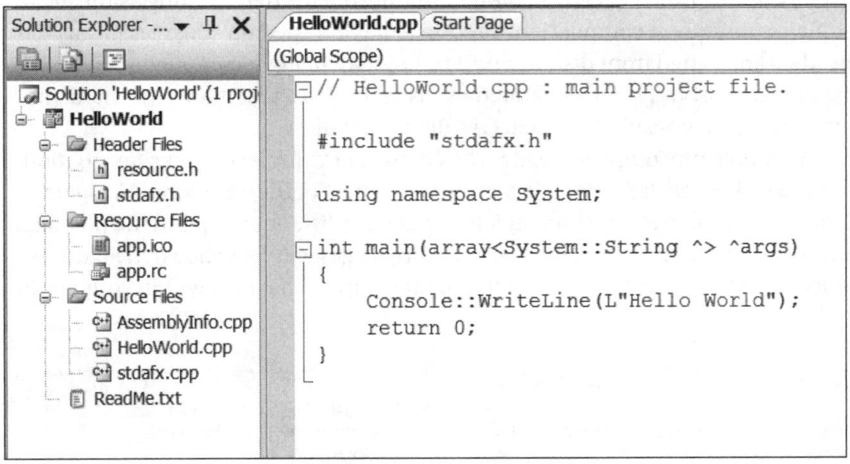

Figure 1-3. *The HelloWorld application as created by the CLR Console Application Wizard*

Let's have a look at those new files.

Resources

These files outfit your application with a snappy little icon and pave the way for future application development. Visual C++ allows you to embed resources in your binary files. They can be bitmaps, icons, strings, and other types. For more information, consult the Visual C++ documentation.

- resource.h

- app.ico

- app.rc

Precompiled Headers

These files improve compilation speed by avoiding multiple compilations of common code:

- stdafx.h

- stdafx.cpp

One topic that surfaces again and again throughout this book is the distinction between declarations and definitions in C++. Unlike C#, class prototypes, called declarations, may be separated from class definitions into distinct files. This improves compilation speed, avoids circular dependencies, and provides an object-oriented abstraction layer for complex projects.

In many C++ projects, it is common that files containing just declarations, called *header files* and terminated with the .h extension, are compiled as a unit at the start of every source file. If the headers are identical across the project, the compiler ends up compiling the same chunk of code with each source file. One optimization provided by Visual C++ is to compile the headers referenced in the stdafx.h file en masse into a binary PCH (precompiled header) file in advance of all other compilation. This is called *precompiling* the headers. As long as the headers are not modified, subsequent compilations of source files are sped up considerably as the precompiled headers are loaded from disk as a unit rather than being recompiled individually. Two files, stdafx.h and stdafx.cpp, are generated by Visual C++ to assist in this mechanism. For more information, again consult the Visual C++ documentation.

It is possible to disable precompiled headers by changing the project properties. To modify the project settings, right-click the HelloWorld project in the Solution Explorer. Navigate to Configuration Properties, and click the plus sign to expand the list. Then expand the plus sign next to C++, and select Precompiled Headers. The Property Pages window, shown in Figure 1-4, appears on the screen, which allows you to configure precompiled headers within your application.

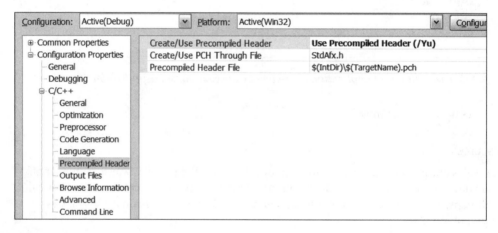

Figure 1-4. *Configuration of precompiled headers from the Property Pages window*

AssemblyInfo.cpp

The file AssemblyInfo.cpp contains all of the attribute information for the assembly. This is similar to the C#-produced AssemblyInfo.cs. This includes, but is not limited to, the copyright, version, and basic assembly description information. The default values are fine for development, but you may not want the copyright for Microsoft Corporation in your assembly when you ship. Figure 1-5 shows an excerpt from a sample AssemblyInfo.cpp.

```
//
// General Information about an assembly is controlled through the following
// set of attributes. Change these attribute values to modify the information
// associated with an assembly.
//
[assembly:AssemblyTitleAttribute("HelloWorld")];
[assembly:AssemblyDescriptionAttribute("")];
[assembly:AssemblyConfigurationAttribute("")];
[assembly:AssemblyCompanyAttribute("Microsoft")];
[assembly:AssemblyProductAttribute("HelloWorld")];
[assembly:AssemblyCopyrightAttribute("Copyright (c) Microsoft 2005")];
[assembly:AssemblyTrademarkAttribute("")];
[assembly:AssemblyCultureAttribute("")];

//
// Version information for an assembly consists of the following four values:
```

Figure 1-5. *An excerpt from AssemblyInfo.cpp*

HelloWorld.cpp

The main source file has a few significant differences as well, as Figure 1-6 shows:

- The main function is defined to accept a managed array of System::String, which is equivalent to the C# Main(string[] Args). This allows you to access command-line arguments.

- The precompiled header file stdafx.h is included to support the use of precompiled headers.

- The literal string "Hello World" is prepended with an L to indicate a wide character string. In native C++, strings are byte arrays by default. When compiling C++/CLI, the compiler attempts to distinguish between wide character strings and byte arrays by context. Whether or not you have an L in this context, a wide character System::String is created.

```
AssemblyInfo.cpp  HelloWorld.cpp  Start Page
(Global Scope)
// HelloWorld.cpp : main project file.

#include "stdafx.h"

using namespace System;

int main(array<System::String ^> ^args)
{
    Console::WriteLine(L"Hello World");
    return 0;
}
```

Figure 1-6. *HelloWorld.cpp*

Window Layout

One of the well-designed features of Visual Studio is the ability to customize the appearance of the IDE by rearranging windows using simple mouse movements. In this section, we learn how to dock and position the Quick Find window.

The Problem with the Find and Replace Window

To invoke Visual Studio's Find and Replace window, press Ctrl-F. The window shown in Figure 1-7 appears.

Figure 1-7. *Visual Studio's Find and Replace window*

Now if you click and hold the title bar, you can move this window around and find text in files quite easily. There is only one big problem with this. Suppose you have a very large file where the same text appears again and again. Then you might find yourself clicking Find Next repeatedly until you find the instance you're searching for. Unfortunately, sometimes after you click Find Next, Visual Studio elects to move the Find and Replace window to the left or right in order to make the text visible, rather than displaying it above or below the dialog box. When the window moves, your mouse cursor is left hovering over where the Find Next button used to be, rather than where it is now. You move the cursor, click again, and there goes the window. One word comes to mind—irritating.

Docking the Window

Luckily, there are a few simple solutions. One nice trick is to use a hotkey to cycle through the results (F3 has this functionality in the standard Visual C++ key bindings; the C# key bindings are different). Another way is to dock the Find and Replace window on one of the fixed frames of the IDE. By default, the Find and Replace window is set to Floating, as shown in Figure 1-8. Right-click the title bar, and select Dockable. Now this window can be part of a window frame.

Figure 1-8. *Right-clicking on the title bar reveals options for displaying the window.*

Now when you click and hold the title bar, you see a small compass in the frame that the cursor is hovering over, as well as reference markers on each of the other window frames. The compass allows you to direct the placement of the window with respect to the frame you are hovering over. Move the window over another frame, and the compass hops to that one.

The Center of the Compass

The compass itself has tabs for the directions (north, south, east, and west) as well as a center box. If you release the mouse over the center box, the window becomes tabbed within the current frame. Go ahead and drop it over the main frame, where the documents are edited. You can see now that it shares a frame with the other main windows. Unfortunately, this is a terrible place for a Find and Replace window, because you have to have the file you're searching in visibly available as well when you search for text, and tabbing does not allow you to do this. Right-click the title bar, and notice that Tabbed Document is checked (Figure 1-9). Click Dockable, and the Find and Replace window returns to the center of the screen.

When you hover over one of the compass direction tabs, the corresponding portion of the target frame is grayed out, so that you can preview the new window arrangement. If you drop the window in the wrong place, you can always either tear it off or manually set it to Dockable or Floating, depending on its state.

My preference is to move the mouse cursor over the bottommost frame, where the Output window is normally located, and then use the compass in order to tab the Find and Replace window on the bottom frame.

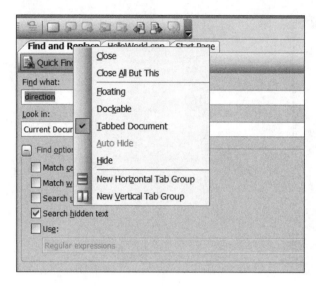

Figure 1-9. *Find and Replace as a tabbed document in the main frame*

Building, Executing, and Debugging

Let's take a quick tour of some key Visual C++ IDE commands (Table 1-2) as we build and test HelloWorld.

Table 1-2. *Common IDE Commands Quick Reference*

C#	C++	Explanation
F3	F3	Find next
F8	F4	Go to the next compilation error in the source
Shift-F8	Shift-F4	Go to the previous compilation error in the source
F5	F5	Execute with debugging
Ctrl-F5	Ctrl-F5	Execute without debugging
F6	F7	Build
F9	F9	Toggle breakpoint
F10	F10	Step over
F11	F11	Step into

Building the Program

Depending on our key bindings, we can use either F6 or F7 to build. If there are any errors, they appear in the Output window at the bottom of the screen, and you can use either F8 or F4 to cycle through them.

In C++, just as in C#, multiple compilation errors are often spurious; the compiler tries to compile beyond the first detected problem and may get lost. Often this allows you to see two or three errors and fix them all in a single editing pass. Just as often, the extra errors are an artifact of the compiler going out to lunch based on incorrect syntax, and fixing the first error or two may make the remainder disappear. I recommend building often.

Executing HelloWorld

The F5 key is the execute command. Since this is a console application, execution spawns a command window that displays "Hello, World" and then quickly closes, which is somewhat unsatisfying. There are several ways around this. One approach is to create another Visual Studio 2005 command prompt, navigate to the debug directory where the executable was created, and run the program manually, as we did earlier. Another way is to add the following call to the end of the `main()` function:

```
Console::ReadLine()
```

This method asks for a line of input from the user and keeps the console window open until the user presses the Enter key.

Another set of solutions presents itself by taking advantage of the built-in Visual C++ debugger. You could either set a breakpoint on the last line of the program using the F9 command, or you could just step through the program line by line. Either way, you can switch to the spawned command prompt to see the output as desired.

Let's try using the debugger.

Using the Visual C++ 2005 Debugger

The debugger is integrated into Visual Studio 2005, so initiating debugging is very simple. Entering any debugging command launches your application under the debugger. The window layout is sure to change, as there are several status windows that are only visible while debugging by default.

■**Note** There are different window configurations for editing and debugging. Each configuration must be customized separately.

The basic debugging commands are F5 (Execute with Debugging), F9 (Toggle Breakpoint), F10 (Step Over Source Line) and F11 (Step Into Source Line).

Stepping Through the Code

A Step command executes a line of code in the program. There are two varieties of the Step command: F10 (Step Over) and F11 (Step Into). These are similar, yet they differ when applied to a function call. F10 executes until the line after the function call, whereas F11 stops execution at the first line of the function body. Of course, using F11 is always dependent on whether debugging information is available for the binary the function came from. Since debugging information for `Console::WriteLine()` is not distributed with Visual C++ 2005, both F10 and F11 step over the function.

Press F10 to begin debugging HelloWorld with Visual C++ 2005. The title bar changes to show "HelloWorld (Debugging)" to indicate debugging mode. In addition, a command window is spawned in a separate window. At this point, it is blank since HelloWorld has yet to display any information.

A small yellow arrow appears on the left edge of the editor window, which indicates the current line of code that is executing. Figure 1-10 shows that execution has stopped at this point, and the debugger awaits the next command.

```
HelloWorld.cpp
(Global Scope)
// HelloWorld.cpp : main project file.

#include "stdafx.h"

using namespace System;

int main(array<System::String ^> ^args)
{
    Console::WriteLine(L"Hello World");
    return 0;
}
```

Figure 1-10. *Debugging HelloWorld*

The arrow indicates that we are beginning execution of the main() function, and the next line to be executed contains the Console::WriteLine() statement.

Press F10 again. The Console::WriteLine() function call executes, and "Hello World" appears in the separate command window.

If you dare to press F10 a couple more times, you create a nightmare on your screen. The first time, you execute over the return function. The next time, you return from the HelloWorld code into the CRT. This module performs important tasks, including initializing your program in Windows, packaging the command-line arguments for your program, and handling the program's exit to Windows. Note that this code calls main() explicitly by name, which explains why every C++ program requires a global function called main().

Completing Execution

Press F5 once to execute the remainder of the exit code and return to the editor. If HelloWorld.cpp is not visible, you can click the tab to reveal the source again. At this point, debugging has completed, and the title bar no longer indicates debugging.

Summary

This chapter provided you with a basic outline of how to create simple C++/CLI applications from the console and more-sophisticated applications using the IDE. I also showed you how basic debugging can be performed in Visual C++ 2005 using the integrated debugger.

In the next chapter, we'll see how you can call C# from a simple C++ program.

CHAPTER 2

■ ■ ■

There's No Place Like Home

I have not ceased being fearful, but I have ceased to let fear control me. I have accepted
fear as a part of life, specifically the fear of change, the fear of the unknown, and I have
gone ahead despite the pounding in the heart that says: Turn back, turn back; you'll die
if you venture too far.

—Erica Jong

In this chapter, we introduce C++'s interoperability features and show you a quick way to combine C# and C++. We begin by developing a card-shuffling class in C#. Next we add a C++ stub that uses the C# class. In Chapter 4, we take it one step further and migrate the entire application to C++. We will return to language integration and interoperability in greater detail in Chapter 19.

Developing the Program

Suppose you've got a perfectly good C# class that you'd like to use with your C++ code. It'd be a shame to have to throw it all away and rewrite it in C++, wouldn't it?

When I was developing the .NET Reflector add-in for C++/CLI, I found myself in this exact situation. During my development, Lutz Roeder, the author of .NET Reflector, was right in the middle of improving the Reflector interfaces and ended up removing a class I needed. To help me out, he sent me a C# file with the deleted code. Rather than being forced to rewrite his code in C++, I added references to his class in my project and went back to work on the add-in.

Deal Me In

It seems that interview questions are always relevant, no matter how many years you've been in the industry. They can be thought-provoking and entertaining. One of my favorites, shuffling a deck of cards, should prove instructive.

On the surface this appears to be an easy problem, but there are several ways you can get into trouble before you even begin coding.

The Process

One of the first times that the interview starts going wrong is when you try to figure out how to represent the deck before you shuffle it. The nightmare would unfold something like this:

YOU: What does the deck look like?

INTERVIEWER: It's random.

YOU: How can I represent the random input? Are you going to give me a list of the cards in their input states?

Let me say that at this point the interviewer will retreat to the cave and repeat the question in some form:

INTERVIEWER: You are given an arbitrary deck of cards, and you need to produce a shuffled deck of cards. That's all I'm going to say.

That's what he says, but he's thinking "no hire." You need to pause a moment here and think about the goal. The goal is to produce a shuffled deck of cards that is perfectly random. The order of the cards when you start shouldn't matter. You can pick any order you like.

Enumerating the Cards

The next hurdle in the interview is getting past the idea of representing the cards as ace through king in four different suits. There is a simple way: identify each card with a number from 1 to 52. It's even easier for programming in C++ and C# if the cards are numbered from 0 to 51 given that arrays are zero indexed in these languages.

Assign an arbitrary order to the suits as well as a number between 0 and 3. Bridge uses alphabetical order, so why not follow suit?

```
namespace CSharp
{
    class Deck
    {
        enum Suit
        {
            Clubs = 0, Diamonds, Hearts, Spades
        }
    }
}
```

You can use the same trick for the cards themselves:

```
namespace CSharp
{
    class Deck
    {
        enum Card
        {
```

```
            Ace=0, Deuce, Trey, Four, Five, Six, Seven,
            Eight, Nine, Ten, Jack, Queen, King
        }
    }
}
```

We thus have two types of information to represent separately: the Card number between 0 and 12, and the Suit number between 0 and 3. A common solution to this problem is to map them to a single number using the following formula:

```
Number = Suit*13+Card
```

Since Card is less than 13, it is clear that (int)(Card/13) ==0, so dividing both sides by 13 gives the Suit, with the remainder being the Card. Thus we have derived the following equations for the reverse transformation:

```
Suit = Number/13
Card = Number%13
```

Number realizes its minimum when Card and Suit are both 0 and its maximum when Card=12 and Suit=3.

```
min(Number) = 0 * 13 + 0 = 0
max(Number) = 3 * 13 + 12 = 51
```

So, we have mapped an arbitrary card (Suit, Card) to a unique number between 0 and 51. For all practical purposes, this problem reduces to that of randomizing the numbers between 0 and 51. You would think that this would be an easy thing, but it turns out not to be trivial, and it's very easy to get it wrong. This is especially disturbing given the proliferation of online gambling.

Note Here's an intuitive algorithm that just doesn't work. Put the cards in an array, and iterate through them, swapping each card with a card in a random position. This does, in fact, mix up the cards quite spectacularly, but it favors certain card sequences and produces an uneven distribution. Can you see why?

Each swap has one chance in 52 of swapping with itself—a trivial swap. One thing you might think about is that if the result of the shuffle is an unshuffled deck, say, {1 2 3 4. . .51}, then there must have been an even number of nontrivial swaps. Now the deck {2 1 3 4. . .51} requires an odd number of nontrivial swaps. That should be a red flag, because our algorithm always executes exactly 52 swaps, which is even, so it seems doubtful that these two decks are generated with equal likelihood.

The Shuffling Algorithm

A sound algorithm mimics what you do when you deal out cards. First, you pick one card at random from the 52 in the deck, then you pick one from the 51 that remain, and so on. In this algorithm, you get an even distribution up to the randomness of the random number generator:

```csharp
namespace CSharp
{
    class Deck
    {
        void Shuffle()
        {
            for (uint u = 52; u > 0; --u)
            {
                Swap(ref Cards[u - 1], ref Cards[RandomCard(u)]);
            }
        }
    }
}
```

The Completed C# Program

This implementation shuffles a deck of cards and "deals" out the first five cards for viewing. We can conclude that the name of the game is five-card stud.

```csharp
using System;
namespace CSharp
{
    public class Deck
    {
        uint[] Cards;
        Random randomGenerator;
        public enum Suit
        {
            Clubs = 0, Diamonds, Hearts, Spades
        }
        public enum Card
        {
            Ace = 0, Deuce, Trey, Four, Five, Six, Seven,
            Eight, Nine, Ten, Jack, Queen, King
        }
        Deck()
        {
            randomGenerator = new Random();
            Cards = new uint[52];
            for (uint u = 0; u < 52; ++u)
            {
                Cards[u] = u;
            }
        }
        void Swap(ref uint u, ref uint v)
        {
            uint tmp;
            tmp = u;
```

```
            u = v;
            v = tmp;
        }
        void Shuffle()
        {
            for (uint u = 52; u > 0; --u)
            {
                Swap(ref Cards[u - 1], ref Cards[RandomCard(u)]);
            }
        }
        uint RandomCard(uint Max)
        {
            return (uint)((double)Max * randomGenerator.NextDouble());
        }
        string CardToString(uint u)
        {
            Suit s = (Suit)(Cards[u] / 13);
            Card c = (Card)(Cards[u] % 13);
            return c.ToString() + " of " + s.ToString();
        }
        public static void Main()
        {
            Deck deck = new Deck();
            deck.Shuffle();
            for (uint u = 0; u < 5; ++u)
            {
                Console.WriteLine(deck.CardToString(u));
            }
            Console.ReadLine();
        }
    }
}
```

A Quick Look at the Code

As in every C# application, the code begins with static Main(). Once there, we create a new Deck, call Shuffle() on it, then display the first five cards. Since WriteLine() is not familiar with how to print cards, we create a function that converts the card to a string and then call WriteLine() with its results. The function CardToString(uint cardnumber) does the trick.

Projects and Solutions

First let's create a simple C# shuffle project. There is nothing particularly unique about this C# project. To create it, select File ➤ New ➤ Project. Navigate through the New Project tree view to create a Visual C# console application named Shuffle. If your system is set up like mine, the console application appears as shown in Figure 2-1.

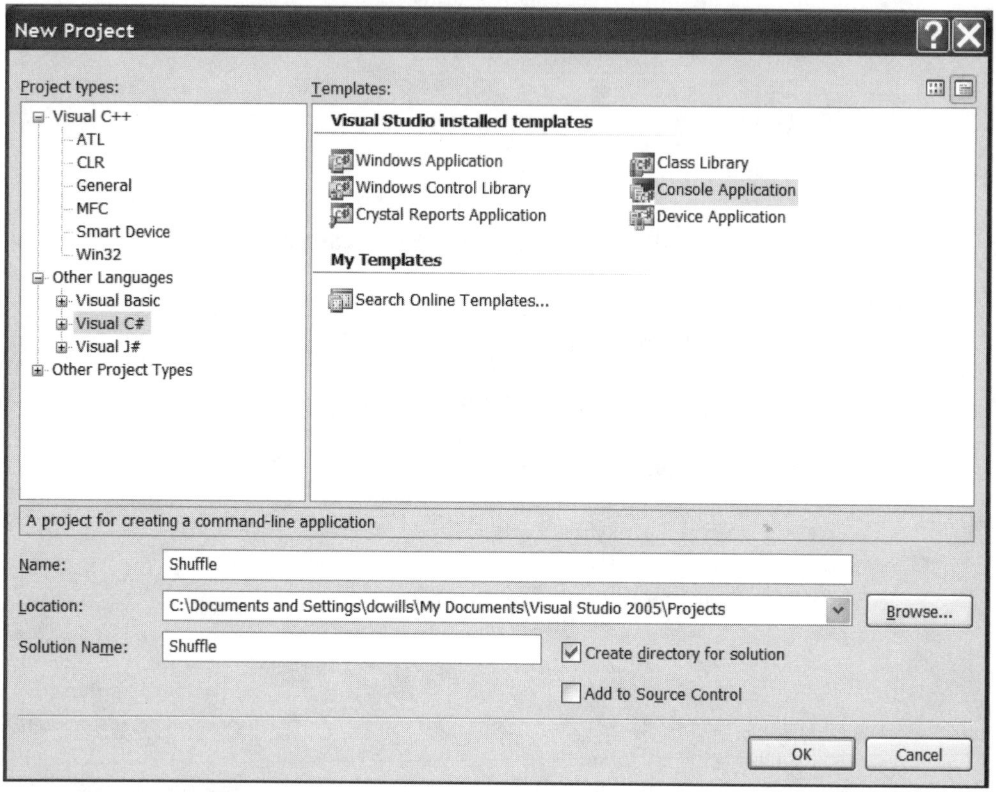

Figure 2-1. *The C# Shuffle console application*

Both the C# and C++ compilers package metadata into modules and assemblies. *Modules* are building blocks of assemblies. *Assemblies* are made up of one or more modules and are units of deployment. Assemblies are deployed as executable files or class libraries. In this first version, the Shuffle project is a standalone executable. Later in this chapter, we will change this executable into a class library without changing a single line of C# code.

A Quick Look

Select Edit ➤ Outlining ➤ Collapse to Definitions. This gives you a bird's-eye view of the code, as shown in Figure 2-2.

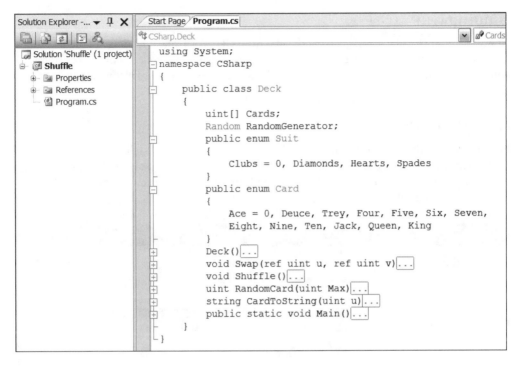

Figure 2-2. *A bird's-eye view of the code*

Placing the cursor over any of the boxes containing an ellipsis pops up a window that displays the collapsed section of the code.

Building and Executing the Project

Select Build ➤ Build Solution to build the project. With the Visual C++ key bindings, this is the F7 key. With the Visual C# key bindings, this is the F6 key. In either case, you can execute it with the F5 key.

You see output similar to the following—your hand may vary:

```
Ten of Diamonds
Deuce of Clubs
Trey of Clubs
Jack of Hearts
Deuce of Spades
```

The Command window now pauses, waiting for you to press Enter because of the `Console.ReadLine()` call.

Hmmm. Pair of deuces—not bad, but not good enough to open.

Binding C++

Now we're going to take this C# class and call it from C++. We'll take advantage of the fact that C++/CLI programs begin with a global function named main(), whereas C# programs start with a class with a static function named Main(). Since these names are distinct, they don't conflict, and we can bind them together seamlessly.

Creating the C++ Project

First we merge the C# program with C++/CLI. To create a C++ project, select File ➤ New ➤ Project. Under Templates, select Visual C++, then CLR, then CLR Console Applications. Name the project CardsCpp, and select Add to Solution from the Solution drop-down list, as shown in Figure 2-3. Then click OK.

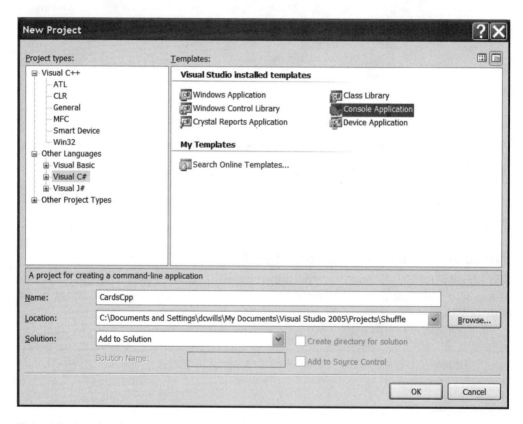

Figure 2-3. *Creating the C++/CLI project*

Setting the Startup Project and Project Dependencies

You should have a new project named CardsCpp. Follow these steps in the Solution Explorer:

1. Right-click the CardsCpp project, and select Project Dependencies. Check the box so that CardsCpp depends on Shuffle. This ensures that the C# project Shuffle is built before the C++ project CardsCpp. We want a dependency in this direction, because we will bring in the completed C# project as a class library DLL and the C++ project will be the master project. See Figure 2-4.

2. Right-click the CardsCpp project again, and select Set as Startup Project.

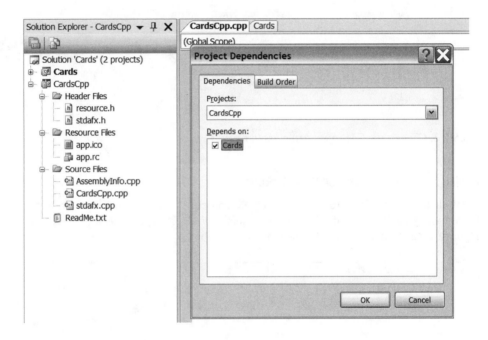

Figure 2-4. *Project Dependencies dialog box*

Making the C# Project a Class Library

Now we'll do a bit of magic and modify the C# application, so that it can be referenced as a class library by the C++ application. Right-click Shuffle in the Solution Explorer, and select Properties. In the Application tab, change the Output Type to Class Library, as shown in Figure 2-5.

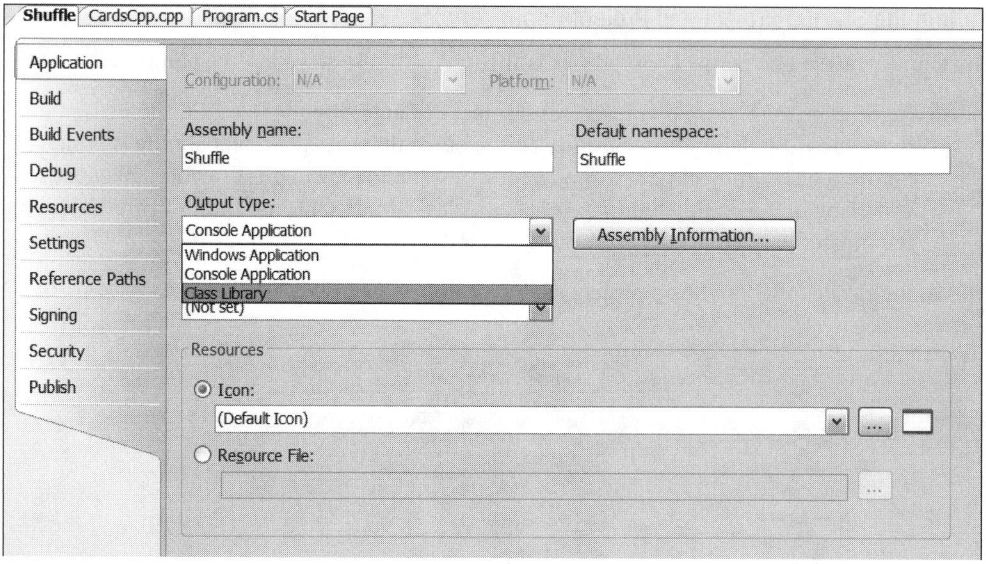

Figure 2-5. *Convert the C# project to a class library.*

Adding a Reference to the C# Class Library

Right-click the CardsCpp project, and select References. Then click the Add New Reference button. Click the Projects tab; the Shuffle project should already be selected, as shown in Figure 2-6. Click OK to add a reference to Shuffle to the C++ project.

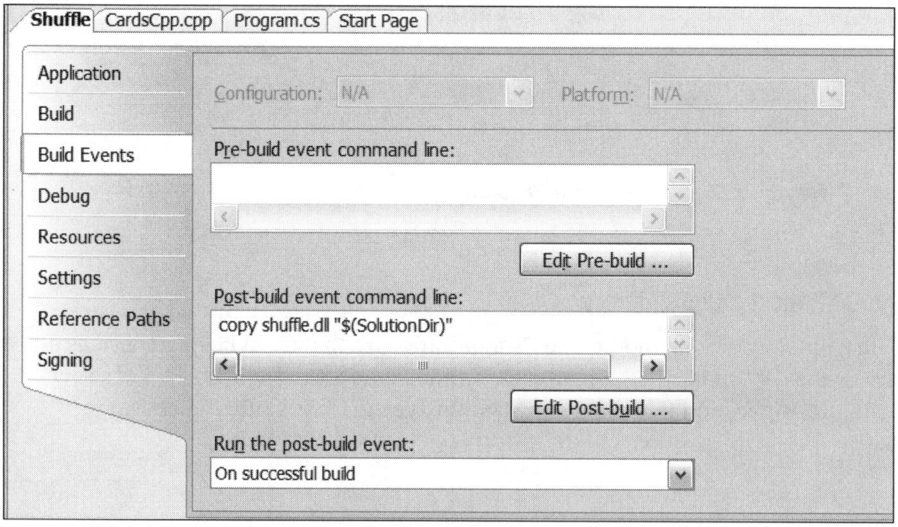

Figure 2-6. *Add a reference to the C# project.*

Creating the C++/CLI Stub

There is one small change to make to the C++ source file, `CardsCpp.cpp`. Replace the following line:

```
Console::WriteLine(L"Hello World");
```

with

```
CSharp::Deck::Main();
```

Note that as you type this, Visual C++ IntelliSense kicks in with a pop-up window and assists you. Just like C# IntelliSense, it is a context-sensitive code engine that helps you discover class members and parameter information as you type. As you can see in Figure 2-7, IntelliSense reveals the methods and fields of the `CSharp::Deck` class. What they are and how they are accessible are determined by the miniature icons to the left of the names. A smaller box adds more information about the selected item as well as XML document comments where available.

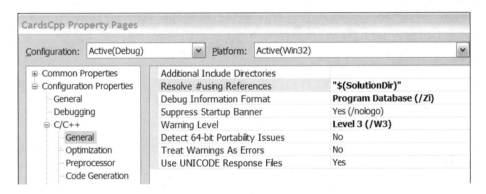

Figure 2-7. *IntelliSense helps you code.*

Your code should now look like Figure 2-8, ready to execute with F5.

```
CardsCpp.cpp  Program.cs  Start Page
(Global Scope)
// CardsCpp.cpp : main project file.

#include "stdafx.h"
#using "Shuffle.dll"
using namespace System;

int main(array<System::String ^> ^args)
{
    CSharp::Deck::Main();
}
```

Figure 2-8. *The finished C++/CLI stub*

Doing the Shuffle Without the IDE

Combining C++ and C# programs is also quite easily done without the IDE, although it doesn't scale to large projects as easily. The IDE puts power at your disposal, but it also adds a layer of complexity. With the IDE, you get the following:

- Editing help and code information, with IntelliSense and browsing

- Project management

- Build management

- Integrated debugging

Basic Command-Line Compilation

Since this is a very small and simple project, we don't need to go through a full IDE setup to show our demonstration.

Use the following bare-bones C++ program with the precompiled headers removed. Create a file called cardscpp1.cpp in the same directory as shuffle.cs:

```
#using "shuffle.dll"
void main()
{
    CSharp::Deck::Main();
}
```

Open a Visual Studio 2005 command prompt and navigate to this directory. Compile and execute this program as follows:

```
csc /target:library /out:shuffle.dll program.cs
cl /clr cardscpp1.cpp
cardscpp1

King of Diamonds
Trey of Clubs
Jack of Hearts
Deuce of Diamonds
Four of Hearts
```

Looks like we should fold this time!

Using a Module

The results of the previous examples are an executable and a separate library in a DLL. Using a module, we can combine them into a single executable. This can only be done using a custom build rule in the IDE; "module" is not a valid output type for a C# project. We'll do it from the command line.

First, we compile the C# class into a module. Then we gather it into a single executable assembly using the C++ compiler.

Create a file called cardscpp2.cpp in the same directory as shuffle.cs:

```
#using "shuffle.netmodule"
void main()
{
    CSharp::Deck::Main();
}
```

Compile the C# into a module, make an executable using C++, and run it:

```
csc /target:module /out:shuffle.netmodule program.cs
cl /clr cardscpp2.cpp
cardscpp2

King of Clubs
Queen of Diamonds
Queen of Spades
Ten of Spades
Ace of Clubs
```

Now that's a winning hand!

Summary

In this chapter, we developed a simple C# program. First, we compiled and ran it standalone from the IDE. Then we changed its output type to a library in order to create a DLL for use by a C++ executable, both from the IDE and the command line. Finally, we created a module from the C# program, which we combined with the C++ in order to create a single executable. This should give you a fairly good introduction to the various ways you can work with C# and C++ under .NET. In Chapter 19, we will revisit these topics and discuss interoperability with native code. But let's not get ahead of ourselves; there are a lot of fundamentals to cover first, and we'll explore syntax differences in the next chapter.

CHAPTER 3

■ ■ ■

Syntax

The pure and simple truth is rarely pure and never simple.

—Oscar Wilde

The previous chapters emphasized the similarities between C# and C++/CLI. Now we touch on the main areas where they differ and begin to understand why. These include additional or different keywords, separators, and operators.

For example, in C++, the additional keyword namespace is required when using a namespace (see Table 3-1).

Table 3-1. *Namespaces in C# and C++/CLI*

C#	C++/CLI
using System.Threading; System.Console.WriteLine("H");	using namespace System::Threading; System::Console::WriteLine("H");

Moreover, where C# uses dot as a general separator, C++ employs several different separators depending on the context as well as the meanings of the items being separated. The most common of these separators are colon-colon (::) and dot (.). The colon-colon separator, or scope resolution operator, is used to qualify identifiers with namespaces, classes, properties, and events and to access static fields and methods. The dot separator, or member access operator, is used to access members of instances of classes.

The paradigms of C++, different separators in different contexts, and of C#, a single separator for all contexts, are consistent with the overall design philosophy of each of the languages. C# favors simplicity, whereas C++ demands a deeper level of specificity in exchange for greater flexibility.

Table 3-2 shows separator differences between C# and C++. I cover all of these separators in detail as the book progresses.

Table 3-2. *Separators in C++*

Separator	Name	Meaning
::	colon-colon	Scope resolution operator, used when the expression to the left of the :: is a namespace, class, property, or event name and the expression to the right of the :: is a namespace, class name, or member of a class
.	dot	Class member access operator, used when the expression to the left of the arrow is a class object
->	arrow	Class member access operator, used when the expression to the left of the arrow is a pointer or handle to a class object
.*	dot star	Pointer to a member operator, used when the expression to the left of the arrow is a class object and the expression to the right of the arrow is a pointer to a member of the same class
->*	arrow star	Pointer to a member operator, used when the expression to the left of the arrow is a pointer to a class object and the expression to the right of the arrow is a pointer to a member of the same class

C# and C++ define classes and structures differently. In addition to one obvious syntactic difference—C++ requires a trailing semicolon after a type definition—significant semantic differences exist. See Table 3-3 for an example comparing classes and structures in C# and C++.

Table 3-3. *Classes and Structures in C# and C++/CLI*

C#	C++/CLI
class R {}	ref class R {};
N/A	ref struct R {};
struct V {}	value class V {};
N/A	value struct V {};
enum E {}	enum class E {};
N/A	enum struct E {};
N/A	class C {};
N/A	struct C{};

In C#, classes and structures are vehicles for implementing *reference types* and *value types* as defined by the CLI. In C++, classes and structures define a *type*—in general, a related collection of fields and methods and subtypes.

C++/CLI introduces two class modifiers, ref and value, which provide a way to map the C++ type specifiers to the CLI types. Together with the class or struct keyword and separated by whitespace, as in ref class, they form a single new keyword, appropriately called a *whitespace keyword.*

Reference types and value types are very important in .NET programming, and it's a good idea to review these types a bit before we continue. There are many practical differences between reference types and value types, but the main differences relate to how they are allocated. A reference type is allocated in two parts. A reference type's data is allocated on the managed heap, while a separate handle to this data is allocated on the stack. A value type is allocated automatically on the stack.

A C# class is a reference type; so is a C# string. A C# struct and most C# built-in types, including int and char, are value types. Value types contained in reference types, either explicitly or implicitly via boxing, become elements of the reference type and are allocated on the managed heap.

C# class (Reference Type)

Suppose you have a C# class named Hello. Allocate an instance using

```
Hello h = new Hello();
```

From the syntax, it appears that you have created a single unified entity of type Hello. Behind the scenes there is much more going on, as data was allocated on the stack as well as the managed heap. An instance of the Hello object was allocated on the managed heap, and a handle to this instance was stored on the stack in the variable h.

C# struct (Value Type)

If Hello is defined as a C# struct, then a completely different operation occurs. The entire instance of Hello is allocated on the stack, and h represents the instance of this object.

Caveat

The fact that reference types are divided between the stack and heap generates some interesting and somewhat unintuitive results when you're assigning values to reference types. When you assign one value type to another, you copy the data associated with one instance of the type to another instance. When you assign one reference type to another, you overwrite the handle to one instance with the handle of another instance. The instances themselves remain unchanged.

Consider the following code in C#:

```
class Hello
{
    int i;
    Hello(int number)
    {
        i=number;
    }
    static void Main()
    {
        Hello h = new Hello(1);
        Hello j = new Hello(2);
        j = h;
        System.Console.WriteLine(j.i);
        h.i = 3;
        System.Console.WriteLine(j.i);
    }
}
```

After compiling and running this code, we get

```
C:\>csc /nologo test.cs
C:\>test
1
3
```

In this program, we allocate two objects of type Hello on the managed heap. The handles to these classes, h and j, are allocated on the stack. We overwrite the handle in j with the handle in h and orphan Hello(2). Hello(2) becomes available for reclamation by the garbage collector. Both h and j now reference the Hello(1) object, and there is no difference between accessing the member field i using h or using j.

In other words, since Hello is a reference type, h and j are handles that point to data on the managed heap. When the assignment j=h occurs, h and j both refer to the same data. Assigning 3 to h.i also affects j.i, and displaying j.i results in the number 3.

Contrast

On the other hand, if Hello were a value type, you would see a different result. Change the declaration of Hello from class to struct:

```
struct Hello
{ /**/ }
```

After compiling and executing the program, we see

```
C:\>csc /nologo test.cs
C:\>test
1
1
```

The results are different this time, since our objects are all allocated on the stack and are overwriting one another.

Lack of Locality

A local inspection of the method Main() is insufficient to determine the results of the program. You cannot determine what result the WriteLine will generate by just looking at the surrounding code. C# requires you to refer to the definition of Hello and discover whether Hello is a class or a struct.

This lack of locality is dangerous and goes against the C++/CLI design philosophy. In C++/CLI, the distinction between reference types and value types is much more explicit. The programmer specifies more precisely what he or she wants to do, which avoids confusion and ultimately makes the code more maintainable. The cost is that the syntax is slightly more difficult.

The C++ Approach

In C++/CLI, handles are typically flagged using the handle punctuator ^. It is also called a *tracking handle*, because it points to an object that may be moved around during garbage collection.

Translating the previous code to C++/CLI, we achieve the following:

```
private ref class Hello
{
private:
    int i;
    Hello(int number)
    {
        i=number;
    }
public:
    static void Main()
    {
        Hello ^h = gcnew Hello(1);
        Hello ^j = gcnew Hello(2);
        j = h;
        System::Console::WriteLine(j->i);
        h->i = 3;
        System::Console::WriteLine(j->i);
    }
};
void main()
{
    Hello::Main();
}
```

After compiling and executing, we get

```
C:\>cl /nologo /clr:pure test.cpp
C:\>test
1
3
```

There are a few obvious syntactic differences from the C# version. However, I'd like to start off by pointing out a semantic difference. In C++/CLI, changing Hello from a reference type to a value type, by changing the whitespace keyword ref class to value class, does not produce different results on compilation and execution.

Changing the type from a reference type to a value type affected where the type was allocated, but it did not change the fact that in the previous code snippet we are treating the data as referenced data. If Hello morphs into a value type, then the compiler generates different IL, so that h and j remain handles to the data on the managed heap, and the result is consistent. Behind the scenes, the value types are boxed—we'll revisit that later in Chapter 6.

Types of Member Access Operators

The other important difference between the C++ snippet and the C# snippet is that C++ handles use a different class member access operator. The syntax is similar to that of pointers in C++, as handles may be considered a special kind of pointer. If you are working with a handle or pointer to an object, you use the arrow member access operator (->) to access the object's members. If you are working with an instance of the object itself, you use the dot member access operator (.). Although it may seem more complicated to have two different types of member access operators, one benefit is that code like our previous example always does what you expect it to, because you are forced to be mindful of what you're doing as you write—and that's a good thing.

Keyword Differences

In this section, we go over the keyword differences between C# and C++. Most of these differences are because of the evolution of the C++ language and the compatibility and disambiguation restrictions for adding to the C++ grammar.

Let's begin with the foreach keyword, shown in Table 3-4.

Table 3-4. *foreach in C# and for each in C++/CLI*

C#	C++/CLI
foreach	for each

In C++/CLI, the keyword for each has a space, and the usage differs slightly from foreach in C#. The converted code appears in Table 3-5.

Table 3-5. *Examples of foreach in C# and for each in C++/CLI*

C#	C++/CLI

<pre>using System;
using System.Collections;
class R
{
 	
    static void Main()
    {
        ArrayList list = new ArrayList(0);
        list.Add("hello");
        list.Add("world");
        foreach (Object o in list)
        {
            Console.WriteLine(o);
        }
    }
}</pre>
	<pre>using namespace System;
	using namespace System::Collections;
	ref class R
	{
	public:
	    static void Main()
	    {
	        ArrayList ^list = gcnew ArrayList(0);
	        list->Add("hello");
	        list->Add("world");
	        for each (Object ^o in list)
	        {
	            Console::WriteLine(o);
	        }
	    }
	};
	void main()
	{
	    R::Main();
	}</pre>

Review

Let's review what you've seen so far. Differences between C# and C++/CLI include the following:

- The additional keyword namespace is used.

- Namespaces are separated by colon-colon (::) instead of a dot (.).

- ref class is used instead of class.

- The punctuator ^ is used to declare handles.

- An arrow (->) is used as a handle member access operator, not a dot (.).

- for each contains a space.

- The class definition ends with a semicolon (;).

- C++/CLI begins programs with a global function named main().

Now let's continue on; you can see that C++/CLI uses the keyword nullptr instead of null in Table 3-6.

Table 3-6. *null and nullptr*

C#	C++/CLI
null	nullptr

These keywords are used as shown in Table 3-7.

Table 3-7. *Usage of null and nullptr*

C#	C++/CLI

<pre>class R
{
    static void Main()
    {
        R r = null;
    }
}</pre>
	<pre>ref class R
	{
	    static void Main()
	    {
	        R^ r = nullptr;
	    }
	};</pre>

There are significant differences between switch and goto in C# and C++, as introduced in Table 3-8.

Table 3-8. *switch, case, and goto in C# and C++*

C#	C++
Does not allow case statements to fall through	Allows case statements to fall through
goto *case_statement*	N/A
goto *label*	goto *label*
switch(string s)	N/A

In C#, if a break or goto is missing from a nonempty case statement, the compiler issues an error. In C++, execution is said to *fall through* from a case to the case below it and continue with the next case.

Both languages support a goto keyword to a user-defined label. C# allows an explicit goto to a case statement. There is no C++ equivalent, and the reason is largely historical. In C, a switch/case/break construct was not so much a formal fork as a macro replacement for goto. The cases are not distinct blocks, but rather labels that act as switch targets. C switches were modeled after assembly language jump tables. C++ retains its heritage. C# attempts to employ a more formal abstraction, where the cases are truly distinct and disconnected entities, so C# naturally does not support fall through. Both abstractions have their respective advantages and disadvantages.

The C# construct switch(string) is not supported in C++. In C++, you must expand your switch statement using if and else. See Table 3-9 for example uses of switch in goto and fall through cases in C# and C++.

Table 3-9. *Usage of switch in C# and C++*

C#	C++
``// switch on a System.String and goto case
string s="1";
switch(s)
{
case "1":
goto case "2";
case "2":
break;
}```	```// equivalent to switch on a System::String
System::String ^s="1";
if(s=="1")
{
}
else if(s=="2")
{
}```
```// fall through case not available```	```// fall through case
int i,j=0;
switch(i)
{
case 1:
j++;
// no break, so case 1 falls into case 2
case 2:
break;
}```

Arrays and Functions

Managed arrays are declared differently in C++/CLI (see Table 3-10).

Table 3-10. *Managed Arrays in C# and C++/CLI*

C#	C++/CLI
reftype [] valuetype []	array<reftype^>^ array<valuetype>^

<pre>class R
{
    static void Main()
    {
        R[] n = new R[5];
        int[] m = {1, 2, 3, 4};
        m[3]=0;
    }
}</pre>
	<pre>ref class R {};
	
	void main()
	{
	    array<R^> ^n = gcnew array<R^>(5);
	    array<int> ^m = {1, 2, 3, 4};
	    m[3]=0;
	}</pre>

Although they both are implemented using System::Array, C++/CLI uses a pseudo-template syntax for their declaration. Managed arrays will be explained in further detail in Chapter 7. Pseudo-template syntax is consistent with the way extensions have been added to the C++ language in the past, such as for the cast operators (see Chapter 16).

In both C# and C++, you can attach modifiers to function arguments. C# and C++/CLI pass parameter arrays, reference parameters, and out parameters differently, as shown in Table 3-11.

Table 3-11. *Function Argument Modifiers*

C#	C++/CLI
params T[]	... array<T> ^
ref	%
out	[System::Runtime::InteropServices::Out] %

We will revisit these later.

The Conversion Operators

The operations performed by the C# operators is and as may be performed by the C++ pseudo-template casting operators static_cast<>() and dynamic_cast<>() (see Table 3-12).

Table 3-12. *C# and C++/CLI Conversion Operators*

C#	C++/CLI
as	dynamic_cast<>()
as	static_cast<>()
is	(dynamic_cast<>()!=nullptr)

Conversion operators will be explained in further detail in Chapter 16.

Memory Allocation

The new operator indicates allocation on the native heap in C++. The gcnew operator was added in C++/CLI to indicate allocation on the managed heap. C# also uses the new operator to allocate value types on the stack. In C++, this is unnecessary, as the C++ syntax for allocating instances of user-defined value types is identical to the syntax for built-in types such as int. See Table 3-13 for a list of keywords used in allocation on the managed heap.

Table 3-13. *Allocation on the Managed Heap in C# and C++/CLI*

C#	C++/CLI
new (reference types)	gcnew
new (value types)	No operator is necessary.

A short example of memory allocation on both the native and managed heaps in C++/CLI follows:

```
value struct V {}; //value type
ref struct R {}; //reference type
struct N {}; //native type
void main()
{
    N n;
    N *pN = new N();
    R ^r = gcnew R();
    V v;
}
```

Memory allocation will be discussed in further detail in Chapter 6.

Accessibility and Visibility

The accessibility and visibility keywords are similar, but the syntax is different. The keyword differences are listed in Table 3-14, and the syntactic differences will be explained in detail in Chapter 8.

Table 3-14. *Basic Protection Mechanisms*

Type Attributes	C#	C++/CLI
Public	public	public:
NotPublic	private	private:
Assembly	internal	internal:
Family	protected	protected:
FamilyOrAssembly	internal protected	protected public:
FamilyAndAssembly	N/A	protected private:

Properties, Events, and Delegates

In Chapter 10, we will discuss properties, events, and delegates, but see Table 3-15 for an introduction.

Table 3-15. *Simple Example of a Property in C# and C++/CLI*

C#	C++/CLI

<pre>class R
{
    private int V;
 	
    public int Value
    {
        get
        {
            return V;
        }
        set
        {
            V = value;
        }
    }
}</pre>
	<pre>ref class R
	{
	private:
	    int V;
	public:
	    property int Value
	    {
	        int get()
	        {
	            return V;
	        }
	        void set(int newV)
	        {
	            V = newV;
	        }
	    }
	};</pre>

Generics

In Chapters 14 through 16, you will learn about generics and templates, but see Table 3-16 for an introduction.

Table 3-16. *Simple Example of a Generic in C# and C++/CLI*

C#	C++/CLI

<pre>public class R<T>
{
    private T m_data;
 	
    public R(T data)
    {
        m_data = data;
        System.Console.WriteLine(m_data);
    }
}
public class R1
{
    static void Main()
    {
        R<int> r = new R<int>(3);
    }
}</pre>
	<pre>generic <typename T> public ref class R
	{
	private:
	    T m_data;
	public:
	    R(T data)
	    {
	        m_data = data;
	        System::Console::WriteLine(m_data);
	    }
	};
	
	int main()
	{
	    R<int> ^r = gcnew R<int>(3);
	}</pre>

Built-in Types

C# and C++/CLI map to the CLI types with different keywords, and the C++/CLI mappings are consistent with native C++ to the extent possible. See Table 3-17 for an introduction before we go into greater detail in Chapter 6.

Table 3-17. *Built-in Types*

C#	C++/CLI
byte	char
sbyte	signed char
short	short
ushort	unsigned short
int	int, long
uint	unsigned int, unsigned long
long	long long
ulong	unsigned long long
single	float
double	double
string	System::String^
object	System::Object^
decimal	System:Decimal
char	wchar_t
bool	bool

Summary

Although the sheer volume of differences between C# and C++ may seem daunting at first, after a while a pattern emerges. Each language is intelligently designed and internally consistent, and C++ syntax will become intuitive quite soon. In the next chapter, we will apply what we're learning by converting a C# program to C++/CLI line by line.

■ ■ ■

C# to C++/CLI

This is like déjà vu all over again.

—Yogi Berra

In this chapter, I show you how to convert a basic C# application to C++/CLI. I cover more advanced conversion methods in greater detail in later chapters.

Let me start by taking apart the elements of the C# shuffling program from Chapter 2 and detailing the necessary changes, one at a time. Rather than pedantically plodding through the code line by line, I'll draw representative samples from the code and present the finished product.

The code from Chapter 2 follows, with line numbers inserted, just so you don't have to flip back and forth:

```
01  using System;
02  namespace CSharp
03  {
04      public class Deck
05      {
06          uint[] Cards;
07          Random randomGenerator;
08          enum Suit
09          {
10              Clubs = 0, Diamonds, Hearts, Spades
11          }
12          enum Card
13          {
14              Ace=0, Deuce, Trey, Four, Five, Six, Seven,
15              Eight, Nine, Ten, Jack, Queen, King
16          }
17          Deck()
18          {
19              randomGenerator = new Random();
20              Cards = new uint[52];
21
22              for (uint u = 0; u < 52; ++u)
23              {
```

```
24                    Cards[u] = u;
25                }
26            }
27            void Swap(ref uint u, ref uint v)
28            {
29                uint tmp;
30                tmp = u;
31                u = v;
32                v = tmp;
33            }
34            void Shuffle()
35            {
36
37                for (uint u = 52; u > 0; --u)
38                {
39                    Swap(ref Cards[u - 1], ref Cards[RandomCard(u)]);
40                }
41            }
42            uint RandomCard(uint Max)
43            {
44                return (uint)((double)Max * randomGenerator.NextDouble());
45            }
46            string CardToString(uint u)
47            {
48                Suit s = (Suit)(Cards[u] / 13);
49                Card c = (Card)(Cards[u] % 13);
50                return c.ToString() + " of " + s.ToString();
51            }
52
53            public static void Main()
54            {
55                Deck deck = new Deck();
56                deck.Shuffle();
57                for (uint u = 0; u < 5; ++u)
58                {
59                    Console.WriteLine(deck.CardToString(u));
60                }
61                Console.ReadLine();
62            }
63        }
64    }
```

We'll begin with the initial declarative blocks and build from there.

Add the Keyword namespace After using

On line 1, add the `namespace` keyword to the `using` statement by changing the following C# code:

```
using System;
```

to this C++

```
using namespace System;
```

The `using` statement, as applied to a namespace, brings all symbols from that namespace into the scope of the `using` statement. In this case, we want to use the `Console` class to output data to the screen. Without a `using` statement, we'd have to tell the compiler explicitly how to find the `Console` class by writing `System::Console` whenever we wanted to use it. This is called *fully qualifying* the name. In C++/CLI, we are required to add the keyword `namespace` to the `using` declaration.

Add the Punctuator ^ to the Reference Type Declarations

On lines 7 and 55, change the reference type declarations by changing the following C# code:

```
Random randomGenerator;
Deck deck
```

to this C++

```
Random ^randomGenerator;
Deck ^deck
```

If you look up the word "Random" in the .NET Framework Class Library reference on MSDN, you find that `Random` is a reference type. How can you tell?

In the C# section of the MSDN page, you find that `Random` is declared as follows:

```
public class Random
```

In the C++/CLI section, you find that `Random` is declared as follows:

```
public ref class Random
```

Both of these declarations indicate a reference type. In this case, `randomGenerator` is actually a handle for an instance of `Random` that is allocated on the managed heap. In C++/CLI, the fact that it is a handle is explicitly indicated using the handle punctuator ^, and the type of `randomGenerator` is `Random^`. In many ways, `randomGenerator` can be thought of as a pointer to an object of type `Random` on the managed heap, but don't take this analogy too far. There are significant differences between handles and pointers in C++, which we discuss in further detail in Chapter 9.

Modify the Built-in Types

On lines 6, 22, 27, 29, 37, 42, 44, 46, and 57, change the C# aliases:

```
uint
string
```

to C++

```
unsigned int
System::String^
```

Since C# and C++ compiled for the CLR both target the CLI, there is always a direct analogue between managed types of one language and managed types of the other language. C++ does not have the abbreviated form uint and requires you to use the expanded unsigned int.

C++ also does not have a built-in type for string, so you need to use System::String^. In C#, you can choose between the built-in alias string and System::String; they are equivalent. The type string is built in to the language, and System.String is the equivalent, which is typically brought in via a using System statement.

■**Note** Why doesn't C++ have standard abbreviated forms for built-in types such as unsigned int? Well, this was proposed to the ANSI Committee on C in 1987 by me, but it was voted down, because "the addition of synonyms for existing types would add identifiers to the set of reserved names without adding functionality." This philosophy is less in vogue today, as evidenced by the fact that C# has a synonym string for System.String. This does not add any functionality—it's just convenient.

So what is the practical difference if string and String are the same? Consider the following C# program, and note the absence of any using statements:

```
public class Hello
{
    static void Main()
    {
        String s;
    }
}
```

Now try to compile it:

```
Microsoft (R) Visual C# 2005 Compiler version 8.00.50727.42
for Microsoft (R) Windows (R) 2005 Framework version 2.0.50727
Copyright (C) Microsoft Corporation 2001-2005. All rights reserved.
g1.cs(5,9): error CS0246: The type or namespace name 'String'
could not be found
(are you missing a using directive or an assembly reference?)
```

As you can see, without the using System statement, the compiler has no idea what String is. If we fully qualify String by changing it to System.String, it will compile.

Note that, since System.String is a reference type, the handle punctuator is used in C++/CLI, so the proper conversion to C++/CLI gives us System::String^. Since we already have using namespace System, it suffices to use String^.

Change the Array Declarations and Type Parameters

On line 6, change the C# array declaration:

```
uint[] Cards;
```

to C++

```
array<unsigned int>^Cards;
```

In this case, the declarations look so different it's difficult to imagine that they indicate the same thing. The goal here is to instruct the compiler that we would like Cards to be a managed array of unsigned integers of unknown length. In Table 4-1, you can see how managed array syntax maps between C# and C++/CLI.

Table 4-1. *Managed Array Declaration in C# and C++/CLI*

C# Array Syntax	C++/CLI Array Syntax
type[] *variable-name*;	array< type >^ *variable-name*;

The first change is the actual syntax used in array declaration. The C++/CLI language uses a syntax that is called *pseudo-template format*, in reference to the fact that it feels like a C++ template but does not exhibit all the characteristics of one. It uses the < and > characters, as in the case of template declaration, instantiation, and usage. In addition, a managed array is stored on the managed heap, so *variable-name* is a handle, and it requires the ^ punctuator.

The second change is the use of the typename unsigned int instead of uint, as explained previously.

Change the Enumeration Declarations

On lines 8 and 12, change the following enumeration declarations from C#:

```
public enum Suit {};
public enum Card {};
```

to C++

```
public:
    enum class Suit {};
    enum class Card {};
```

To get the syntax correct for this enumeration declaration, we have to make three small changes. Note that to make things more interesting, I added accessibility to our translation problem. First of all, in C++/CLI, accessibility indicators for nested types, class fields, and methods, like public, are not item specific; they are context specific. In the C# version, the keyword public indicates that the specific enum Suit has public accessibility. In the C++/CLI version, the keyword public: within a class indicates that all types, methods, and fields from that point forward have public accessibility. If we neglected to add the keyword public to the next enum declared after Suit, it would gain the default accessibility of a C# class, which is private. On the other hand, in the C++/CLI version, absent an accessibility keyword, the succeeding enum declaration would gain the contextual accessibility level, which in this case is public because of the explicit use of public: before enum. When dealing with accessibility at a global scope, the C++ language also has a public keyword that is item specific.

The second change is that C++/CLI managed enumerations, which are the analogue of C# enumerations, require the additional keyword class to distinguish them from native C++ enumerations.

The final change is one we have seen several times before—that C++/CLI type definitions are terminated by a trailing semicolon after the closing curly brace. Enumerations are types; namespaces are not. The easy way to remember this is that if you can make one, you need a trailing semicolon. You can instantiate a type, but not a namespace.

Change the Object Allocations and Instantiations

On lines 19, 20, 22, 37, and 55, change the following C# code:

```
randomGenerator = new Random();
Cards = new uint[52];
uint u;
```

to C++

```
randomGenerator = gcnew Random()
Cards = gcnew array<unsigned int>^(52);
unsigned int u;
```

These expressions map from C# to C++/CLI fairly easily, and it's really just a matter of getting used to the differences. The primary difference is that C++ distinguishes allocations on the native heap from allocations on the managed heap by requiring the keyword gcnew rather than the keyword new. If you happen to use the wrong one, the compiler is usually polite enough to issue an error message to remind you.

Change the Pass by Reference Parameters

On lines 27 and 39, change the following C# code:

```
void Swap(ref uint u, ref uint v)
Swap(ref Cards[u - 1], ref Cards[RandomCard(u)]);
```

to C++

```
void Swap(unsigned int %u,unsigned int %v)
Swap(Cards[u - 1], Cards[RandomCard(u)]);
```

We need to modify both the Swap() function declaration as well as all uses of Swap(). Instead of the C# keyword ref, C++/CLI uses the % punctuator to indicate a tracking reference. In C++/CLI, the punctuator is only used in the function declaration, not on function usage.

In Table 4-2, I list the correspondences between C# and C++, including the C++ implementation of the C# out keyword.

Table 4-2. *Parameter Passing in C# and C++/CLI*

C#	C++/CLI

ErrorCode GetData(ref int data)
{
 	
}
	using namespace System::Runtime::InteropServices;
	ErrorCode GetData(int %data)
	{
	
	}

ErrorCode GetResult(out int result)
{
    return GetData(ref result);
}
	ErrorCode GetResult ([Out] int %result)
	{
	    return GetData(result);
	}

C++ does not have an out keyword, but its behavior can be duplicated using the [System::Runtime::InteropServices::Out] attribute.

Change the Class Member Access Operators for Handles

On lines 44, 56, and 59, we modify the class member access operators in C#:

```
randomGenerator.NextDouble()
deck.Shuffle()
deck.CardToString(u)
```

to C++

```
randomGenerator->NextDouble()
deck->Shuffle()
deck->CardToString(u)
```

Handles and pointers access their members using the -> class member access operator. As discussed earlier, randomGenerator is a handle, and accessing the data on the managed heap requires the -> class member access operator.

Change the Separators for Namespaces and Static Accesses

On lines 59 and 61, we change the following separators in C#:

```
Console.WriteLine()
Console.ReadLine()
```

to C++

```
Console::WriteLine()
Console::ReadLine()
```

The . class member access operator is reserved for instantiations, which indicate that you are accessing the data directly rather than through a handle or pointer indirection. The :: separator, the scope resolution operator, is used for qualification of namespaces and static members.

Change the Class Declarations

On line 4, we change the class declarations in C#:

```
class
struct
```

to C++

```
ref class
value class
```

In C++, struct differs from class only in the accessibility and inheritance protection mechanisms. In addition, neither corresponds to the CLI reference and value types. The whitespace keywords ref class and value class (as well as ref struct and value struct) were added to C++ in order to represent these types.

Add the Function main()

C++ programs begin with a global function called main(). C# programs begin with a public static member function called Main(). Since these functions have different signatures, they can coexist in a C++ program, and we can add a global main() function that calls the C# Main() method. This is the simplest way to add the function main() without changing the remainder of the code:

```
void main()
{
    CPP::Deck::Main();
}
```

The completed program follows:

```
using namespace System;
namespace CPP
{
    public ref class Deck
    {
        array<unsigned int>^Cards;
        Random^ randomGenerator;
        enum class Suit
        {
            Clubs = 0, Diamonds, Hearts, Spades
        };
        enum class Card
        {
            Ace=0, Deuce, Trey, Four, Five, Six, Seven,
            Eight, Nine, Ten, Jack, Queen, King
        };
        Deck()
        {
            randomGenerator = gcnew Random();
```

```
                Cards = gcnew array<unsigned int>(52);
                for (unsigned int u = 0; u < 52; ++u)
                {
                    Cards[u] = u;
                }
            }
            void Swap(unsigned int %u,unsigned int %v)
            {
                unsigned int tmp;
                tmp = u;
                u = v;
                v = tmp;
            }
            void Shuffle()
            {
                for (unsigned int u = 52; u > 0; --u)
                {
                    Swap(Cards[u - 1],Cards[RandomCard(u)]);
                }
            }
            unsigned int RandomCard(unsigned int Max)
            {
                return(unsigned int)((double)Max * randomGenerator->NextDouble());
            }
            String^ CardToString(unsigned int u)
            {
                Suit s = (Suit)(Cards[u] / 13);
                Card c = (Card)(Cards[u] % 13);
                return c.ToString() + " of " + s.ToString();
            }
        public:
            static void Main()
            {
                Deck^ deck = gcnew Deck();
                deck->Shuffle();
                for (unsigned int u = 0; u < 5; ++u)
                {
                    Console::WriteLine(deck->CardToString(u));
                }
                Console::ReadLine();
            }
    };
}
void main()
{
    CPP::Deck::Main();
}
```

Place this code in a file called `cardsconverted.cpp`, compile, and run:

```
C:\>cl /nologo /clr:pure cardsconverted.cpp
cardsconverted
C:\>cardsconverted
Four of Diamonds
Ten of Spades
Ace of Spades
Ace of Hearts
Trey of Spades
```

That's openers and more. Time to bet; I'm not bluffing.

Summary

In this chapter, we went through the simple shuffling program of Chapter 2, took it apart line by line, and converted it to C#. Since it is so easy to combine different languages in .NET, you won't need to do this often. You'll be able to create modules and class libraries in C# and C++/CLI, or even Visual Basic, and bind them all together without changing the individual source files. Still, the lesson of actually going through the steps of a conversion is quite valuable.

In the next chapter, we'll explore some tools that will help you program more effectively in C#, C++, and .NET.

∎∎∎∎

Tools

When all else fails, clean your tools.

—Robert Pirsig

In this chapter, we'll acquaint ourselves with a few of the tools that make .NET development easier in both C# and C++.

Lutz Roeder's .NET Reflector

One of the most powerful tools for .NET development available today is Lutz Roeder's .NET Reflector.[1] This program is an invaluable tool for understanding .NET assemblies. It allows you to decompile .NET executables as well as libraries into IL, C#, C++/CLI, and other languages. It is currently freely available at `www.aisto.com`.

What Is Reflection?

A .NET assembly is far more than just a sequence of instructions for execution. It contains descriptions and attributes about the contents of the assembly, collectively called the *metadata*. In .NET parlance, *reflection* is the ability for the program to read and analyze the metadata of another assembly at runtime. When a program reads its own metadata, it is a bit like looking in the mirror, so the term "reflection" seems appropriate. The namespace `System::Reflection` is devoted to the .NET's class library, which implements the primary reflection mechanisms. There are two others: CCI, which allows you to access information that `System::Reflection` cannot, and the `IMetadata` API. All of these mechanisms complement each other.

---

1. .NET Reflector is copyrighted by Lutz Roeder. All images and references are used with permission.

Reflection allows you to discover all metadata information about a type without needing to instantiate it. This includes but is not limited to the following items:

- Name

- Fields

- Methods

- Visibility

- Attributes

Reflection enables you to discover all sorts of characteristics of these items. These include field modifiers (initonly, literal, etc.), method types (generic or not), properties, and events. Reflection even allows you to create types on the fly using Reflection::Emit.

Lutz Roeder's .NET Reflector

Lutz Roeder's .NET Reflector implements a reflection mechanism independent of the mechanism implemented in the .NET framework. It is designed to churn the metadata and CIL into a higher level of abstraction through decompilation. This paradigm is slightly different, as it is not called from within the program itself, so it is not technically a mirror; it is rather like a voyage through the looking glass itself. You launch .NET Reflector, specify which assembly or executable you want to view, and then have a look inside. While the class library in System::Reflection is primarily used for runtime analysis or processing, .NET Reflector excels at examining an assembly after it is packaged.

Decodes the Base Class Library Assemblies

The Base Class Library (BCL) is what we call the rich set of assemblies shipped with the .NET Framework. This program works on all of the BCL .NET assemblies, so you can peek inside any of the Microsoft DLLs to assist your programming efforts. I find this especially useful when I'm trying to figure out which DLLs must be referenced or resolved via #using in a program in order for it to compile correctly. For example, the System::Collections::Generic namespace is divided into two parts, one part in mscorlib.dll and the other in System.dll. It's quite easy to discover which classes are implemented in which DLLs using .NET Reflector. For example, if you're using System::Collections::Generic::List<T>, you do not need to reference any DLL, because mscorlib.dll is implicitly and automatically referenced in every C++/CLI program. On the other hand, if you're using System::Collections::Generic::Stack<T>, you do need to either add a reference to System.dll in your project settings or add the following line to your code:

```
#using "System.dll"
```

In either case, the following line is required as well if you want to refer to Stack<T> or List<T> without the explicit namespace qualification:

```
using namespace System::Collections::Generic
```

The keywords #using and using are not the same; they have different purposes in C++/CLI. It's a bit confusing, but that is how the language is defined.

#using is a type of *compiler directive*, meaning it instructs the compiler how to do something when compiling. In the case of #using, it instructs it to add a reference to that .NET assembly like what is done with /reference on the C# compiler's command line. using is a keyword that is part of the language, and using namespace brings symbols into scope.

Viewing the Metadata and CIL, or Into the Abyss

I've mentioned that .NET Reflector "allows you to peek inside" programs and "decode assemblies," but I did not explain exactly what that means. Assemblies, whether compiled as executables or dynamically linked libraries, contain far more than executable code. This collection of information is called metadata and, ideally, is a self contained package that describes everything it needs to know to work with this assembly.

Years ago, programs themselves were merely a combination of executable code and data. The only program that was capable of executing another program was the operating system itself, which acted as an information router, defining how to pass information between specialized components, such as device drivers designed to work with hardware components and higher level programs that wanted to communicate with these device drivers.

Over time, operating systems and programs evolved. Programs were designed to exchange information with other programs. In the Windows universe, this initially took the form of the clipboard for passive exchanges and OLE[2] for active exchanges. Programs evolved to contain more than just executable code; programs were bound to resource files, which contained localization and globalization information, so that not only could they be translated to other languages but could also work with foreign character sets, different currencies, ways of dealing with time, and other culture-specific information.

The .NET Framework represents a paradigm shift that really offloads much of these responsibilities to the operating system, or in this case, the .NET Framework, which can be thought of as an extension of the operating system.

Binding as much information as possible about an assembly into a single file and organizing it intelligently as a collection of many types of data, or metadata, are key elements of the success of the .NET Framework.

Extensible Class Browser

Both the Microsoft .NET Framework IL Disassembler (ildasm.exe) and Dependency Walker (Depends.exe), shipped with Visual Studio, allow the user to examine or understand the aspects of metadata. ILDasm allows you to look at the Common Intermediate Language (CIL) as well as the metadata. CIL constitutes the executable instructions that make up the program. Lutz Roeder's .NET Reflector is a class browser that is able to display the CIL for all methods inside your assemblies. It also goes one step further and is able to decompile the CIL into semiordinary C#, Visual Basic, and Delphi.

---

2. OLE was a precursor of COM and stands for "Object Linking and Embedding."

One of the beautiful things about this program is that it has a well-defined code model and accepts third-party add-ins. An add-in to decompile CIL into C++/CLI was written by Jason Shirk and me. It is freely available on my web site, www.sandpapersoftware.com.

■**Note** Dozens of programs have already been written to do amazing things with .NET Reflector. You can find them by visiting Lutz's site at www.aisto.com/incoming/reflector/addins.

From C# to C++/CLI

You can use Lutz's .NET Reflector as an educational tool to learn C++/CLI's syntax. It is also possible to use this as a tool to convert from C# to C++/CLI. Doing so is much less satisfying, because Reflector decompiles what is literally in the metadata to a high-level format; oftentimes there are artifacts in the CIL created by compilation or syntactic conveniences in the languages themselves. The algorithm to do this is simple and uses the following steps:

1. Create a C# program.

2. Compile the program.

3. Load the program in .NET Reflector.

4. View any class definition or procedure using the C++/CLI add-in.

Installing and Loading .NET Reflector and the C++/CLI Add-in

The first step is to go to Lutz Roeder's web site, www.aisto.com, and install .NET Reflector. Next, go to www.mybadhairday.com, and install the C++/CLI add-in for .NET Reflector.

There are two files contained in the latest drop:

- cppclilanguage.dll: This is the actual add-in. Put it anywhere you like. Edit the .cfg file or use the View ➤ Add-Ins menu to install this DLL.

- reflector.config.exe: This configuration file loads reflector.exe with the 2.0.50727 version of the .NET Framework. This file must reside in the same directory as reflector.exe.

.NET Reflector (reflector.exe) only requires .NET version 1.0 to execute, but the cppclilanguage.dll add-in requires .NET 2.0. If you attempt to load it with 1.0 or 1.1, you get an error pop-up, as shown in Figure 5-1.

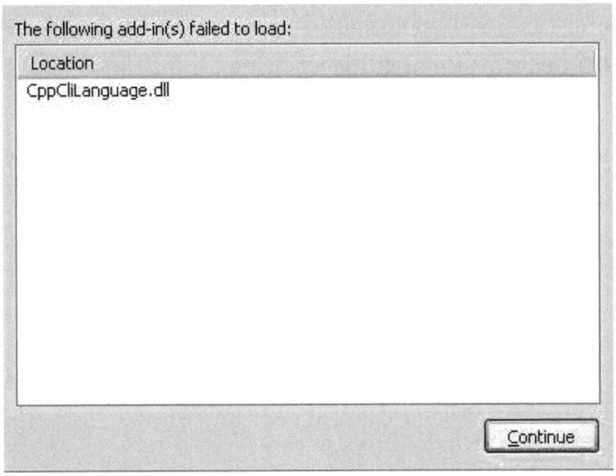

Figure 5-1. *C++/CLI add-in fails to load with .NET Framework version 1*

If you double-click on the CppLanguage.dll line, a more substantial error message appears, as shown in Figure 5-2.

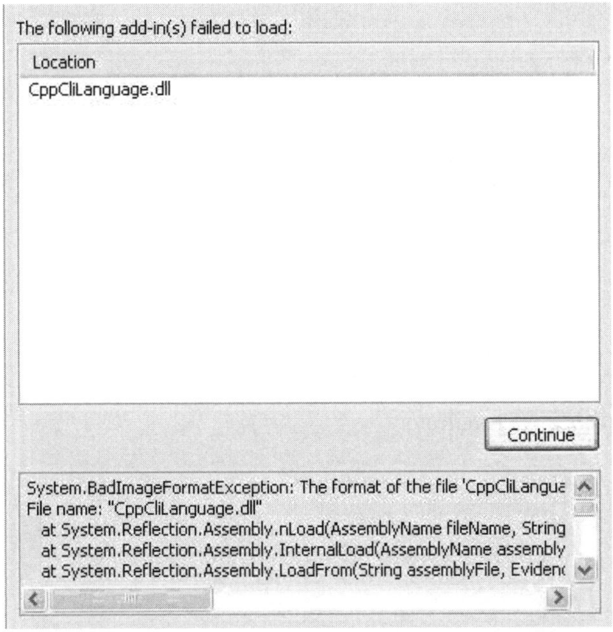

Figure 5-2. *Exception generated by the .NET Framework*

Executing .NET Reflector

Let's do a sample run through with .NET Reflector. Compile the following C# program:

```
struct S
{
}
class R
{
    public static void Main()
    {
        R r = new R();
        S s = new S();
    }
}
```

C# View

Using .NET Reflector, open the executable using File ➤ Open (see Figure 5-3). Navigate to the Main() routine by clicking on the plus signs. Expand the {}, which correspond to the global namespace. Then expand R, navigate to Main(), and double-click. Make sure the drop-down window shows C# as the decompilation view.

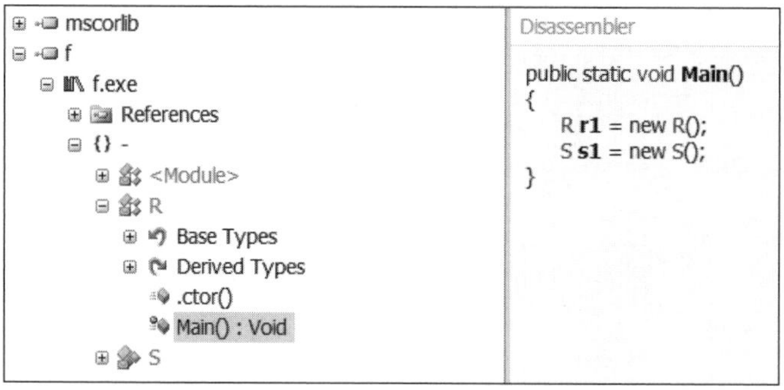

Figure 5-3. *C# view of the sample code using .NET Reflector*

C++/CLI View

Now change the drop-down view to C++/CLI. The view should switch to look like the one shown in Figure 5-4.

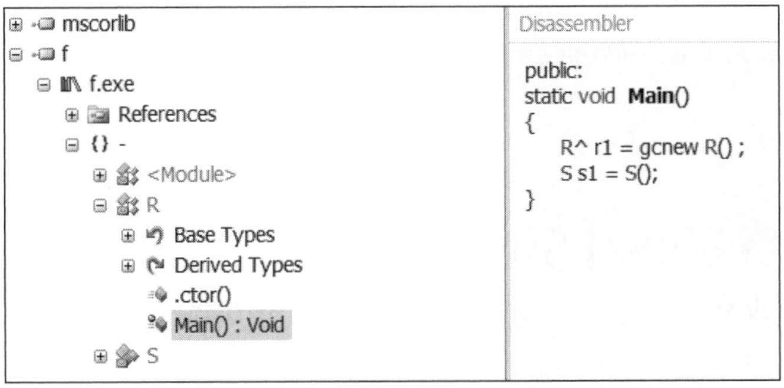

Figure 5-4. *C++/CLI view of the sample code using .NET Reflector*

As you can see, value types and reference types are declared and initialized differently in C++/CLI; this will be discussed in greater detail in Chapter 6.

Instant C++

Instant C++[3] is a useful C# to C++/CLI translator, available from Tangible Software Solutions (www.tangiblesoftwaresolutions.com). This company offers an easy to use, affordable translator for legacy C# projects. This software not only converts isolated C# code snippets to C++/CLI but translates complete projects.

For example, suppose we convert the previous sample using the Snippet Converter (see Figure 5-5).

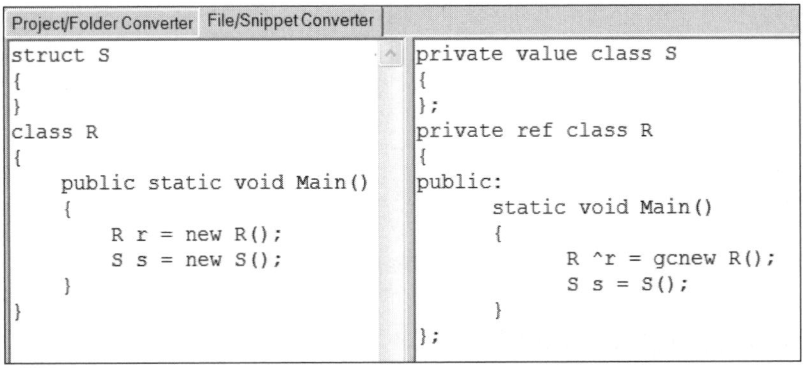

Figure 5-5. *Conversion from C# to C++/CLI using Instant C++*

---

3. Instant C++ is copyrighted by Tangible Software Solutions. All images and references are used with permission.

This snippet is ready to compile, save the necessary global `main()`, which all C++ programs require. Just add the following line, and the program compiles in C++:

```
void main() { R::Main();}
```

Tools Shipped with Visual Studio

A number of extremely useful tools ship with Visual Studio. I introduce two of my favorites in this section.

Microsoft .NET Framework IL Disassembler (ILDasm)

`ildasm.exe` is a metadata and CIL viewer, like .NET Reflector, that cuts at a more basic level. To use ILDasm from the Visual Studio 2005 command prompt, just enter the following:

```
ildasm <assembly name>
```

You can also launch it from the Tools menu in the IDE. In either case, you are greeted with a window similar to the one shown in Figure 5-6.

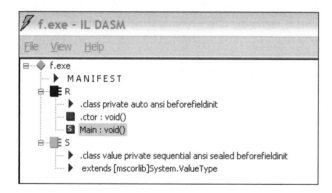

Figure 5-6. *ILDasm's view of the test executable*

Clicking the plus sign expands the definitions under each class.

Dependency Walker (Depends)

`Depends.exe` is a dependency walker for Windows binaries. It works with .NET assemblies as well as native Win32 binaries. It is an invaluable tool for tracking down missing DLLs as well as working through manifest issues. To use Depends, enter the following command from the Visual Studio 2005 command prompt:

```
depends <binary name>
```

You will see a window similar to the one shown in Figure 5-7.

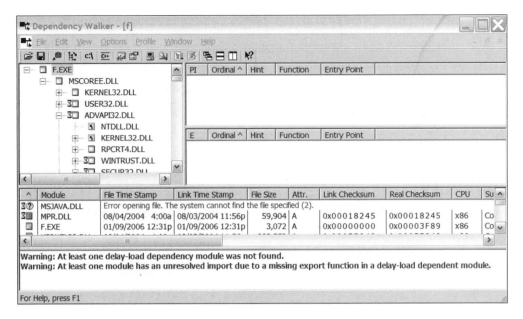

Figure 5-7. *Dependency Walker*

As you can see, it appears that I have some sort of dependency on MSJAVA.DLL that is not resolved. Wonder what caused that?

More Visual Studio Tools

No matter how clever you are, your productivity is limited by the quality of your tools. Though it's beyond the scope of this book to introduce you to all of the tools shipped with Visual Studio 2005, here are a few more worth investigating:

- PEVerify.exe: The Portable Executable Verifier determines whether an assembly meets the requirements for verifiable code.

- SN.exe: The Strong Name utility digitally signs assemblies.

- GACUtil.exe: This utility deals with the global assembly cache, a machinewide code cache for assemblies that are shared between multiple applications on a computer.

- NMake.exe: The Make utility carries out the build process from the command line.

- MT.exe: The Manifest tool is for processing manifests.

- RC.exe: The Resource Compiler is for processing .rc files.

- ResGen.exe: The Resource Generator converts resources between formats.

- CLRVer.exe: The CLR Version tool determines the versions of the CLR installed on a machine.

- `where.exe`: This tool allows you to track down a file using an environment variable.

- `windiff.exe`: This tool allows you to compare different versions of the same text file visually.

- `guidgen.exe`: This tool generates unique global identifiers.

- `TLBImp.exe`: The Type Library Conversion tool is used for importing classes from type libraries.

Summary

Now we have the tools that we need to dig deeper into the C++/CLI and .NET implementation. Without further ado, let's go attack data types in the next chapter.

CHAPTER 6

■ ■ ■

Data Types

The game's afoot.

—William Shakespeare, Henry V

In this chapter, we dig deeper into the CLI type system as well as the implementation of C++/CLI in Microsoft Visual C++ 2005. You should already have a firm base in C# classes, structures, and interfaces from your previous programming experience, and we want to build on that knowledge to expose differences between C# and C++/CLI.

C# Types vs. C++ Types

The C# language was designed specifically to target the CLR. Therefore, all of its data types map directly to CLI types. C++/CLI not only defines data types for the CLI but also defines data types for use in native C++. All of these data types are defined using the keywords class and struct. These keywords had a preexisting meaning in C++ before C# was devised. In C++, class defines a native type, which can be thought of as a general collection of related fields and methods. A C++ struct is the same as a C++ class except that the default accessibility is public for all members, and a C++ struct inherits publicly from its base classes.

In C#, class defines a CLI reference type descended from System::Object that has a specific set of characteristics and limitations. A C# struct defines a CLI value type that has a different set of characteristics.

In order for C++/CLI to implement the CLI types, new keyword combinations were added to the language. The class qualifiers ref and value are prepended to the keywords class and struct to create the new whitespace keywords ref class and value class. These indicate managed types as defined by the CLI. Table 6-1 illustrates the correspondences.[1]

---

1. A future version of C++/CLI may implement mixed types; a *mixed type*, according the C++/CLI specification, is "either a native class or a ref class that requires object members, either by declaration or by inheritance, to be allocated on both the CLI heap and the native heap."

Table 6-1. *C++, C#, and CLI Type Comparision*

C++ Type	C# Type	CLI Type	Default Accessibility	Stored In
ref class	class	reference	private	managed heap, stack
ref struct	N/A	reference	public	managed heap, stack
value class	struct	value	private	native heap, managed heap, stack
value struct	N/A	value	public	native heap, managed heap, stack
class	N/A	N/A	private	native heap, stack
struct	N/A	N/A	public	native heap, stack

The C++ struct Keyword

Let me reiterate that the struct keyword is not used in C++/CLI to indicate either a C# class or a C# struct. A struct in C++ is the exact same thing as a class, except that it has public, rather than private, accessibility and inherits publicly by default. This is also true of ref struct and value struct. Other than with respect to protection mechanisms, they are identical to ref class and value class.

A C++ struct is extremely useful. Whenever I wish to prototype a quick class or method and don't want to worry about protection, I use a C++ struct rather than a C++ class. I'm going to delve deeper into protection mechanisms in Chapter 8.

Native Classes

As mentioned previously, C++/CLI also has native classes. Unlike a ref class and a value class, which map directly to CLI defined types, a *native class* is an unmanaged type that does not have a CLI mapping. Native classes, elements of classic C++, will be discussed further in Chapter 18.

Value Types and Reference Types

Value types and reference types are allocated, accessed, and copied with the same syntax; declaring these types as either struct or class is the main difference. As shown previously, having the same syntax can lead to unintended consequences when instances of these types are assigned. Value types are copied in their entirety, whereas only handles to the reference type are actually copied during an assignment. In C#, except for the initial declaration where you declare struct or class, the syntax is identical for value types and references types. C# hides the distinction between value types and reference types from the programmer, which can be both good and bad. C++/CLI, on the other hand, does not hide these details and distinguishes between value types and reference types. A quick review of memory allocation during program execution is a great place to start understanding the different concepts.

Dynamic Memory Pools

During the execution of a C# program, new items are allocated in one of two places: the stack or the managed heap. C++/CLI adds a third pool, the native heap, which will be discussed further in Chapter 18 during the discussion on native C++.

The Managed Heap

When you call new on a C# class, the class data is allocated sequentially in a continuous block in the managed heap. When the CLR calculates that you have no more references to an object, the object becomes a candidate for garbage collection.

Over time, multiple object allocations and orphaned objects can cause a single large continuous block of free memory to become fragmented into allocated memory and bubbles of unreferenced memory. A subsequent call to the allocation mechanism might not be able to find a sufficiently large contiguous block of memory to contain the new data, even though the total free memory in the system is larger than the desired amount. In this case, the CLR is able to collect the garbage and rearrange memory within the managed heap. In this process, similar to defragmenting a hard disk, in-use memory is moved to combine available memory bubbles to create larger contiguous blocks of memory. It is called *garbage collection*, because available bubbles of memory are not valid data, they are effectively "garbage," and combining available bubbles involves essentially collecting the garbage.

The Stack

In the CLI, the other primary memory buffer used for dynamic allocation of data is the program stack. A *stack* is a memory buffer that grows in a single direction and shrinks in the opposite direction. New allocations can only be made at the top of the stack, and only the memory at the top of the stack may be freed. Allocating memory on the stack is called *pushing*, and freeing memory off the stack is called *popping*. In computer science parlance, the stack is a First-In, Last-Out (FILO) buffer, which means that the first data you push onto the stack is the last data you pop off.

At first glance, using a stack seems to be overly restrictive and not as useful as you might like. In reality, a stack is particularly useful for making function calls and essential for recursive calls. All processors today are speed optimized for using stacks. In C# and C++, the program stack is where return addresses for procedure calls are stored as well as value types and the handles to the reference types. Because of the way that stacks are allocated and deallocated, stacks never become fragmented, and garbage collection is never necessary, thus the restrictive nature of a stack realizes performance benefits.

The Native Heap

Native C++ has a third and final memory area for dynamic allocation called the native heap. Allocations on the native heap are made using the new keyword. C++/CLI applications can use the native heap as well as the managed heap and stack for memory allocation. We will discuss this further in Chapter 18.

Garbage Collection

Recall that when the managed heap becomes fragmented, objects must be moved around to create larger contiguous blocks of memory in a process called *garbage collection*. As will be discussed further in Chapter 20, specific instances of reference types may be excluded from garbage collection by a process known as *pinning*, but this can have negative performance implications.

Let me reiterate: In-use memory is moved. This means that if you have a reference type in your program, it may be moved without your knowledge.

When you use a reference type, it is made of two parts: the data itself, which is allocated on the managed heap, and a handle to the data, which is allocated on the stack. I'll explain the stack in detail later in this chapter, but for now, suffice it to say that the stack does not move in the same way.

When garbage collection is performed, the data in the managed heap is moved to make larger contiguous blocks free for allocation, and at the same time, any handles that point to this data must continue to point to this data after garbage collection is complete. If you like, you can think of handles as pointers, and visualize the pointers to the instances of data on the managed heap being updated each time the data is moved. It does not matter how this is actually implemented within the CLR, but if the garbage collection mechanism is working correctly, your handles will continue to track your data after garbage collection is complete.

Initialization

As I mentioned previously, C# hides the implementation differences between reference types and value types. Consider the following C# example:

```
struct V
{
}
class R
{
    static public void Main()
    {
        V v = new V();
        R r = new R();
    }
}
```

In this example, we have a simple value type V and a reference type R. The procedure Main() is a public static function that allocates a V as well as an R. When you compile this example code and examine the resulting executable using ildasm.exe, you find the following CIL within the Main() method:

```
.method public hidebysig static void  Main() cil managed
{
  .entrypoint
  // Code size       16 (0x10)
  .maxstack  1
  .locals init (valuetype V V_0, class R V_1)
```

```
  IL_0000:  nop
  IL_0001:  ldloca.s   V_0
  IL_0003:  initobj      V
  IL_0009:  newobj     instance void R::.ctor()
  IL_000e:  stloc.1
  IL_000f:  ret
} // end of method R::Main
```

As you can see from the CIL, the value type V is initialized with the initobj instruction, which initializes V on the stack. initobj is used to initialize a value type when there is no constructor. The reference type R is initialized by the newobj instruction, which calls R's constructor, allocates R's data on the managed heap, and returns a handle to this data. These are extremely different operations.

The C++/CLI equivalent

Let's look at the equivalent code in C++/CLI:

```
value class V
{
}
ref class R
{
    static public void Main()
    {
        V v = V();
        R^ r = gcnew R();
    }
}
```

As you can see, gcnew is not used when v is allocated, which makes sense, because we don't want to allocate v on the managed heap. It is allocated on the stack, and the C++/CLI code reflects that. The CIL also reflects this, as it uses initobj rather than newobj to instantiate v. Granted, gcnew could have been used to allocate an instance of V on the managed heap. This operation is called *boxing*. We discuss boxing later in this chapter. For the sake of this example, we want to allocate it on the stack.

■**Note** If you use .NET Reflector on the example, you find it easy to switch between viewing a method as C#, C++/CLI, or CIL.

We can see from this simple example that where C# attempts to hide the implementation from the user to ease programming, C++/CLI remains loyal to the implementation and maps directly to the CIL.

Uninitialized Declarations

C# has declaration syntax for uninitialized value types but requires them to be initialized before they can be used. Consider the following C# code:

```
struct V
{
    public int i;
}
class R
{
    static public void Main()
    {
        V v;
        System.Console.WriteLine(v.i);
    }
}
```

If you attempt to compile this, you get the following error:

```
h.cs(10,34): error CS0170: Use of possibly unassigned field 'i'
```

C# blocks you from using uninitialized memory. Similar syntax in C++/CLI produces different results:

```
private value class V
{
public:
    int i;
};
private ref class R
{
public:
    static void Main()
    {
        V v;
        System::Console::WriteLine(v.i);
    }
};
```

This seemingly similar code compiles and runs without error and produces the following result:

```
0
```

Let's pass it through .NET Reflector to look at Main() and figure out what code the C++/CLI compiler generates. Figure 6-1 shows .NET Reflector's view of the code.

```
public:
static void Main()
{
    V v1 = V();
    Console::WriteLine(v1.i);
}
```

Figure 6-1. *.NET Reflector's view of the translation of an uninitialized declaration to C++/CLI*

As you can see from the figure, C++ does in fact initialize v, and running the program produces 0 as a result of the default initialized value of int being zero.

Initialization Variants

Let's summarize the preceding discussion by using .NET Reflector to analyze the following code:

```
value struct V
{
    V(int i)
    {
    }
};
ref struct R
{
    static public void Main()
    {
        V v1;
        V v2(1);
        V v3 = V(2);
    }
};
```

Figure 6-2 shows what the compilers generate. Note that the variables are renamed in the IL.

C#

C++/CLI

```
public static void Main()          public:
{                                  static void Main()
    V v4 = new V();                {
    V v3 = new V(1);                   V v4 = V();
    V v1 = new V(2);                   V v3 = V(1) ;
    V v2 = v1;                         V v1 = V(2) ;
}                                      V v2 = v1;
                                   }
```

Figure 6-2. *Initialization of value types in C++/CLI*

As you can see from the figure, all variants of V are initialized in some manner by C++.

Fields

Consider the following C# code:

```
using System.Collections;
class R
{
    ArrayList a = new ArrayList();
    static void Main() {}
}
```

If we employ Instant C++ to convert this snippet to C++/CLI, it reports that we have some work to do by hand:

```
//TODO: INSTANT C++ TODO TASK: C++ does not allow initialization
of non-static fields in their declarations:
        ArrayList ^a = gcnew ArrayList();
```

Think for a moment about what this result means. This correct diagnostic is saying that the variable a is a nonstatic field and thus cannot be initialized here. Every nonstatic member belongs to some instance, so this kind of initialization would need to be made for every instantiation of the class. The class R has no instantiation to which this declaration belongs. If it were static, we would share a single ArrayList for all instantiations, but it is not static. One of these objects is allocated for each instantiation of class R. Fields should be initialized in a constructor, but there is no explicit constructor declared for class R. In fact, C# does a bit of sleight of hand here and creates a constructor implicitly to initialize the variable a.

Let's employ .NET Reflector to see the constructor C# generated for this snippet; Figure 6-3 shows the constructor.

```
Disassembler

public R()
{
    this.a = new ArrayList();
}
```

Figure 6-3. *The implicitly generated constructor*

As you can see, a constructor was generated that initializes the variable a. If we now switch to C++/CLI mode, we can view the constructor we need to write in order to convert this snippet, as shown in Figure 6-4.

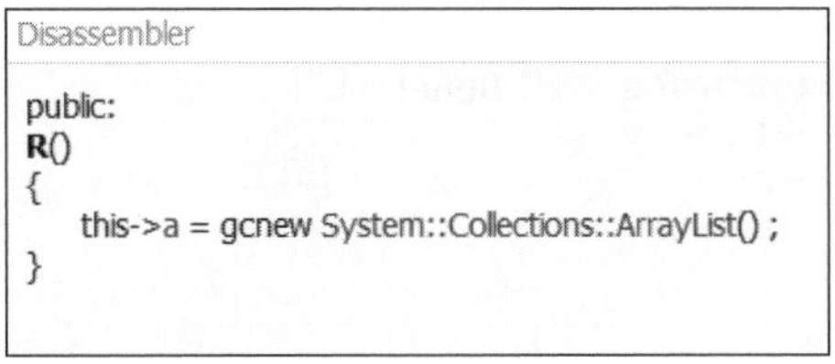

```
Disassembler

public:
R()
{
    this->a = gcnew System::Collections::ArrayList() ;
}
```

Figure 6-4. *The C++/CLI version of the constructor*

Note that this version of the C++/CLI Reflector add-in qualifies ArrayList with the namespace System::Collections. We don't need to use this if we have the using statement in the code, as follows:

```
using namespace System::Collections;
```

We now can use this accumulation of knowledge to craft the conversion of the C# code:

```
using namespace System::Collections;
ref class R
{
    ArrayList ^a;
    static void Main() {}
public:
    R()
    {
        this->a = gcnew ArrayList();
    }
}
```

Multiple Constructors

As you learned previously, we need to move object initialization code into the class's constructor. What happens if the class has more than one constructor? What does C# do?

Consider the following C# snippet:

```
class R
{
    class R1 {}
    R1 rA = new R1();
    R(int i) {}
    R() {}
    static void Main() {}
}
```

In this case, rA needs to be initialized once for each object, and two different constructors are available. See Figure 6-5 to look at these constructors using .NET Reflector.

private:
R(int i)
{
    this->rA = gcnew R::R1() ;
}
	private:
	R()
	{
	    this->rA = gcnew R::R1() ;
	}

Figure 6-5. *Class initialization with multiple constructors*

As you can see from the figure, C# copies the initialization code to both constructors independently.

Static Initialization

Let's now consider a broader example that builds on the previous examples by using both static and normal initializations. Consider the following C# code:

```
class R
{
    class R1
    {
    }
    struct V1
    {
    }
    V1 vA = new V1();
    R1 rA = new R1();
    V1 vB;
    R1 rB;
    static V1 vC = new V1();
    static R1 rC = new R1();
    R()
    {
        vB = new V1();
        rB = new R1();
    }
    static public void Main()
    {
        R r = new R();
    }
}
```

Even though this class already has a constructor, C# still moves initializations around for the CIL to operate correctly. We can employ .NET Reflector to discover which initializations were moved during compilation, which guides us on how to make an equivalent C++/CLI program. Figure 6-6 shows the members of class R as displayed in .NET Reflector.

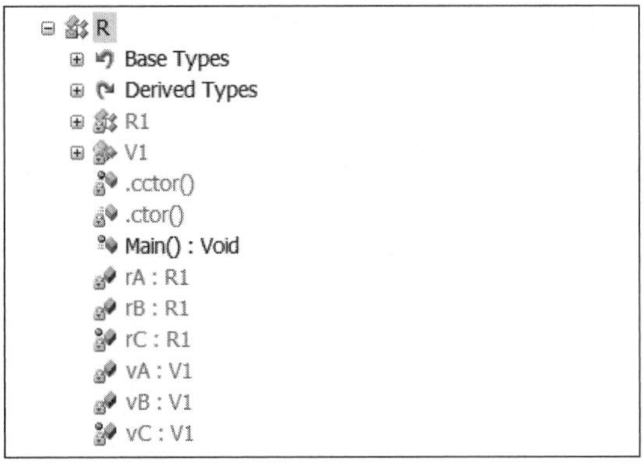

Figure 6-6. *Class R in .NET Reflector*

As you can see, not only does R have a constructor, which is represented as .ctor, it also has a static constructor, which is represented as .cctor.

Static Constructors

A *constructor*, more verbosely called an *instance constructor*, is called each time an instance of a class is created. A *static constructor*, also known as a *class constructor* or a *type initializer*, is called only once, before any instances of the class are created. It is used for one-time initialization of data common to all instances.

Now let's get back to examining the code and peek at the constructor and static constructor. Both of these constructors are relocation targets of the C# compiler. The instance constructor gets all instance initializations, and the static constructor gets all static initializations. First let's examine the constructor shown in Figure 6-7.

```
private:
R()
{
    this->vA = R::V1();
    this->rA = gcnew R::R1() ;
    this->vB = R::V1();
    this->rB = gcnew R::R1() ;
}
```

Figure 6-7. *Class R's constructor*

Similar to what you learned previously, the initializations for vA and rA are moved to the constructor. No surprises there. How about the static constructor shown in Figure 6-8?

```
static R()
{
    R::vC = R::V1();
    R::rC = gcnew R::R1() ;
}
```

Figure 6-8. *Class R's static constructor*

Similar to the move of vA and rA, vC and rC are moved to the static constructor. This makes sense as well, because if regular initializations are moved to the constructor, then static initializations should be moved to the static constructor. C++/CLI moves the static initializations to the static constructor automatically, so we can let the compiler create it implicitly. C++/CLI is able to do this, because there is at most one static constructor in a class, though there may be multiple instance constructors in a class.

Now we can construct the final C++/CLI code and finish this aspect of the topic of initialization:

```
ref class R
{
    ref class R1
    {
    };
    value class V1
    {
    };
    V1 vA;
    R1 ^rA;
    V1 vB;
    R1 ^rB;
    static V1 vC = V1();
    static R1 ^rC = gcnew R1();
    R()
    {
        vA = V1();
        rA = gcnew R1();
        vB = V1();
        rB = gcnew R1();
    }
public:
    static void Main()
    {
        R ^r = gcnew R();
    }
};
```

Alternatively, in C++/CLI, vC and rC could be initialized using an explicit static constructor as follows:

```
private:
    static R()
    {
        vC = V1();
        rC = gcnew R1();
    }
```

The static constructor is executed before any instantiations of the class R are performed. Consider the following application:

```
using namespace System;
ref struct R
{
    static R()
    {
        Console::WriteLine("Static Constructor");
    }
    R()
    {
        Console::WriteLine("Constructor");
    }
};
int main()
{
    R ^r;
    Console::WriteLine("in main()");
    r = gcnew R();
}
```

This program has the following output:

```
Static Constructor
in main()
Constructor
```

This output shows that the static constructor for R was called before any R objects were instantiated.

Boxing

Since there are two major categories of types in .NET, value and reference, it is not surprising that we occasionally need to perform some type of conversion between them.

Oftentimes, we need to pass a value type to a method that requires a reference type. This task is potentially daunting, as value types are stored on the stack, whereas reference types are stored on the managed heap. Java has wrapper classes to solve this kind of problem; the CLR provides boxing.

The process of couching a value type as a reference type is called *boxing*. Boxing returns a System::Object^ that references a copy of the value data and can be used to refer to the data while allocated on the managed heap. Boxing is generally automatic and implicit.

The inverse operation, retrieving the original value type from the boxed object is called *unboxing*. Unlike boxing, unboxing must be done explicitly. This is intuitive, because all value types become a single boxed object, so the CLR knows exactly what to do. On the other hand, given a boxed object, the CLR cannot determine which value type is contained therein without an explicit cast.

Method Boxing

Many CLR methods accept reference types as parameters. For example, `Console::WriteLine()` accepts either a built-in type or a reference type as parameter.

Example of Boxing and Unboxing

Consider the following example of boxing and unboxing. In this sample, we take a value type V, box it into an `Object`, and send it to `Console::WriteLine()` as an `Object`. Next, we unbox it explicitly to a V and send it to `Console::WriteLine()` again, which boxes it implicitly. Therefore, the following example contains both implicit and explicit boxing, as well as explicit unboxing:

```
using namespace System;
value struct V {};
ref struct R
{
    static void Main()
    {
        V v;
        Object ^o = v;
        Console::WriteLine(o);
        v = (V) o;
        Console::WriteLine(v);
    }
};

int main()
{
    R::Main();
}
```

The results of this program follow:

```
V
V
```

Delving into the IL, we can see the CIL boxing operations:

```
.method public hidebysig static void Main() cil managed
{
    // Code Size: 47 byte(s)
    .maxstack 1
    .locals (
            V v1,           //this is ldloc.0
            object obj1)    //this is ldloc.1
```

```
      L_0000: ldnull          // 0
      L_0001: stloc.1         // obj1 = 0
      L_0002: ldloca.s v1     //
      L_0004: initobj V       // v1 = V()
      L_000a: ldloc.0         // get v1
      L_000b: box V           // box it (explicit)
      L_0010: stloc.1         // obj1 = boxed(v1)
      L_0011: ldloc.1         // get obj1
      L_0012: call void [mscorlib]System.Console::WriteLine(object)
      L_0017: ldloc.1         // get obj1
      L_0018: unbox V         // unbox obj1 of type V
      L_001d: ldobj V         // get V
      L_0022: stloc.0         // v1 = unboxed
      L_0023: ldloc.0         // get v1
      L_0024: box V           // box it (implicit)
      L_0029: call void [mscorlib]System.Console::WriteLine(object)
      L_002e: ret
}
```

You don't need to be an expert in CIL to see what is going on here, especially since I have annotated the individual instructions.

Unboxing Dangers

Since unboxing is explicit, there is the danger of a programmer unboxing an object to the wrong type, which generally causes the CLR to throw an exception. Consider the following example:

```
using namespace System;
using namespace System::Collections;
ref struct R
{
    static void Main()
    {
        ArrayList^ a = gcnew ArrayList();
        int i=3;
        double d=4.0;
        a->Add(i);
        a->Add(d);
        for each(int j in a)
        {
            Console::WriteLine(j);
        }
    }
};
void main() { R::Main();}
```

In this example, we implicitly box an int and a double by adding them to an ArrayList(). The for each loop unboxes these values into an int, causing an exception when the double is unboxed. The results to the screen follow:

```
Unhandled Exception: System.InvalidCastException: Specified cast is not valid.
    at R.Main()
    at mainCRTStartup(String[] arguments)
```

Safe Unboxing

In C#, you can fix the preceding code by using the keyword is as follows:

```
using System;
using System.Collections;
class R
{
    public static void Main()
    {
        ArrayList a = new ArrayList();
        int i = 3;
        double d = 4.0;
        a.Add(i);
        a.Add(d);
        foreach(Object o in a)
        {
            if(o is int)
            {
                int i1 = (int)o;
                Console.WriteLine(i1);
            }
            else
            {
                double d1 = (double)o;
                Console.WriteLine(d1);
            }
        }
    }
}
```

In this code, you can see the check to see if the object is a boxed int (o is int). To perform the same trick in C++/CLI, you use dynamic_cast<>() as follows:

```
using namespace System;
using namespace System::Collections;
ref struct R
{
    static void Main()
    {
        ArrayList^ a = gcnew ArrayList();
        int i=3;
        double d=4.0;
        a->Add(i);
        a->Add(d);
        for each(Object ^o in a)
        {
            if(dynamic_cast<int^>(o) != nullptr)
            {
                int i1=(int)o;
                Console::WriteLine(i1);
            }
            else
            {
                double d1=(double)o;
                Console::WriteLine(d1);
            }
        }
    }
};
void main() { R::Main();}
```

The casting operators are revisited in more detail in Chapter 16.

Constructor Forwarding

C# has a special syntax that allows you to defer initialization of objects between constructors. This is called *constructor forwarding*, or delegating constructors, and is not supported in the current version of C++/CLI.[2] Here is a C# example of constructor forwarding:

```
class R
{
    R(int i) {}
    R() : this(0) {}
    public static void Main() {}
}
```

---

2. This feature was recently voted into the C++0x working draft in April 2006, paper N1986.

In this example, the R() constructor forwards construction to the R(int) constructor and continues construction in the R() method. There is no trick to doing this in C++/CLI. Sometimes programmers attempt to get around this by using the following incorrect syntax:

```
ref struct R
{
    R(int i)
    {
    }
    R()
    {
        R(0);
    }
};
void main()
{
    R^ r = gcnew R();
}
```

This code does not work for the following reason: when the R() constructor calls R(0), it does not instruct the compiler to forward construction to the R(int) constructor. Rather, it creates a temporary copy of R, initialized with 0, which is discarded upon exit from the method. Figure 6-9 shows the R() constructor using .NET Reflector.

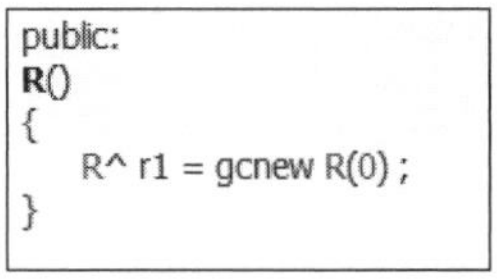

```
public:
R()
{
    R^ r1 = gcnew R(0);
}
```

Figure 6-9. *A failed attempt at constructor forwarding in C++/CLI*

As you can see, the compiler creates a temporary of type R with a 0 as an initialization parameter, which does not accomplish the same thing as C# constructor forwarding. The recommended paradigm in C++ is for each constructor to call a common method.

C# Partial Classes

C# allows the definition of a single class to span multiple files using the partial keyword. C++/CLI has no direct analogue, as it supports a different paradigm. As alluded to previously, C++ allows you to place a class declaration in a single header file and implement the class members in multiple C++ files, but this has nothing to do with the concept of partial classes.

Reference Types on the Stack

A less-often-used feature of C++/CLI is the ability to declare and use a reference type as if it were a stack variable like a value class. This is strictly syntactic sugar and is not needed for standard C++/CLI programming. Even though the memory is still physically allocated on the managed heap, the compiler makes the object observe the semantics of an object allocated on the stack.

Basic Types

Let's look at Table 6-2, which contains the built-in C# types, to see how they map to C++/CLI.

Table 6-2. *Mapping Basic C# Types to C++/CLI*

C#	C++/CLI	Size	Type	Signed	Marshal	Example
sbyte	char	1	SByte	Yes	No	–1, 'A'
byte	unsigned char	1	Byte	No	No	3u, 0xff
short	short	2	Int16	Yes	No	–1
ushort	unsigned short	2	UInt16	No	No	3u
int	int or long	4	Int32	Yes	No	–1l
uint	unsigned int or unsigned long	4	UInt32	No	No	3u, 3ul
long	long long	8	Int64	Yes	No	–1ll
ulong	unsigned long long	8	UInt64	No	No	3ull
single	float	4	Single	Yes	No	4.0f
double	double	8	Double	Yes	No	3.0
string	System::String^	N/A	String	N/A	No	"A"
object	System::Object^	N/A	Object	N/A	No	N/A
decimal	System:Decimal	16	Decimal	Yes	No	N/A
char	wchar_t	2	Char	No	Yes	L'A'
bool	bool	1	Boolean	N/A	Yes	true

Basic Type Differences

One important thing to note is that some of the common C# types have no analogue in C++/CLI or are slightly different in C++/CLI and require some level of marshaling for conversion.

Missing Keywords

The string, object, and decimal keywords in C# have no corresponding built-in type in C++/CLI. Does this mean we can't use these types in C++? Not at all. In fact, since both C# and C++/CLI target the CLI, we can always resort to specifying the CLI target type by name and using that instead.

Marshaling Required

What is marshaling? In general, a *marshaler* is a program that translates or packages data between two programs. A marshaler may be required in a number of circumstances where two programs cannot operate seamlessly on a single instance of data. The C++/CLI types wchar_t and bool have marshaling attributes attached to them in the metadata for proper consumption from C# and other .NET languages. Attributes will be discussed in greater detail in Chapter 20. Until then, let's look at some marshaling attributes in the metadata.

Consider the CIL for the following simple C++/CLI method. Note that Hello() takes a wchar_t as a parameter and returns a bool; both of these types are marshaled:

```
ref class R
{
    bool Hello(wchar_t ch)
    {
        return true;
    }
};
```

Figure 6-10 shows the C# view of the Hello() method using .NET Reflector.

```
[return: MarshalAs(UnmanagedType.U1)]
private bool Hello([MarshalAs(UnmanagedType.U2)] char ch)
{
    return true;
}
```

Figure 6-10. *C# view of Hello()*

As you can see, the MarshalAs(UnmanagedType.U1) return attribute is added to the bool return value, and MarshalAs(UnmanagedType.U2) is added to the char value (which corresponds to the wchar_t).

The UnmanagedType enum is a member of System::Runtime::InteropServices and indicates the kind of data being marshaled. If you look at mscorlib.dll in .NET Reflector and glance at this enum, you discover that U1 is 4 and U2 is 6.

Now let's look at the C++/CLI version of Hello() using .NET Reflector shown in Figure 6-11.

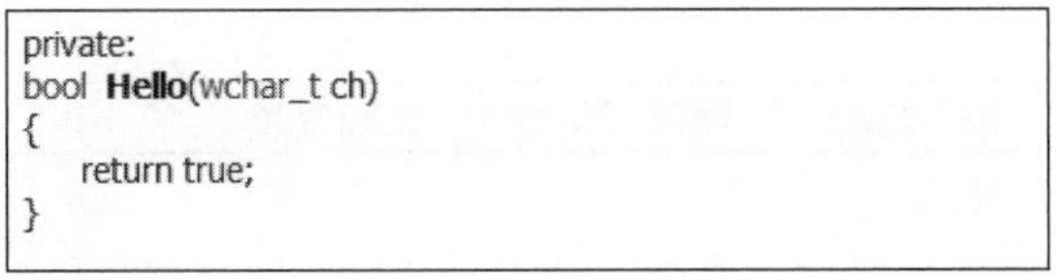

```
private:
bool Hello(wchar_t ch)
{
    return true;
}
```

Figure 6-11. *C++/CLI view of Hello()*

Wait—where has the marshaling gone? Well, when we wrote the C++/CLI add-in, we realized that use of a wchar_t or a bool always emits a MarshalAs attribute, so these attributes are suppressed from the output. On the other hand, if you wanted to communicate something nonstandard, like the following:

```
using namespace System::Runtime::InteropServices;
ref class R
{
    [returnvalue: MarshalAs(UnmanagedType::Bool)]short Hello(wchar_t ch)
    {
        return (short)true;
    }
};
```

then the C++/CLI .NET Reflector add-in would not suppress the marshal attributes, because they differ from the default. We can see this in Figure 6-12.

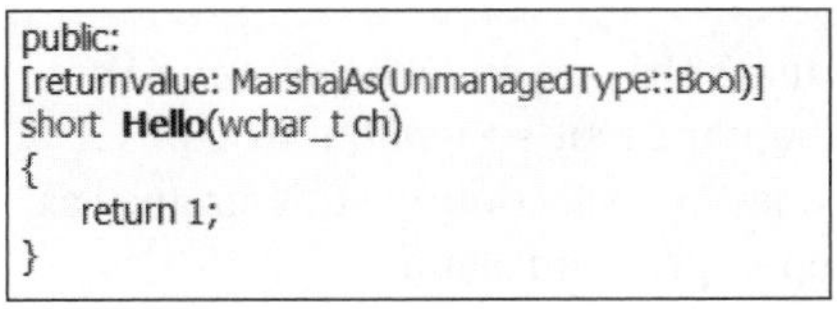

```
public:
[returnvalue: MarshalAs(UnmanagedType::Bool)]
short Hello(wchar_t ch)
{
    return 1;
}
```

Figure 6-12. *C++/CLI Hello() with special marshaling*

As you can see from the screenshot, the special marshaling we have added for our short conversion to unmanaged bool displays clearly in .NET Reflector.

Table 6-3 lists the various strengths and weaknesses of the C++ class types.

Table 6-3. *Feature Limitations by Class Type*

Feature	Native Class	Ref Class	Value Class	Interface
Assignment operator	X	X		
Class modifier	X	X	X	
Copy constructor	X	X		
Delegate definitions	X	X	X	X
Default constructor	X	X		

Continued

Table 6-3. *Continued*

Feature	Native Class	Ref Class	Value Class	Interface
Destructor	X	X		
Events		X	X	X
Finalizer		X		
Function modifiers	X	X	X	X
initonly field		X	X	X
Literal field		X	X	X
Member of delegate type		X	X	
Override specifier	X	X	X	
Parameter arrays	X	X	X	X
Properties		X	X	X
Reserved member names	X	X	X	X
Static constructor		X	X	X
Static operators	X	X	X	X

Summary

That concludes our introduction to classes and class types.

If you didn't understand everything in this chapter, that's OK—*go on to the next one.* You see, the goal of this chapter is not to drill in the details about the type system but to expose you to a little bit more of what is going on behind the scenes. We will continue this strategy as the book unfolds and come back to the important concepts again and again.

Next let's look at that all-important basic data structure, the array.

■■■

Arrays

Give me a place to stand, and I will move the earth.

—Archimedes of Syracuse

In this chapter, we will deal with C++ arrays, beginning with syntactic differences. C++/CLI offers two types of arrays:

- Native arrays that are elements of classic C++

- Managed arrays that are identical to C# arrays, though with different syntax

One of the first things you notice about managed arrays in C++ is that their declarations are completely different, and that's not a bad thing. When two languages are as similar as C# and C++, you can get a false sense of security and end up writing incorrect code that can come back to haunt you. You might use a keyword in C++ that has a different meaning in C#, such as class, and expect it to act the same way. Alternatively, you might have trouble remembering seemingly esoteric syntactic differences, such as whether a semicolon is required after a particular closing curly brace. With managed arrays, this is unlikely to happen, since the C++ declaration syntax is completely different from the C# declaration syntax.

Within C++, native and managed arrays differ in both declaration and implementation. Because of the constraints of extending a well-defined array structure for C++ in a language-compatible fashion, the C++/CLI syntax for managed arrays turned out to be somewhat complex. Never fear though—after a while, the syntax feels quite intuitive.

Native Arrays

A *native array* is always a single buffer in which array elements are arranged contiguously. This is true no matter the rank or dimension. An array is a buffer, and array indices are shortcuts to calculating the offset within this buffer. In other words, every usage of an array in native C++ could be simulated through the use of a single, one-dimensional buffer and a bit of mathematics. Because of this, many authors treat native C++ arrays as if they always have a rank or dimension of one. Higher dimensional native arrays are always rectangular; the number of elements in any given dimension is always a constant.

Oftentimes in native C++, you find programmers accessing buffers using both pointers and arrays, and this can be quite confusing. In addition, accessing C++ array buffers directly through direct calculation and casts may not be type safe.

Managed Arrays

Managed arrays are different. *Managed arrays* are full-fledged .NET citizens descended from System::Array. Multidimensional arrays can either be rectangular or jagged. *Rectangular arrays* have a constant number of elements for each dimension. You can think of them as rectangles or blocks.

Jagged arrays are arrays in which the number of elements of a particular dimension can vary; you can think of a jagged array as an array of arrays, each with its own declaration and definition.

Managed Array Details

Managed arrays are declared using a kind of pseudo-template syntax. You do not need to become an expert on templates to understand how to declare and use managed arrays in C++. The syntax is borrowed from template syntax, but arrays are not templates and cannot be specialized.

To use managed arrays, you need to learn only this particular syntax, either by definition or example (I will be sure to provide a lot of examples).

Managed arrays are declared and defined using the array context-sensitive keyword followed by the type of the array element in angle brackets, followed by the number of elements in the array in parentheses. Rectangular arrays of a rank greater than one can be declared, as well, in a slightly more-sophisticated manner by including the rank inside the angle brackets and the individual definitions within the parentheses. I will describe in detail the declaration, definition, and use of jagged arrays later on in this chapter.

The built-in definition of a managed array looks something like the following:

```
namespace cli
{
    template<typename Type, unsigned int dimension = 1>
    ref class array : System::Array
    {
    public:
        array(unsigned int size);
    };
}
```

A Simple Example

Let's consider an example and wrap it in a function to use it. First let's look at how to declare, allocate, and initialize a simple managed array in C++/CLI.

Declaration

Here's a C# array:

```
int [] a = new int[] {1,2,3,4};
```

The same statement in C++/CLI follows:

```
array<int>^ a = gcnew array<int>(4) {1,2,3,4};
```

Now let's go over this a bit. First of all, consider the following expression:

```
array<int>^ a
```

This expression declares a as a handle, because of the ^ punctuator, to an array of integer type. The number of elements within this array is not part of the declaration of a.

The next part is

```
gcnew array<int>(4)
```

The gcnew keyword is used, because we want to allocate an array on the managed heap. Remember, gcnew is the equivalent of the new keyword in C# for allocations on the managed heap. This statement means "allocate an array of four integers on the managed heap." The new keyword in C++ is used for allocations on the native heap. If you mistakenly use the new keyword in this context, the compiler issues an error like the following:

```
t.cpp(3) : error C2750: 'cli::array<Type>' : cannot use 'new'
on the reference type; use 'gcnew' instead
        with
        [
            Type=int
        ]
```

The last part of the allocation looks like this:

```
{1,2,3,4}
```

In C++ jargon, this is called an *aggregate initialization* and is used to define the elements of the newly allocated array. Aggregate initialization is also supported in the C++ language without gcnew to provide for a less-verbose array initialization syntax:

```
array<int>^ a = {1,2,3,4};
```

Adding Usage

Now let's examine this declaration in the context of a simple, yet illuminating, standalone example. We can declare, allocate, and initialize the array as described previously and use a simple for each loop to display the values of the array on the console. In order to compile this snippet, use the Visual Studio 2005 command prompt, and enter the following code:

```
cl /clr test.cpp
int main()
{
    array<int>^ a = gcnew array<int>(4) {1,2,3,4};
    for each(int i in a)
    {
```

```
            System::Console::Write(i);
        }
        System::Console::WriteLine();
}
```

When executed, this snippet displays the four elements of the array, {1,2,3,4}, as expected:

1234

Arrays as Parameters and Return Values

Similar to C#, in C++/CLI, an array may be passed as a parameter to a method as well as returned from a method as the method's return value.

Passing an Array to a Method

Standard parameter lists are a good example of arrays passed as parameters to a method. When a C# or C++/CLI console application is executed, an array of the command-line arguments is passed to the unique entry point, which is either a class's static Main() method in C# or main() in C++/CLI.

In C#, parameter lists passed to Main() are declared as follows:

```
public static void Main(string [] args) {}
```

This line indicates that Main() takes an array of string type as a parameter. The C++/CLI equivalent looks like the following, using the pseudo-template syntax:

```
public:
static void Main(array<String^>^ args) {}
```

This seemingly completely different statement does the same thing as its C# counterpart. Let's break it down bit by bit.

First of all, string is the C# alias for System::String. Note that String has a capital "S" in this context. This is a reference type, so it requires the ^ punctuator. Let's proceed, assuming we have added

```
using namespace System;
```

to the top of the file, so the System:: prefix is not required to resolve String. Next, we get the C# keyword string mapped to the C++/CLI expression String^.

Continuing to assemble the pseudo-template syntax on the fly, we have array<String^> for the string array, and since args is really a handle to an array allocated on the managed heap, we end up with array<String^>^ args. Now, you might ask how we know that args is a handle and not the array itself. Remember that in C++ handles refer to objects on the managed heap, and .NET arrays are always allocated on the managed heap and never on the stack. Only value types are allocated on the stack, and System::Array is a reference type.

Returning an Array from a Method

Similar to C#, in C++/CLI a method can have an array as a return value. In actuality, the array itself is not being returned; rather, a handle to the array on the managed heap is returned. C++/CLI clearly reflects this. Consider the following C# snippet:

```
static string[] GetStrings()
{
    string[] strings = {"1", "2"};
    return strings;
}
```

The equivalent C++/CLI is constructed as follows:

```
static array<String^>^ GetStrings()
{
    array<String^>^strings = {"1", "2"};
    return strings;
}
```

As you can see, an array is allocated on the managed heap within the GetStrings() function, and a handle to this array is the return value of the method.

Passing a Variable Number of Parameters

In C#, a variable number of parameters may be passed to a method and converted to an array using the params keyword. The C++/CLI equivalent of the params keyword is an ellipsis (. . .). There may be, at most, one parameter array for a method, and it must be the last parameter. The parameter array is declared, similar to C#, using the array type preceded by the parameter array construct, which in C++ is the ellipsis.

Example

Suppose you wanted to write a method that returns the sum of an arbitrary number of integers in C#. You might end up with something like the following:

```
class R
{
    static int Sum(params int [] Arr)
    {
        int r = 0;
        foreach(int i in Arr)
        {
            r+=i;
        }
        return r;
    }
    static void Main()
    {
```

```
        int[] Arr2 = {1,2,3,4,5};
        System.Console.WriteLine(Sum(Arr2));
        System.Console.WriteLine(Sum(1,2,3,4));
    }
}
```

The method Sum() takes an array of integers as its single parameter. It accepts either an array of integers or an arbitrary sequence of integers, which are bundled into an array automatically by the compiler.

In the example, Main() calls Sum() twice. The first time Sum() is called with an explicitly declared and initialized array of integers. The second time Sum() is called using a sequence of integers as arguments, which are bundled into an array by the compiler.

Here is some similar C++/CLI with translated array and params syntax:

```
ref struct R
{
    static int Sum(... array<int> ^Arr)
    {
        int r = 0;
        for each(int i in Arr)
        {
            r+=i;
        }
        return r;
    }
    static void Main()
    {
        array<int> ^Arr2 = {1,2,3,4,5};
        System::Console::WriteLine(Sum(Arr2));
        System::Console::WriteLine(Sum(1,2,3,4));
    }
};
void main() {R::Main();}
```

Note that the params keyword has been changed to the ellipsis, and the array declarations, allocations, and initializations have been converted. The C++ language already supports something similar in native code. The ellipsis was chosen to implement .NET param arrays, because it is a natural extension of the language that feels familiar to the C++ programmer. In native code, a function taking an indeterminate number of variables uses the ellipsis. This function, known as a *vararg function*, looks something like the following:

```
int printf(char *format, ...);
```

The first parameter is used as a placeholder in memory from which to access the rest of the parameters by their offsets. The compiler provides a library of functions to help you extract and use the arguments inside your function body. By contrast, .NET param arrays feel natural and are easy to grasp by the programmer, since all support is built into the language instead of accessed in a library.

Type Safety and Implicit Conversions

C# and C++/CLI parameter arrays are both type safe. If you have a method that accepts a parameter array of integers, it just doesn't make sense to pass it an element of type System::String. In this case, you get a diagnostic. But what about other conversions that are not so obvious, like passing a 3.0f float instead of an integer 3? Suppose we have the following C# program:

```
class R
{
    static void Test(params int [] Arr)
    {
        foreach(int i in Arr)
        {
            System.Console.WriteLine(i);
        }
    }
    static void Main()
    {
        Test(1, 2, 3, 4.2f);
    }
}
```

Here we attempt to assemble an array of integer type using a floating point number. If you try to compile this with the C# compiler, you see the following diagnostic:

```
Microsoft (R) Visual C# 2005 Compiler version 8.00.50727.42
for Microsoft (R) Windows (R) 2005 Framework version 2.0.50727
Copyright (C) Microsoft Corporation 2001-2005. All rights reserved.

t.cs(12,9): error CS1502: The best overloaded method match
for 'R.Test(params int[])' has some invalid arguments
t.cs(12,23): error CS1503: Argument '4': cannot convert from 'float' to 'int'
```

As you can see, the compiler recognizes that 4.2f is not an integer and issues a diagnostic. Let's look at the translated example in C++/CLI:

```
void Test(... array<int> ^Arr)
{
    for each(int i in Arr)
    {
        System::Console::WriteLine(i);
    }
}
void main()
{
    Test(1,2, 3, 4.2f);
}
```

Now let's attempt to compile it, though we probably do not expect this to succeed:

```
C:\>cl /clr:pure t.cpp
Microsoft (R) C/C++ Optimizing Compiler Version 14.00.50727.42
for Microsoft (R) .NET Framework version 2.00.50727.42
Copyright (C) Microsoft Corporation.  All rights reserved.

t.cpp
Microsoft (R) Incremental Linker Version 8.00.50727.42
Copyright (C) Microsoft Corporation.  All rights reserved.

/out:t.exe
/clrimagetype:pure
t.obj
```

We are surprised again! It turns out that C#'s rules for implicit conversions are stricter than those of C++/CLI. C++ allows an automatic conversion from float to int, because this was allowed in C, and C++ is an extension of C.

If we attempt to execute the program now, we see the results:

```
C:\>t
1
2
3
4
```

The float 4.2f was truncated to 4 without a diagnostic. This seems to be a bit of a bad thing, so Microsoft Visual C++ added a level-two diagnostic to warn you about conversions which can truncate data.

■**Note** Warnings are enabled using the /W{n} command-line option, where n varies from 0 (no warnings) to 4 (strict warnings). The default in the compiler is n=1, although projects created using the Visual C++ IDE get a warning level of n=3.

If you now recompile at warning level 2, you see the following:

```
C:\>cl /clr:pure /W2 t.cpp
Microsoft (R) C/C++ Optimizing Compiler Version 14.00.50727.42
for Microsoft (R) .NET Framework version 2.00.50727.42
Copyright (C) Microsoft Corporation.  All rights reserved.

t.cpp
t.cpp(10) : warning C4244: 'argument' : conversion from
'float' to 'int', possible loss of data
Microsoft (R) Incremental Linker Version 8.00.50727.42
Copyright (C) Microsoft Corporation.  All rights reserved.

/out:t.exe
/clrimagetype:pure
t.obj
```

This gives you the diagnostic you need.

The complete list of automatic conversions and their priorities are listed in detail in the C++ standard.[1] In general, it's a good idea for your code to compile cleanly at level 3. Level 4 warnings, the highest level of warnings generated by the compiler, are often spurious and can be taken on advisement. Still, it is worthwhile to compile your code at level 4 at least once before every release and be able to justify any warnings that you choose to ignore.

Summary

Parameter arrays are type safe, but we always have to be on the lookout for conversions, especially the kind where data might be lost, as C#'s conversion rules are more strict than C++'s conversion rules. We'll revisit conversions in Chapter 11.

Sophisticated Example

Here's a more sophisticated example of the usage of managed arrays in C++/CLI. In this case, we're trying to answer a common algorithm question: given a sequence, how can you find the subsequence with the largest sum?

This is an ideal place to use parameter arrays, because we would like to call the method with several different examples, each with an arbitrarily long sequence.

At first glance, you might imagine yourself making many passes over the same array, starting at a different index to discover the largest partial sum. It turns out that an efficient one-pass algorithm exists; the insight you need to find it is to realize that once a partial sum becomes negative, it cannot make any sum going forward larger, so there's no reason to continue adding to this sum. Many people go wrong with this question, because they either don't realize the one-pass nature of the problem or don't deal effectively with the special case when all of the numbers are negative.

---

1. Standard conversions are covered in chapter 4 of the C++ standard, ISO/IEC 14882:2003(E).

I won't go into the following program line by line, as it is short enough to be an excellent study piece and serve as an example of C++/CLI arrays in action:

```cpp
using namespace System;
void  MaxSubSequence(...array<int>^Sequence)
{
    int MaxStart, MaxEnd, MaxSum, Sum, Start;
    for each(int j in Sequence)
    {
        Console::Write("{0} ", j);
    }
    MaxSum = Int32::MinValue;
    Start = 0;
    Sum = 0;
    for(int i=0; i<Sequence->Length; i++)
    {
        // don't carry negative sums forward
        if(Sum<0)
        {
            Sum = 0;
            Start = i;
        }
        Sum += Sequence[i];
        // is our new sum better?
        if(Sum > MaxSum)
        {
            MaxSum = Sum;
            MaxStart = Start;
            MaxEnd = i;
        }
    }
    Console::Write(" has subsequence: ");
    for(int j=MaxStart; j<= MaxEnd; j++)
    {
        Console::Write("{0} ", Sequence[j]);
    }
    Console::WriteLine();
}

int main()
{
    MaxSubSequence(1,1,-1,-4,5,-3,6,7,-17,3,5,-2,8);
    MaxSubSequence(1,1,-1,-4,5,2,6,7);
    MaxSubSequence(-5,1,-3,-4);
    MaxSubSequence(-5,-2,-3,-4);
    MaxSubSequence(-5,1,1,1,-1,-3,1,1);
    MaxSubSequence(-10,2,3,-2,0,5,-15);
}
```

Let's give it a try:

```
1 1 -1 -4 5 -3 6 7 -17 3 5 -2 8  has subsequence: 5 -3 6 7
1 1 -1 -4 5 2 6 7  has subsequence: 5 2 6 7
-5 1 -3 -4  has subsequence: 1
-5 -2 -3 -4  has subsequence: -2
-5 1 1 1 -1 -3 1 1  has subsequence: 1 1 1
-10 2 3 -2 0 5 -15  has subsequence: 2 3 -2 0 5
```

And that's correct.

Higher Dimensional Arrays

Both C# and C++/CLI allow the allocation and initialization of multidimensional managed arrays. As mentioned previously, there are two types of multidimensional arrays:

- *Rectangular arrays*: These are rectangles, or blocks, in which the number of elements per dimension is constant.

- *Jagged arrays*: These are arrays of arrays. Each subarray has a different dimension, although the type of each subarray must be identical.

Basics

A short C# program follows that shows rectangular and jagged arrays in action:

```
using System;
class R
{
    static void Main()
    {
        int[,] Rect = new int[3,4];
        for(int i=0; i<3; i++)
        {
            for (int j=0;j<4;j++)
            {
                Rect[i,j]=i+j;
            }
        }
        int [][] Jagged = new int[3][];
        for(int i=0; i<3; i++)
        {
            Jagged[i] = new int[i+1];
            for(int j=0; j<i+1; j++)
            {
                Jagged[i][j]=i+j;
```

```
                }
            }
        }
}
```

The first array, Rect, is a 3×4 rectangular array of 12 elements. It is declared with the following syntax:

```
int[,] Rect = new int[3,4];
```

The C++/CLI equivalent, using pseudo-template syntax follows:

```
array<int, 2>^ Rect = gcnew array<int, 2>(3, 4);
```

This line says that we are allocating a two-dimensional array of integer type. The second array is jagged and contains three arrays of varied length. It is declared with the following syntax:

```
int [][] Jagged = new int[3][];
```

The C++/CLI equivalent, using the pseudo-template syntax, follows:

```
array<array<int>^>^ Jagged = gcnew array<array<int>^>(3);
```

The C++/CLI code says that Jagged is a reference to an array of references to arrays of integer type. Here is the entire snippet in equivalent C++/CLI; note that the usage of array elements is identical:

```
using namespace System;
ref struct R
{
    static void Main()
    {
        array<int, 2> ^Rect = gcnew array<int, 2>(3,4);
        for(int i=0; i<3; i++)
        {
            for (int j=0;j<4;j++)
            {
                Rect[i,j]=i+j;
            }
        }
        array<array<int>^> ^Jagged = gcnew array<array<int>^>(3);
        for(int i=0; i<3; i++)
        {
            Jagged[i] = gcnew array<int>(i+1);
            for(int j=0; j<i+1; j++)
            {
                Jagged[i][j]=i+j;
```

```
        }
      }
    }
};
void main() {R::Main();}
```

Differences

One of the major differences between rectangular arrays and jagged arrays is the ability to isolate a single row of the array. For example, suppose Rect and Jagged are defined as in the previous example. What happens if we attempt to use the following syntax to recall the length of the first row?

```
int k = Rect[0]->Length;
```

The compiler issues the following diagnostic:

```
t.cpp(23) : error C3262: invalid array indexing: 1 dimension(s)
 specified for 2-dimensional 'cli::array<Type,dimension>^'
        with
        [
            Type=int,
            dimension=2
        ]
t.cpp(23) : error C2227: left of '->Length' must point to
 class/struct/union/generic type
            type is 'int'
```

This correct diagnostic is attempting to say that Rect requires two indices rather than one, and that Rect[0]->Length doesn't resolve to anything (because it is not a subarray). On the other hand, the following code

```
int k = Jagged[0]->Length;
```

is perfectly valid and results in k=1. Jagged[i] is an array in its own right. In fact, we could even pass it as an argument to the MaxSubSequence() method defined previously, as follows:

```
MaxSubSequence(Jagged[0]);
```

Real World Example of a Jagged Array

People tend to have more trouble visualizing uses for jagged arrays in our structured and organized world. As an example, though, students each have some kind of recorded information for each homework assignment and test, whether that information is a grade or just an indication that the test was not taken, but different classes have different numbers of students, and students have taken different numbers of classes. Jagged arrays are ideal for representing data structures where the number of elements of a subitem varies from item to item.

Suppose we were keeping track of major works by renowned painters. There is often little correlation between the number of surviving paintings by an artist and the influence of the artist. Michelangelo only has one surviving easel painting, but attempts to dismiss his influence would certainly be misguided.

Consider the following example of jagged arrays:

```cpp
using namespace System;
ref struct Painting
{
    String ^artist;
    String ^name;
    int date;
    Painting(String ^artist, String ^name, int date)
    {
        this->artist = artist;
        this->name = name;
        this->date = date;
    }
    virtual String ^ToString() override
    {
        return String::Format("{0} ({1})", name, date);
    }
};
ref struct R
{
    static void Main()
    {
        array<array<Painting^>^>^ ^Painters =
        {
            {
                gcnew Painting("Leonardo da Vinci", "Mona Lisa", 1505)
            },
            {
                gcnew Painting("Marc Chagall", "I and the Village", 1911),
                gcnew Painting("Marc Chagall", "La Mariee", 1927)
            }
        };
        for each(array<Painting^>^ painter in Painters)
        {
            Console::WriteLine("Paintings by {0}", painter[0]->artist);
            for each(Painting ^painting in painter)
            {
                Console::WriteLine("    {0}",painting);
            }
        }
    }
};
void main() {R::Main();}
```

In this example, we create a jagged array of Painters. Each element of Painters is a sub-array of Painting by the corresponding painter, and their lengths differ.

If we compile and execute this, we see the following:

```
C:\>cl /nologo /clr:pure test.cpp
test.cpp
C:\>test
Paintings by Leonardo da Vinci
    Mona Lisa (1505)
Paintings by Marc Chagall
    I and the Village (1911)
    La Mariee (1927)
```

Summary of Managed Arrays of Higher Dimensions

Rectangular arrays are blocks of the defined type that are allocated, defined, and accessed as such. Jagged arrays are arrays of arrays, and reflect this as well.

Native Arrays

Native arrays may also be used in C++/CLI, but it is best to discuss the use of native arrays within the context of pointers and other native structures in Chapters 9 and 18.

Summary

It's all about how you handle your data—that's the key to programming. By now, you should be feeling pretty confident with built-in types and arrays. Stay tuned for queues, trees, and more. The list goes on and on!

In the next chapter, we'll begin to delve into the object-oriented features of C++ in the context of polymorphism and protection.

CHAPTER 8

■ ■ ■

Polymorphism and Protection

We have met the enemy and he is us.

—Walt Kelly (Pogo)

Both C# and C++ are object-oriented languages, which means that both languages support the creation of objects that encapsulate not only data but associated methods or operations on that data. Both languages also provide mechanisms to relate different objects to one other, ranging from operator overloading to inheritance, interfaces, and parametric polymorphism. Both languages provide mechanisms to restrict and control the access to data, ranging from limitations on accessibility and visibility to canning and filtering data using properties.

In this chapter, we will discuss some of these mechanisms, insofar as they differ from those of C#.

Polymorphism

Polymorphism, from the Greek *poly morphos*, meaning "many shapes," is common jargon in many of the sciences and is rapidly moving into the vernacular. In object-oriented programming, polymorphism refers to the way objects can be grouped and classified, so that an object may either be treated as a different object, a member of a group of objects, or accessed in terms of defined characteristics. The following list highlights some important concepts in polymorphism:

Inheritance: "Inheritance" refers to treating objects as different objects. This is done by allowing an object, or class in general terms, to draw data and characteristics from other classes, called *base classes*. For example, a `GoldenRetriever` object might have a base class of `Dog`. In this case, `GoldenRetriever` objects can be treated as if they are `Dog` objects, because they are.

Interfaces: "Interfaces" refers to considering objects in terms of their characteristics; interfaces allow you to organize objects according to what they can do rather than what they are. For example, `Car` and `Dog` objects can both make noise. It is often much simpler to represent that both of these objects support the `MakeNoise` interface rather than making them both inherit from a common `NoiseMaker` base class. Inheriting from the `NoiseMaker` class would be problematic, as not all animals speak but many do. For example, giraffes have no vocal chords, but rabbits squeak and growl; cars are required by law to have horns, but the horns may be broken.

Generics: Treating objects as groups of objects (in CLI) is done via parametric polymorphism, or generics. In this case, Kennel<Animal> could represent an Animal within a Kennel. Specializations of the behavior of individual Animals within a Kennel can be accomplished using constraints. Generics work best with types that are opaque to the generic class and types that implement multiple interfaces that the generic class supports.

Templates: "Templates" refers to treating objects as groups of objects (in C++ only). Templates are similar to generics in that they allow code to be written for a group of objects, but they also allow object-specific code or specializations (both full and partial) to deal with differences between objects. Templates are generally more powerful and more complex than generics.

Inheritance

Inheritance is a common subject in elementary C# books. Consistent with the goals of this text, in this section, I try to focus on the differences between inheritance in C# and inheritance in C++.

In general, C# implements the CLI inheritance model. C++ implements this model too, but it builds on and extends it in several ways. Some of these extensions are supported on the CLI and compile in safe or pure modes. Others are beyond the CLI and must be implemented using native C++.

Multiple and Virtual Inheritance

In C#, each class can only inherit from a single base class. C++ supports *multiple inheritance*, which means that a class can have more than one base class. Multiple inheritance certainly adds a level of complexity that was avoided by the CLI. Let's consider a short example.

Suppose you have a Mule object. Well, a Mule object can be thought of as a Horse as well as a Donkey, right? After all, a Mule is a product of a male Donkey and a female Horse, thus you might have the following valid native C++:

```
class Horse {};
class Donkey {};
class Mule : Horse, Donkey {};
```

In order to compile this, let's use the /c option to indicate that we just want to compile, not create, an executable; that way we skip the overhead of linking, which we do not care about for the purpose of observing the compilation, and avoid the linker error that indicates we have not defined the global function main():

```
cl /c /clr:pure /nologo test.cpp
```

Now we know we can create a Mule object and treat it either as an instance of Horse or Donkey. Here's where things start to get tricky.

Aren't horses and donkeys both animals? Let's add that to the code:

```
class Animal {};
class Horse : Animal {};
class Donkey : Animal {};
class Mule : Horse, Donkey {};
```

In this case, for a given `Mule`, how many instances of `Animal` are created? How many should be created? Perhaps with some object paradigms, you would like to have two common base classes. In this case, there really is only one `Animal` that is the `Mule`, and we'd like to represent this in the code. C++ allows you to define your class hierarchy using both of these paradigms. If we want just a single `Animal`, as we do in this case, we can inherit virtually using the `virtual` keyword. Otherwise, we leave it as is. *Virtual inheritance* tells the compiler to include only one subobject of each type in a class hierarchy. Suppose we want to feed the mule lunch, and `Lunch` consists of an `Apple` object and a `Carrot` object. In this case, the relation between `Lunch` and `Apple` is not an is relationship; rather `Lunch` contains `Apple` and `Carrot`, and they are two pieces of `Food`. In this case, we do not want to use virtual inheritance. Let's look at the completed C++ program:

```
using namespace System;
class Animal
{
public:
    Animal()
    {
        Console::WriteLine("Animal");
    }
};
class Horse : virtual Animal {};
class Donkey : virtual Animal {};
class Mule : Horse, Donkey {};
class Food
{
public:
    Food()
    {
        Console::WriteLine("Food");
    }
};
class Apple : Food {};
class Carrot : Food {};
class Lunch : Apple, Carrot {};
void main()
{
    Mule m;
    Lunch l;
}
```

As you can see, Horse and Donkey both inherit virtually from Animal. Let's try it out:

```
C:\>cl /nologo /clr:pure test.cpp
test.cpp
C:\>test
Animal
Food
Food
```

We accomplished the goal of creating a single animal and serving him two pieces of food.

Private and Protected Inheritance

Unlike C#, access to base classes can be restricted by inheriting via private or protected inheritance. These are discussed in the section titled "Protection Mechanisms."

The CLI and Multiple Inheritance

The CLI allows a type of multiple inheritance using interfaces. Suppose we attempt to use reference types instead of native types for our Food class hierarchy:

```
ref class Food {};
ref class Apple : Food {};
ref class Carrot : Food {};
ref class Lunch : Apple, Carrot {};
```

Let's compile this code:

```
C:\>cl /c /nologo /clr:pure test.cpp
test.cpp
test.cpp(4) : error C2890: 'Lunch' : a ref class can only have one non-interface
base class
        the ref class 'Apple' is a base class of 'Lunch'
        the ref class 'Carrot' is a base class of 'Lunch'
```

Error 2890 states that we cannot do this, and in a way, it's a blessing. Having your objects inherit from multiple objects can make your code hard to understand, and interfaces allow you to do many of the same things without the confusion.

Interfaces

Rather than dealing with an object based on what it is and implying what it does based on that, an interface defines what an object is able to do.

Interfaces Are Specifications

Interfaces embody a specification of what classes must implement to support an interface; think of it as a contract if you will. The only methods that interfaces are allowed to implement are static methods. Interfaces are similar to abstract classes, which are described and distinguished later in this chapter.

A Class May Inherit From Multiple Interfaces

Not only can interfaces be inherited, but a single class may inherit from multiple interfaces in addition to inheriting from a single base class. This allows you to create an object that has several well-defined ways or interfaces in which you can use it but is still clearly ordered within the class hierarchy, because it has a single, unique base class. This paradigm works well for the vast majority of object-oriented applications.

Interfaces May Inherit From Other Interfaces

Because interfaces may inherit from other interfaces, objects can define a basic contract for communicating with an object. This also allows for the possibility of a more elaborate level of communication if the object supports a more-advanced version of a contract.

A Value Type May Inherit From an Interface

The CLI does not allow value types to inherit from other classes, but it does allow value types to inherit interfaces. Value types, by default, are *sealed classes*, which means that they cannot be inherited and thus cannot be extended. We will revisit sealed classes later in this chapter.

A Simple Example

Let's go back to the animal farm and see what we can do with interfaces. Suppose we want to create objects of types Dog and Cat and say that they can do things like eat and sleep. It seems reasonable to make Eat and Sleep interfaces. We could then use Eat and Sleep as the base classes for Dog and Cat as follows:

```
using namespace System;
interface class Sleeps
{
    void GoToSleep();
};
interface class Eats
{
    void Feed();
};
ref struct Cat : Eats, Sleeps
{
    virtual void GoToSleep()
    {
        Console::WriteLine("Cat is Catnapping");
    }
    virtual void Feed()
    {
        Console::WriteLine("Cat is Eating");
    }
```

```
};
ref struct Dog : Eats, Sleeps
{
    virtual void GoToSleep()
    {
        Console::WriteLine("Dog is Sleeping");
    }
    virtual void Feed()
    {
        Console::WriteLine("Dog is Eating");
    }
};
void main()
{
    Cat ^c = gcnew Cat();
    Dog ^d = gcnew Dog();
    c->Feed();
    c->GoToSleep();
    d->Feed();
    d->GoToSleep();
}
```

■**Note** In C++, types can inherit and restrict access to base class members, which sets their default accessibility. This inheritance can be public, private, or protected. Any C++ struct, interface, or CLI type inherits public by default. Using struct for everything ensures that we don't run into any protection issues. We will revisit inheritance later in this chapter.

Here are a couple of important things to notice about this example:

- C++/CLI uses interface class rather than just interface to declare an interface, similar to its use of enum class instead of enum.

- The use of the virtual keyword is the same as in C#, which allows the derived class to either implement or override methods. In polymorphism jargon, the topmost (base) method is the *implementation*, and derived methods are *overrides*.

This is a pretty basic example, but it's not as simple as we'd like it to be. Since Cat and Dog each support the Eats and Sleeps interfaces, they are each forced to implement the GoToSleep() and Feed() functions. Another inefficiency is that the implementations for Feed() are practically identical between the two animals.

A logical solution would be to create an Animal class that could contain the default behaviors for each of these interfaces. Dog and Cat could then inherit from Animal. But what is to prevent someone from instantiating an Animal? We never want that to happen; we only want to be able to instantiate Dog and Cat. The next section on abstract classes will help.

Abstract Classes

An *abstract class* is a class that cannot be instantiated. Interfaces answer the question, "Does this class do this?" Abstract classes answer the question, "Is this class a kind of that?" Abstract classes are used quite often; some examples follow:

- Use an abstract class when creating a class that has default behavior for interfaces but should never be instantiated. Our Animal example fits into this category.

- Use an abstract class when creating a class that, by its nature, is never instantiated, because it is made up of a collection of static methods. System::Console is this type of class and contains static methods such as Write() and WriteLine(). Don't bother to even try to instantiate an object of type Console—you won't be able to.

Let's make Animal an abstract class and outfit it with default methods for the interfaces. We can also apply a small trick. Let's use ToString() to get the name of the animal, so we don't have to hard code it into the routine. Here is the new code:

```
using namespace System;
interface class Sleeps
{
    void GoToSleep();
};
interface class Eats
{
    void Feed();
};
ref struct Animal abstract: Eats, Sleeps
{
    virtual void GoToSleep()
    {
        Console::WriteLine("{0} is Sleeping", ToString());
    }
    virtual void Feed()
    {
        Console::WriteLine("{0} is Eating", ToString());
    }
};
ref struct Cat : Animal
{
    virtual void GoToSleep() override
    {
        Console::WriteLine("{0} is Catnapping", ToString());
    }
};
ref struct Dog : Animal
{
};
void main()
```

```
{
    Cat ^c = gcnew Cat();
    Dog ^d = gcnew Dog();
    c->Feed();
    c->GoToSleep();
    d->Feed();
    d->GoToSleep();
}
```

This code is vastly improved and much easier to maintain. The abstract keyword after the class name Animal indicates that Animal is an abstract class. Dog contains no methods at all and uses the default Animal behavior for all interfaces. Cat contains only the method that needs to be different and uses the default behavior for Eats::Feed(). Since the GoToSleep() function already existed in Animal, we are forced to add the keyword override to indicate how we want to replace this method. The keyword new is also a possibility; we discuss this later in the chapter.

Just one thing is disturbing about the example as it relates to our previous discussion of System::Console. In the example, we are not able to instantiate an object of type Animal, but we are able to derive a class Dog from Animal and instantiate it, and Dog uses all of Animal's methods. In a way, Dog is a clone of Animal that is not abstract. This seems like a backdoor method of instantiating a System::Console, and we don't want to allow that—if only there was a way to indicate that a class cannot serve as a base class for any other classes. Your wish is my command.

Sealed Classes

Recall that a sealed class is a class that cannot be extended through inheritance. For example, let's see what happens when you have a sealed class named Base, and you try to derive from it:

```
class Base sealed {};
class Derived : Base {};
```

Now let's compile it:

```
C:\>cl /clr:pure /nologo test.cpp
test.cpp
test.cpp(2) : error C3246: 'Derived' : cannot inherit from 'Base' as it has been
declared as 'sealed'
        test.cpp(1) : see declaration of 'Base'
```

Just as we expected; it cannot be extended, because it's a sealed class. Now let's see what happens when you declare a class as both abstract and sealed.

Static Classes

Let's use .NET Reflector to peek in mscorlib.dll, and look up the declaration of System::Console:

```
public ref class Console abstract sealed
{
};
```

Declaring a class as both abstract and sealed further limits the class. It only is allowed to have static members, nested types, literal fields, and typedefs. The C# equivalent for abstract sealed classes is to define a static class. If you switch the view in .NET Reflector to C#, you see the following:

```
public static class Console
```

Declaring Console as both abstract and sealed, or as static in C#, allows it to be the container for static methods, and it can be neither instantiated nor derived from. It is interesting to note that this can be achieved in C++ by just using a namespace to scope and contain a group of global functions. Of course, you might be thinking, "But can global functions be exported outside the assembly?" You are right to wonder; the answer is that they cannot. When used in a class, the keyword static in the C# language is just syntactic sugar. If you look at the CIL in .NET Reflector, you see the abstract and sealed descriptors in the metadata. These are analogous to the C++ language's context-sensitive keywords, so if you plan to export your contained group of functions from a C++ assembly, don't use a namespace; just use an abstract sealed class. C++ is a language of flexibility, giving you the freedom to achieve your goals in different ways, depending on your requirements, which in this case is the encapsulation level of your group of functions.

Methods

Methods in the base and derived classes commonly have the same name and perform the same function. In the previous example, we have a method GoToSleep(), which is implemented in the base class and reimplemented in the derived class. If you create an instance of the derived class and you treat it like a derived class, it almost goes without saying that you would prefer to use the derived version of the method. But what happens when you treat the derived class as an instance of the base class? This is quite common in object-oriented programming; for example, you might want to create a Menagerie from a collection of Animal. How can you tell the compiler which implementation of the common method to use?

Virtual Methods

In short, a *virtual method* is a base class method that can be changed by a derived class's implementation. If a method is not marked as virtual, treating the derived class as an instance of the base class revives the base class implementation.

The use of virtual methods gives you the ability to choose whether an implementation of a method in a derived class replaces the implementation in the base class. In both C# and C++, you can create virtual methods. There are few differences beyond syntax between virtual methods in C# and C++, but I would like to review this topic here, as it seems to be either glossed over or not explained sufficiently in many texts.

Let's consider a somewhat contrived example, just for entertainment.

Example of Virtual and Nonvirtual Methods

Animal is a base class, and John is a derived class. John is a normal human, and when you ask him to say hello, he says, "Hello." On the other hand, if you treat John like an Animal, he is reduced to the level of an animal and can only mutter "ugh." He's still John no matter how you treat him, and his name does not change:

```
using namespace System;
ref struct Animal
{
    virtual String ^ Name()
    {
        return "Animal";
    }
    String ^Hello()
    {
        return "ugh";
    }
};
ref struct John : Animal
{
    virtual String ^ Name() override
    {
        return "John";
    }
    String ^Hello()
    {
        return "Hello";
    }
};
void main()
{
    John ^j = gcnew John();
    Console::WriteLine("{0} says {1}", j->Name(), j->Hello());
    Console::WriteLine("Oh no! He's an Animal! ");
    Animal ^a = j;
    Console::WriteLine("{0} says {1}", a->Name(), a->Hello());
}
```

In this example, we have two methods in each of the base and derived classes: Name() and Hello(). The method Name() is virtual. It is declared in both classes with the virtual keyword, and the keyword override is used in the derived class as well (more on that later). Since it is virtual, John's implementation of Name() replaces that of Animal's for all instances of John.

On the other hand, Hello() is not marked virtual, so when we treat instances of John as John, we see John's implementation of Hello(), and when we treat instances of John as Animal, we see Animal's implementation of Hello(). This gives us the desired result:

```
C:\>cl /clr:pure /nologo test.cpp
C:\>test
John says Hello
Oh no! He's an Animal!
John says ugh
```

In this way, we are able to pick and choose which methods are replaced in the base by the implementation of the method in the derived class.

Working with Methods

C++/CLI has several ways of overriding virtual methods. Each of these was created with a specific paradigm in mind. I'd like to go over some of the paradigms and reveal the motivation where appropriate. This allows us to see how the implementation affects the required syntax and how the compiler helps us do the right thing and issues diagnostics when potentially dangerous situations occur.

Nonvirtual Methods in Base and Derived Classes

In this case, we have a plain vanilla method in both the base and derived classes. We followed this paradigm before with the Hello() method in both John and Animal. The key thing to note here is that, although the derived implementation hides the base implementation when working with an instance of the derived class, the base implementation is revived when the same instance is cast to the base class. In addition, accessing the base method from the derived class is still possible using the Base:: qualification prefix, similar to the way we specify and access a definition inside a namespace:

```
using namespace System;
ref struct Base
{
    void Method()
    {
        Console::WriteLine("Base::Method");
    }
};
ref struct Derived : Base
{
    void Method()
    {
        Console::WriteLine("Derived::Method");
    }
    void MethodBase()
    {
        Base::Method();
    }
};
void main()
```

```
{
    Derived ^d = gcnew Derived();
    Console::Write("from the Derived class: ");
    d->Method();
    Console::Write("from the Derived class: ");
    d->MethodBase();
    Base ^b = d;
    Console::Write("from the Base class: ");
    b->Method();
    Console::Write("from the Base class: ");
    d->Base::Method();
}
```

Let's compile this and give it a try:

```
C:\>cl /clr:pure /nologo test.cpp
C:\>test
from the Derived class: Derived::Method
from the Derived class: Base::Method
from the Base class: Base::Method
from the Base class: Base::Method
```

The output shows clearly that we are able to access both the derived and base methods from the derived class, and the base method from the base class. Is it possible to access the derived method from the base class?

Virtual Methods in Base and Derived Classes

Let's start this subtopic with a similar code sample:

```
using namespace System;
ref struct Base
{
    virtual void Method()
    {
        Console::WriteLine("Base::Method");
    }
};
ref struct Derived : Base
{
    virtual void Method() override
    {
        Console::WriteLine("Derived::Method");
    }
    void MethodBase()
    {
        Base::Method();
```

```
    }
};
void main()
{
    Derived ^d = gcnew Derived();
    Console::Write("from the Derived class: ");
    d->Method();
    Console::Write("from the Derived class: ");
    d->MethodBase();
    Base ^b = d;
    Console::Write("from the Base class: ");
    b->Method();
}
```

This code generates the following output:

```
C:\>cl /clr:pure /nologo test.cpp
C:\>test
from the Derived class: Derived::Method
from the Derived class: Base::Method
from the Base class: Derived::Method
```

Now this output is extraordinary. Changing the method to virtual changed only the third output line; in Base, Method() has been replaced with Derived::Method() for implicit calls. It is still possible to call the original Base::Method() explicitly, as seen in the second line. In fact, the first line of the following code always calls the original Base::Method(), regardless of whether it is found in the base or derived classes, because it fully qualifies the name:

```
void Test()
{
    Base::Method();
    Method();
}
```

The first call, Base::Method(), calls the base class implementation. The second call, Method(), calls either Derived::Method() or Base::Method(), depending on where this method is implemented and whether we are using virtual functions.

Note that the override keyword is added to the declaration of Method() in the derived class.

If you do not include a keyword here, you are greeted with the following diagnostic:

```
C:\>cl /clr:pure /nologo test.cpp
test.cpp
test.cpp(15) : error C4485: 'Derived::Method' : matches base ref class
method 'Base::Method', but is not marked 'new' or
 'override'; 'new' (and 'virtual') is assumed
        test.cpp(4) : see declaration of 'Base::Method'
```

```
Specify 'override' (and 'virtual') to override the ref class virtual method
Specify 'new' (and 'virtual') to hide the ref class virtual method with a
new virtual method
Position for 'new' and 'override' keywords is after method parameter list
```

This diagnostic is fairly complicated, but it pretty much distills to the fact that either the keyword override or the keyword new is required in this context.

The Keywords new and override

To prevent unexpected results when a derived class hides a virtual method from a base class, the compiler requires an explicit keyword, new or override, to indicate how you wish the method to hide the base class method.

The rationale for the override keyword is fairly straightforward, and we've seen its use several times in this chapter. The override keyword is used when you want the base class's implementation to be overridden by the derived class's implementation.

On the other hand, the keyword new is completely different. This keyword is used to say that you are specifying this method to act at as the virtual method for this class as a base class for another class. It effectively begins a new virtual chain and discards the old one.

An example follows:

```cpp
using namespace System;
ref struct Base
{
    virtual void Method()
    {
        Console::WriteLine("Base::Method");
    }
};
ref struct Derived : Base
{
    virtual void Method() new
    {
        Console::WriteLine("Derived::Method");
    }
};
ref struct Derived2 : Derived
{
    virtual void Method() override
    {
        Console::WriteLine("Derived2::Method");
    }
};
void main()
{
    Derived2 ^d2 = gcnew Derived2();
    d2->Method();
    Derived ^d = d2;
```

```
    d->Method();
    Base ^b = d;
    b->Method();
}
```

Let's look at this code sample. It has three classes, Base, Derived, and Derived2. Derived is also a base class for the Derived2 class. When you use an instance of Derived2 and call Method(), you get Derived2's implementation. When you cast this instance to Derived, you get Derived2's implementation as well, since the override keyword is used on Derived2 to override Derived's version of Method(). However, when you further cast to Base, you go beyond the Derived::Method() virtual chain, because the new keyword is used on Derived to say how Method() should be treated with respect to Base. The result is that Base::Method()'s call is used, since Derived2::Method doesn't override Base::Method.

Here is the output, which reflects this:

```
C:\>cl /clr:pure /nologo test.cpp
C:\>test
Derived2::Method
Derived2::Method
Base::Method
```

You might ask, "What possible paradigm would require you to use such a construction?" It seems difficult and unpredictable without a thorough examination of each method's declaration. As it turns out, you don't have to look far to find a reasonable need for this sort of construction.

Suppose you are writing code that uses a third party's base class library. Suppose you are making objects derived from one of the third-party objects, called Component.

As far as you know, Component looks something like the following:

```
ref struct Component
{
};
```

You create your own components that are more complicated, so you derive other subclasses from it. You add a method to it, called Act(), which does not exist (yet) in the base class library. You add a more-advanced version to your advanced component that overrides the base version. You end up with something like the following:

```
ref struct MyBasicComponent : Component
{
    virtual void Act() {}
};
ref struct MyAdvancedComponent : MyBasicComponent
{
    virtual void Act() override {}
};
```

Suppose this works fine over several generations of your code. You have shipped your interface, and others are relying on your routine named Act(). Then, your third party announces that it has upgraded its base class library and fixed several nagging issues. You purchase it and attempt to recompile, and you discover that a version of Act() has been released for the basic component.

You now have the following choices:

- Rename every instance of Act() in your code, so that it doesn't conflict, thereby confounding your customers and breaking their implementations of your interface.

- Override the third party's version of Act(), so that its internal routines call your version of Act(). This is done using the override keyword.

- Ignore the third-party version of Act(), as it either does not do the same thing or replacing the third-party version with yours would be inappropriate. Peaceful coexistence is possible, and you can always call the other version of Act() using Component::Act() or by casting your object to Component. This is done using the new keyword.

The first option is usually unreasonable, but the other two independently justify the need for their respective keywords.

Overriding With Different Method Names

What if the third-party base class library comes out with a new method you want to override, but you have already given a different name in your code?

You could add code to chain to the third-party method, or you could use the named override syntax. The *named override syntax* replaces the keyword override with the qualified name of the method you are replacing and allows you to override the base class's implementation even if it was named differently. Here is how it is used:

```
using namespace System;
ref struct Component
{
    virtual void ActOut()
    {
        Console::WriteLine("Component::ActOut");
    }
};
ref struct MyBasicComponent : Component
{
    virtual void Act() = Component::ActOut
    {
        Console::WriteLine("MyBasicComponent::Act");
    }
};
ref struct MyAdvancedComponent : MyBasicComponent
{
    virtual void Act() override
    {
        Console::WriteLine("MyAdvancedComponent::Act");
```

```
    }
};
void main()
{
    MyAdvancedComponent ^ac = gcnew MyAdvancedComponent();
    ac->Act();
    MyBasicComponent ^bc = ac;
    bc->Act();
    Component ^c = bc;
    c->ActOut();
}
```

As you can see, ActOut() is replaced by Act() in the declaration of
MyBasicComponent::Act().

Let's see what happens when we try to execute this:

```
C:\>cl /clr:pure /nologo test.cpp
C:\>test
MyAdvancedComponent::Act
MyAdvancedComponent::Act
MyAdvancedComponent::Act
```

As you can see, all versions of both Act() and ActOut() are replaced with the most-advanced component's Act() method, declared in MyAdvancedComponent.

Virtual Methods Summary

You should now have a pretty good idea of the possibilities inherent in virtual methods. Using the new and override keywords, it is possible not only to create a virtual chain of methods but to chain the virtual chains themselves, even if the names of the methods differ.

Accessing Base Class Fields and Methods

In C#, when you want to access base class methods and fields, you use the base keyword. Since native classes in C++ support multiple inheritance, such syntax would be either ambiguous or inconsistent for C++/CLI. C++/CLI adopts the C++ syntax and requires you to specify the name of the base class using the full qualification syntax. We did this a little in the previous examples; let's review it more explicitly here.

Consider the following C# sample:

```
using System;
class Base
{
    public int i;
}
class Derived : Base
{
    public new int i;
```

```
    public void Access()
    {
        base.i = 3;
        i=4;
        Console.WriteLine("Base i = {0}, Derived i = {1}",base.i, i);
    }
    public static void Main()
    {
        Derived d = new Derived();
        d.Access();
    }
}
```

Note the following important points:

- The variable i is declared using the keyword new in Derived, the derived class, to indicate that it hides the variable i in Base, the base class. The override keyword is not used in this context.

- The variable i in the base class is accessed from the method Access() using the expression base.i.

Let's compare and contrast the following C++/CLI version:

```
using namespace System;
ref struct Base
{
    int i;
};
ref struct Derived : Base
{
    int i;
    void Access()
    {
        Base::i = 3;
        i=4;
        Console::WriteLine("Base i = {0}, Derived i = {1}",Base::i, i);
    }
    static void Main()
    {
        Derived ^d = gcnew Derived();
        d->Access();
    }
};
void main() {Derived::Main();}
```

The following points are important to note about this code:

- The variable i in Derived does not require the keyword new. It hides the base class version implicitly.

- The variable i in the base class is accessed from the method Access() using the syntax Base::i. Therefore, the name of the base class is named explicitly. This has several advantages with native classes, as it allows you to not only choose between various base classes but to access grandparent classes with ease.

Protection Mechanisms

Like C#, C++ has several protection mechanisms to manage the accessing of data:

- *Visibility*: This mechanism affects whether the top-level types within your assembly may be used by external assemblies.

- *Accessibility*: Accessibility affects whether constructs may access methods and fields within a given type.

- *Restricted inheritance*: This feature, which does not exist in C# or in the CLI object model, allows you to override the accessibility of a native C++ derived type.

Visibility

The visibility of a nonnested class, struct, interface, delegate, or enum determines whether it can be seen outside its parent assembly. The visibility of a class is set by prepending the visibility keyword to the class definition. The default visibility for a nonnested type is private, for example:

```
public ref class R {};      //visible outside the assembly
private ref class S {};      //visible only within the assembly
ref class T {};               //defaults to private visibility
```

Table 8-1 maps the C# visibility keywords to the C++/CLI visibility keywords for top-level types; the name from the System::Reflection::TypeAttributes namespace is included.

Table 8-1. *Visibility Keywords in C# and C++/CLI for Top-Level Types*

Top-Level Types	TypeAttributes	C#	C++/CLI
Visibility limited to the current assembly	NotPublic	internal	private
Visible to external assemblies as well the current assembly	Public	public	public

Table 8-2 maps the C# visibility keywords to the C++/CLI visibility keywords for nested types.

Table 8-2. *Visibility Keywords in C# and C++/CLI for Nested Types*

Nested Types	TypeAttributes	C#	C++/CLI
Public visibility	NestedPublic	public	public:
Private visibility	NestedNotPublic	private	private:
Visible only to methods from types within its assembly	NestedAssembly	internal	internal:
Visible to methods within its own type and subtypes	NestedFamily	protected	protected:
Visible to methods that are within either its own assembly or its own type or subtypes	NestedFamilyOrAssembly	internal protected protected internal	public protected:
Visible to methods that are within its own assembly and within its own type or subtypes	NestedFamilyAndAssembly	N/A	private protected:

A C++/CLI code sample for nested types follows:

```
public ref class publicClass
{
public:
    ref class NestedPublic
    {
    };
private:
    ref class NestedPrivate
    {
    };
internal:
    ref class NestedAssembly
    {
    };
protected:
    ref class NestedFamily
    {
    };
private protected:
    ref class NestedFamilyAndAssembly
    {
    };
public protected:
    ref class NestedFamilyOrAssembly
    {
    };
};
```

Accessibility

Accessibility is often confused with visibility. Visibility determines which types are visible; *accessibility* governs which fields and methods may be accessed within a visible type.

There are several different accessibility indicators; they are constructed with a keyword followed by a colon.

In C#, accessibility is declared for each member. If you do not declare accessibility for a member in C#, the accessibility becomes `private` by default.

In C++, accessibility is modal, and accessibility is set independently of any member. All subsequent members are given the accessibility of the preceding accessibility declaration. If no accessibility is declared within a type in C++, the default becomes `public` for `struct` and `private` for `class`.

In summary, C# accessibility is set for each item, and C++ accessibility is set by an accessibility declaration that affects all further members. C++/CLI accessibility is defined just like nested types (see Table 8-2).

■**Note** `class` has `private` accessibility by default; `struct` has `public` accessibility by default.

Inheritance

In C++, you can also affect accessibility of base class members via inheritance. Public and protected members of the base class may be accessed as if they were members of the derived class. Members of the base class that are private are inaccessible to the derived class no matter how the derived class inherits.

■**Note** CLI types, including reference and value types, always inherit `public`.

You declare how a derived class should inherit by specifying one of the following keywords before the name of the base class:

`public`: Members of the base class that are `public` or `protected` are treated as if they are `public` or `protected` members of the derived class, respectively. Every member of the base class retains its accessibility in the derived class.

`private`: Members of the base class that are `public` or `protected` are treated as if they are `private` members of the derived class. Every member of the base class becomes `private` in the derived class.

`protected`: Members of the base class that are `public` or `protected` are treated as if they are `protected` members of the derived class.

As you can see, inheritance can only reduce the accessibility of a member, never increase it. Allowing greater accessibility in a derived class than in the base class would defeat the purpose of protection and class encapsulation.

A derived `class` inherits `private` by default, and a derived `struct` inherits `public` by default, with the following major caveat: CLI types always inherit `public` by default.

For example, consider the following:

```
ref struct Base
{
    int var;
};
ref class Derived : Base
{
public:
    void Test()
    {
        var = 3;
    }
};
void main()
{
    Derived d;
    d.var = 3;
}
```

In this example, `Derived` inherits publicly from `Base`, since they are both reference types, and reference types always inherit publicly. The member `var` is public in the base class, so it is accessible in the derived class no matter how the derived class inherits. All that is in question is whether it is accessible via the instance variable `d` in the function `main()`.

Let's give it a try:

```
C:\>cl /c /clr:pure /nologo test.cpp
C:\>
```

No diagnostic appears, so we were successful. Now let's attempt to inherit privately with these reference types. Change the following line:

```
ref class Derived : Base
```

to

```
ref class Derived : private Base
```

Now let's try it again:

```
C:\>cl /c /clr:pure /nologo test.cpp
test.cpp(6) : error C3628: 'Derived': managed classes only support public
inheritance
test.cpp(17) : error C2247: 'Base::var' not accessible because 'Derived' uses
'private' to inherit from 'Base'
```

```
test.cpp(3) : see declaration of 'Base::var'
test.cpp(5) : see declaration of 'Derived'
test.cpp(2) : see declaration of 'Base'
```

As you can see, managed (CLI) types always inherit publicly.

Now change the following code:

```
ref struct Base
ref class Derived : private Base
```

to make these types native and remove the private keyword:

```
struct Base
class Derived : Base
```

And let's try it again:

```
C:\>cl /c /clr:pure /nologo test.cpp
test.cpp
test.cpp(17) : error C2247: 'Base::var' not accessible because 'Derived' uses
'private' to inherit from 'Base'
        test.cpp(3) : see declaration of 'Base::var'
        test.cpp(5) : see declaration of 'Derived'
        test.cpp(2) : see declaration of 'Base'
```

In this case, Derived is a class, and a C++ class inherits privately by default.

There are a couple ways to fix this. We can change Derived from a class to a struct, or add the public keyword before the name of the base class. Alternatively, we could cast d to an instance of Base and access the variable in that manner.

Here's a revamped example:

```
struct Base
{
    int var;
};
struct Derived : Base
{
public:
    void Test()
    {
        var = 3;
    }
};
int main()
{
    Derived d;
    static_cast<Base&>(d).var = 4;
    System::Console::WriteLine("{0}", d.var);
}
```

Let's run it:

```
C:\>cl /clr:pure /nologo test.cpp
C:\>test
4
```

In this example, we inherit publicly from Base, since we changed Derived to a struct. In addition, we can also access the base class variable using a cast, as shown in the function main(). We will revisit the case operators in Chapter 16.

Declaring ref struct and ref class

As you have seen, declaring a reference type or value type using the struct keyword instead of the class keyword affects the default accessibility of the type. It does not affect inheritance, because in the CLI object model, all inheritance is public. It also does not affect the visibility of a type.

For example, consider the following short code sample:

```
ref class R
{
    static void Main() {}
};
void main()
{
    R::Main();
}
```

If you try to compile this, you get the following result:

```
C:\>cl /clr:pure /nologo test.cpp
test.cpp(7) : error C3767: 'R::Main': candidate function(s) not accessible
```

Now change R to a ref struct rather than a ref class as follows:

```
ref class R
{
    static void Main() {}
};
```

The program now compiles fine. We can examine the generated metadata and CIL using .NET Reflector (see Figure 8-1).

```
private ref class R
{
    // Methods
    public:
    R()
    {
    }
    public:
    static void Main()
    {
    }
};
```

Figure 8-1. *ref struct R under .NET Reflector*

As you can see from .NET Reflector, type R still has private visibility (`private ref class R`), but the default accessibility is public (see the first `public:` in `//Methods`). Therefore, changing to a `ref struct` affects accessibility but not visibility.

For the purposes of accessibility and visibility, the following code:

```
ref struct R
{
};
```

is equivalent to this:

```
private ref class R
{
public:
};
```

Overload Resolution

One important distinction between visibility and accessibility is that if a method is visible, it is considered for overload resolution even if it is inaccessible. In so doing, it may potentially hide another viable overload. For example, consider the following example:

```
class Base
{
public:
    int f(int i)
    {
        return i;
    }
};
class Derived : public Base
{
};
class Hello : Derived
{
    void test()
    {
```

```
        f(3);
    }
};
```

In this example, f(3) resolves to Base::f(int i). On the other hand, look what happens when we modify Derived to add an inaccessible function:

```
class Derived : public Base
{
private:
    int f(int i)
    {
        return i;
    }
};
```

Now we try to compile it:

```
C:\>cl /clr:pure /nologo test.cpp
test.cpp
test.cpp(21) : error C2248: 'Derived::f' : cannot access private member declared in
class 'Derived'
        test.cpp(12) : see declaration of 'Derived::f'
        test.cpp(9) : see declaration of 'Derived'
```

The potentially accessible method in Base is completely hidden by the inaccessible method in Derived. The work-around is to access Base's method by fully qualifying its name—Base::f(3).

Hide by Name and Hide by Signature

One key difference between method accessibility in C# and C++ is that C# hides by signature, whereas C++ hides by name. The distinction is as follows: If a method in a derived class has the same name as a method in a base class, the base class method is hidden, because C++ implements "hide by name." In C#, the base class method is visible if it has a different signature, meaning it takes a different set of function parameters.

Hide by Signature

Consider the following C# sample:

```
using System;
class Base
{
    public void f(int i)
    {
        Console.WriteLine("Base.f()");
    }
```

```
}
class Derived : Base
{
    public void f(char c)
    {
        Console.WriteLine("Derived.f()");
    }
    static void Main()
    {
        Derived d = new Derived();
        d.f(3);
    }
}
```

When we compile and execute it, we get the following:

```
C:\>csc /nologo test.cs
C:\>test
Base.f()
```

The compiler first gathered the list of viable candidates and then selected the best match given the passed function arguments. In this example, this list of viable candidates included both versions of f(), since they have different signatures; f(int) is the best match. This example shows that C# is "hide by signature," as Base.f and Derived.f have different signatures.

Hide by Name

Let's look at a similar sample using C++/CLI:

```
using namespace System;
ref struct Base
{
public:
    void f(int i)
    {
        Console::WriteLine("Base.f()");
    }
};
ref struct Derived : Base
{
    void f(wchar_t c)
    {
        Console::WriteLine("Derived.f()");
    }
    static void Main()
    {
        Derived ^d = gcnew Derived();
```

```
        d->f(3);
    }
};
void main() { Derived::Main(); }
```

Note that this code is more or less identical, and we could expect to see similar results:

```
C:\>cl /clr:pure /nologo test.cpp
C:\>test
Derived.f()
```

Again, the compiler first gathered the list of viable candidates and then chose the best match given the passed function arguments. In this example, the list of viable candidates included only the derived version of f(), since both the base and derived version of f() have the same name. Then the only remaining candidate is chosen, and an implicit conversion from int to wchar_t is done (wchar_t is C++/CLI's alias for System::Char, which is char in C#). Derived::f() is the only, and thus the best, match available.

As for which design is better, one can make an argument either way. The key thing when converting code from C# to C++ is to watch out for this difference. Automatic translators from C# to C++, and vice versa, cannot easily handle this kind of difference, and the translated code may compile without error, even though the resulting program might produce different results.

Summary

In this chapter, we covered polymorphism and protection to learn about writing clean objected-oriented code. You should now have a good working knowledge of the key type differences between C# and C++. I suggest you use .NET Reflector on the .NET BCLs to explore a little and look at how various common methods are implemented.

In the next chapter, we'll look at coding in C++ from the opposite angle by having a look at pointers and unsafe code.

PART 2

■■■

Details

CHAPTER 9

▪▪▪

Pointers and Unsafe Code

It is not enough that you should understand about applied science in order that your work may increase man's blessings. Concern for the man himself and his fate must always form the chief interest of all technical endeavors; concern for the great unsolved problems of the organization of labor and the distribution of goods in order that the creations of our mind shall be a blessing and not a curse to mankind. Never forget this in the midst of your diagrams and equations.

—Albert Einstein

Since its inception, the use of pointers has been the best and worst of C and ultimately C++ (though many would argue that the esoteric use of C++ templates has given pointers a run for their money). No other feature gives you the power to strip away the veneer of your programming language and get to the core, and no other feature is as prone to generating hidden bugs that can go undetected for years.

The C# View: A Blessing and a Curse

The designers of C# and the .NET Framework have done a lot of work to make the use of pointers unnecessary in day-to-day programming. Most common tasks can now be written as safe, verifiable code. The entire garbage collection system was designed with the obsoletion of pointers in mind. Reference types, implemented as allocated data and a pointer to data in .NET, appear as a single entity in C#. Type safety on handles is also enforced to avoid pointer issues.

Verifiable code is preferable, because it allows the execution system to know the types of all allocated items at all times; it guarantees a common exception handling system for all types; and it provides a leak-free, common-memory, managed-memory allocation system.

Despite all of this, the designers of C# restrained themselves from omitting pointers from C# altogether.

The use of pointers in C# is supported in code that uses the unsafe keyword and is compiled with the /unsafe compiler option. C++, on the other hand, supports pointers as a part of its primary programming model. It's an interesting fact that C# is verifiable by default and requires a keyword or compiler option to compile otherwise, and C++ is not verifiable by default and uses a compiler option to compile verifiable.

Pointers: A Definition and a Caveat

So, what is a pointer anyway? A *pointer* is a data type that contains the address of another data type. It seems fairly harmless, but there is a catch: Suppose you set a pointer to point to an instance of a type. The idea is that you then can refer to the instance using the pointer alone. You can pass this pointer to other methods, and every method is working on what it considers to be a pointer to an instance of the data type; this usually works fine. Things start to go wrong when, perhaps, the data goes out of scope or one of the holders of the pointer changes the data it points to in a way the others do not expect, so rather than pointing to an instance of the data on the stack, it ends up pointing to stack data from a completely different method. Then, a method that uses the pointer isn't really writing to a data instance; it's writing garbage.

The most common way for pointer bugs to occur is when the pointer and data go out of sync; then, the contract between the pointer and data, which says that the pointer points at valid data, is broken. Perhaps the pointer is old, or the data no longer exists, and the pointer points nowhere. Alternatively, the pointer could start off as the only way to access the data, as is common when using new, and the pointer later goes out of scope and access to the data is lost. Without a garbage collection mechanism, this results in an unreferenceable or orphaned data object and a memory leak.

The following presents a war story from a friend as an example.

HOW TO BRING A 5,000,000-FAULT–TOLERANT SERVER TO ITS KNEES BY PAUL CAYLEY

I assume that all folks reading this book either know what memory leaks are, and, perhaps, may have actually caused a few in their day. Memory leaks are commonplace and happen despite the best efforts of bright people. When I heard that Java would bring about the end of memory leaks, I was not sure if I should be ecstatic that one of programming's greatest banes was now a thing of the past or skeptical. "Skeptical" seems to be the correct answer, as trade publications are full of advertisements for tools to eliminate Java memory leaks.

Why are memory leaks so hard to eliminate? There are lots of reasons. I think the biggest one is design-time decisions that are opaque downstream. Memory allocation and deallocation happen at different times and in different places. Architects and designers don't adequately anticipate how their code will be used. Worse yet, some even assume that others will read their documentation and inline comments and correctly understand the cryptic wisdom and caveats contained therein. (Of course, this supposes that programmers document their code, which may or may not be the case.)

Of course, silliness and sloppiness may also play a role. Programmers can just lose track of what they are doing or have done. And because some people write poor code—which may end up linked to your code, call your bits, or even be your bits—memory may be leaked by the byte or by the bucketful! Let's look at some examples.

Remember Microsoft Outlook? The early versions of Outlook leaked about 100KB of memory per hour, just sitting there. So if you were in the habit of turning on your machine and leaving it on for weeks on end, you had to exit and restart Outlook every few days. If you didn't, after about a week, your system would be slow and unpredictable.

Unfortunately, most programmers expect things to work more often than not, and error checking is sometimes incomplete or omitted altogether. Some programs may continue moving forward, piddling bits and generating faults, after `malloc()` returns empty-handed. The steps in this scenario follow:

1. Outlook leaks memory to the point that other programs and/or the OS become starved.

2. Calls to `malloc()` start failing in new and unusual places.

3. Even though memory is freed by exiting Outlook, things are no longer stable.

4. You bring up the Task Manager to kill the lingering Outlook Messaging Application Programming Interface (MAPI) pump, but things are iffy still.

5. You rename `outlook.exe` to `lookout.exe` as a reminder and reboot.

No big deal, you had to reboot your workstation—unless, of course, you are in a terminal server environment where a single box hosts a number of user sessions. Then you have the added fun of a number of instances of Outlook harmoniously working together to leak lots and lots of memory. And when you reboot, everyone has to start over—happy, happy, joy, joy!

Let's look at another scenario of a long-running process—system status monitors. In this scenario, you have a big, fault-tolerant server that supports a mission-critical application. Not only do you pay $500,000 for a box with multiple power supplies, RAID drives, redundant networks, and such, but you even shell out $50,000 for some system monitoring tools. This system is going to run 24×7 into the next decade. Then a service pack for the OS is shipped, and a new code path is exposed. The monitoring application works fine and does not leak any memory. Unfortunately, the OS API that retrieves OS status updates does leak memory, so every time you call through this API, a record set is returned, and 50 bytes or more of memory are lost. In about 3 months, the monitoring software will do its job and reboot the bulletproof, gold-plated server.

In short, memory leaks are evil. Computers are good. But is there ever good without evil?

Valid Targets and Syntax

In C#, pointers may be set to the address of a value type or to another pointer. In addition, pointers may be freely cast to other pointers.

Since objects in the managed heap are moved around by the garbage collector at seemingly arbitrary intervals, .NET languages must restrict pointers to objects on the managed heap. C# pointers are primarily designed to work with pointers or value types, which reside on the stack. C++/CLI and C# both allow you to temporarily fix the location of an object on the managed heap, although they use different syntaxes. Blocking the garbage collection mechanism, even for a short while, might seem risky, but it's quite useful for making calls to native APIs, called InterOp. We will revisit each of these topics in Chapters 19 and 20.

Common Pointer Operators

The C# pointer operators are listed in Table 9-1. All of these operators exist and have the same definition and usage in C++.

Table 9-1. *Common Pointer Operators in C++ and C#*

Operator	Meaning
&	Take the address of a value. This is the address of the operator in C++ nomenclature.
*	Get the value that a pointer or reference points to. This is the dereference operator in C++. When you use it, you are dereferencing a pointer.
->	ptr-> is an alias for (*ptr). ptr-> is the member-access operator. This is a handy shortcut when ptr points at an instance of a C# struct or value type, and you want to access a member of the structure.

Example of Pointer Usage

A few short examples of pointer usage in both C# and C++/CLI follow.

Declare a pointer to an integer:

```
int *ptr;
```

Assign the address of an integer to an integer-pointer:

```
int i;
ptr = &i
```

Assign a value to the original integer by dereferencing the pointer:

```
*ptr = 3;
```

At this point, the integer i is assigned the value of 3. Now let's wrap this functionality in a program and give it a try.

Verifiable Code and Pointer Usage in C#

Since pointer usage is unverifiable, C# limits the usage of pointer operators to blocks marked with the unsafe keyword. In addition, the /unsafe command-line option must be specified when compiling. This can either be done directly from the command line or by checking the appropriate box in the Project Properties dialog box's Build tab in the Visual Studio IDE. For example, look at the following program, called test.cs:

```
class R
{
    static void Main()
    {
        int i;
        unsafe
        {
```

```
            int *ptr = &i;
            *ptr = 3;
        }
        System.Console.WriteLine(i);
    }
}
```

To compile and run this program, do the following; the /nologo option suppresses the copyright message:

```
csc /unsafe /nologo test.cs
test
```

You should receive the following output:

3

As you can see, the /unsafe command option is used to instruct the compiler to accept usages of the unsafe keyword. If you neglect to compile with the /unsafe option, you see the following diagnostic, if the compiler is doing its job:

```
test.cs(12,9): error CS0227: Unsafe code may only appear if compiling with /unsafe
```

Side Effects of Writing Unsafe Code

There are a few interesting side effects of writing unsafe code. Since it is possible to initialize variables indirectly using pointers, the use of unsafe code affects the compiler's ability to detect uninitialized variables. For example, consider the following C# fragment:

```
int i;
System.Console.WriteLine(i);
```

If you compile this in the context of a program, you see the following diagnostic:

```
test.cs(9,29): error CS0165: Use of unassigned local variable 'i'
```

If you wrapped this code in an unsafe block and added a pointer reference as follows:

```
unsafe
{
    int i;
    int *p = &i;
    System.Console.WriteLine(i);
}
```

the compiler compiles this without a diagnostic even though the variable i remains uninitialized.

If you then execute this block, you see the default value for an uninitialized variable:

```
C:\>test
0
```

In this case, it's not a big deal, but you can see how using unsafe blocks and pointers limits the compiler's ability to help you write solid code.

Pointer Usage in C++

C++ pointers are similar to C# pointers, with many of the same restrictions. The base syntax is identical, which is not surprising given the history and evolution of the languages. There are some important differences, all of which attest to the power of C++:

- C++ does not require the use of the unsafe keyword within the source.

- C++ has four compilation options; C# has safe and unsafe.

- C++ allows pointers to arrays.

- C++ allows pointers to native functions.

- C++ allows pointers to members independent of the instance.

- C++ allows you to mix and combine pointers to arrays, pointers to pointers, pointers to members, and pointers to native functions in the same declaration.

Since the goal of this chapter is to introduce pointers and related concepts, let's postpone discussion of the advanced aspects until Chapters 18 and 19. After all, you don't want to spend too much time trying to decode a valid C++ declaration like the following one before you are ready!

```
void (**(*(*p)(int, char))[])(int);
```

Verifiable Code in C++

The /clr switch determines how your C++ code is compiled to target the CLR. It governs how strict the compiler needs be in disallowing constructs such as pointers and nonmanaged types as well as determining whether your code is compiled to run under the CLR in .NET or as a standalone native executable.

Here are the ways you can compile your code in C++:

- /clr:safe produces an IL-only, verifiable output file and can be used with only managed types and managed code.

- /clr:pure produces an IL-only output file (and no native executable code) and can be used with only managed and native types and managed code.

- `/clr` produces a mix of native and IL files. Managed and native types and managed code and native code are allowed.

- `<default>` indicates that no option is specified. The program compiles for native execution.

In addition, two other options are provided for compatibility with Visual C++ 2002 and 2003:

- `/clr:oldSyntax` accepts the managed extensions syntax from Visual C++ 2002 and 2003.

- `/clr:initialAppDomain` indicates the use of the initial AppDomain[1] behavior of Visual C++ 2002.

In general, C# produces verifiable code by default but is able to use pointers and unverifiable code using the `unsafe` keyword or command-line option. C++ expects you to define the target executable on the command line, as C# and C++ tend to reflect different paradigms rather than verifiable code with optional optimizations, or tweaks, as in C#. The direct equivalent to C# compilation in C++ is `/clr:safe`, but this model does not allow you to take advantage of much of the true power of C++. For that reason, I prefer using `/clr:pure` in general and switching to `/clr:safe` or `/clr` as needed.

Now let's take the exact same pointer usage as the C# example and convert it to C++/CLI:

```
ref struct R
{
    static void Main()
    {
        int i;
        int *ptr = &i;
        *ptr = 3;
        System::Console::WriteLine(i);
    }
};
void main() {R::Main();}
```

As you can see, C++ pointer usage in the program is identical to the C# version. Since pointers are not verifiable, or safe, we should compile this as `pure`. Enter the following line:

```
cl /clr:pure test.cpp
```

This compiles into a CLR executable that writes 3 to the console, just like the C# version.

On the other hand, if you try to compile this as `safe`, you see the following (the `/nologo` option suppresses the copyright message):

```
cl /clr:safe /nologo test.cpp
test.cpp
test.cpp(6) : error C4956: 'int *' : this type is not verifiable
```

---

1. For detailed information about `clr:initialAppDomain`, refer to the Visual C++ documentation.

If you attempt to compile this code without the `clr` flag in any form, you receive a more esoteric message:

```
cl /nologo test.cpp
test.cpp
test.cpp(2) : error C2143: syntax error : missing ';' before '<class-head>'
test.cpp(2) : error C4430: missing type specifier - int assumed. Note: C++ does not
support default-int
test.cpp(8) : error C2653: 'System' : is not a class or namespace name
test.cpp(8) : error C3861: 'WriteLine': identifier not found
```

If you do not specify the `/clr` option, the compiler compiles this code as native C++. In native C++, `ref` is not a keyword, so the compiler does not know that it indicates anything special, and what you get follows the old computer science rule of garbage-in, garbage-out from the compiler. It is always a good idea to double-check the setting of the `clr` flag in either the IDE or the makefile when the compiler appears to spit out seemingly nonsensical diagnostics.

BEHIND THE SCENES

In the previous example, it's quite instructive to understand what the parser is doing. When it sees the keyword `class`, it realizes that, because classes can only be declared in certain places, whatever came before should have already completed, so it outputs the following diagnostic:

```
test.cpp(2) : error C2143: syntax error : missing ';' before '<class-head>'
```

Note that this occurs on line 2, because the parser continues to the open curly bracket before making a judgment on the expression.

```
error C4430: missing type specifier - int assumed. Note: C++ does not
support default-int
```

The next error message is a carryover from traditional C, which allowed you to declare a variable or function without specifying the type. The type would then be identified as `int` by default. This behavior was called, not surprisingly, `default-int`.

Therefore in traditional C, the following declaration was valid:

```
ref;
```

This line declared `ref` to be a global variable of type `int`.

C++ Handles

In the CLR, reference types are divided into two entities: the objects on the managed heap and a handle to those objects. C# obscures this division and provides syntax that allows you to work with a handle as if it is the object itself. C++/CLI, on the other hand, treats the handle as if it is a pointer to the object on the managed heap. In doing so, it uses the pointer syntax outlined in this chapter.

Let's review that syntax here. First let's declare a reference type and a value type:

```
//declare a reference type
ref struct R { int i; };
//declare a value type
value struct V { int j; };
```

Now let's instantiate them (in the context of a method):

```
V v;
R ^ r = gcnew R();
```

The variable v has been allocated on the stack. The variable r is also allocated on the stack, and it is a handle, or managed pointer, to an R object allocated on the managed heap.

Suppose now we want to access the field variable j within V. We would use the . field-access operator and write the following:

```
v.j = 3;
```

In Chapter 3, I showed that for reference types you needed to use the -> member-access operator instead. Previously, I also mentioned that ptr-> is an alias for (*ptr). Let's see how this all comes together.

Set the field i to 3 using pointer syntax:

```
r->i = 3;
```

The equivalent in regular syntax follows:

```
(*r).i = 3;
```

In this case, the variable r is living on the stack and is a handle, or pointer, to an R object on the managed heap:

```
(*r)
```

This expression indicates that the pointer should be dereferenced, which means "go to the object pointed to by the variable r." In other words, this expression returns the actual object on the managed heap. Adding the .i accesses the field itself, which is the same as C# or as a stack-allocated value type in C++.

Of course, using the -> operator is simpler, but knowing the syntax is important.

C++/CLI Address Operators

We have learned that the & operator is used to take the address of a value type or pointer type. Specifically, in C#, this means that it can take the address of a variable on the stack. If you use this operator to take the address of a variable that is not on the stack in C++, you will get a diagnostic. To test this out, we need to use the expression (*r) to get an object on the managed heap. Let's use the address of operator to determine its address and see what happens:

```
&(*r);
```

If you try to compile it, you see the following diagnostic:

```
C:\>cl /clr:pure /nologo test.cpp
test.cpp
test.cpp(12) : error C3072: operator '&' cannot be applied to an instance of a
ref class
        use the unary '%' operator to convert an instance of a ref class to a
handle type
```

Error 3072 is the important diagnostic here, as it says that the address of the operator cannot be used on an object in the managed heap.

To allow you to take the address of an object on the managed heap, C++/CLI introduces the % operator. This operator is the equivalent of the & operator for objects on the managed heap.

In summary, Table 9-2 shows the correspondence among native and managed pointers in C++/CLI.

Table 9-2. *Native to Managed-Pointer Operator Correspondence in C++/CLI*

Operator	Stack / Native Heap	Managed Heap
Address	&	%
Pointer declaration	*	^
Dereference	*	*
Example	value struct V{ int i; }; V v; V * pV = &v; v.i; pV->i;	ref struct R{ int i; }; R ^r1 = gcnew R(); R ^r2 = %(*r1); R r; R ^r3 = %r; r1->i; (*r2).i;

As you can see, there are different address and pointer-declaration operator syntaxes, depending on whether the target is on the managed heap, native heap, or stack. On the other hand, there is only a single dereference operator, because dereferencing a pointer is unambiguous. In any case, you end up with an expression that represents the object either on the stack or the managed heap.

Complex Examples

A more-sophisticated example follows that shows how to take the addresses of pointers. Note that, since pointers and handles are allocated on the stack, we use the & address operator in both cases:

```
static void Main()
{
    V v;
    V *pV = &v;
    R ^ r;
    R ^ * phR = &r;
}
```

This example has the following interesting and more-advanced declaration for phR:

```
R ^ * phR
```

In this case, phR is a pointer to a handle to an R object. This may seem a little strange at first, but you'll grow accustomed to it. Note the following details:

- *phR is an R^ pointer.

- **phR is an R object.

Here's another interesting construct:

```
V ^hV = %v;
```

Is this correct? It says, "Give me a handle to a value type living on the managed heap." But don't value types live on the stack? This shouldn't compile, should it? It turns out that this compiles just fine. Why?

Let's use .NET Reflector to investigate the following sample:

```
static void Main()
{
    V v;
    V ^hV = %v;
}
```

We end up with the code shown in Figure 9-1.

```
public:
static void Main()
{
    ValueType^ modopt(V) modopt(Runtime::CompilerServices::IsBoxed^) local1 = nullptr;
    local1 = ((ValueType^ modopt(V) modopt(Runtime::CompilerServices::IsBoxed^)) V());
}
```

Figure 9-1. *A handle to a V is created via boxing.*

As you can see from the metadata using .NET Reflector, a boxed version of the value type V is automatically created on the managed heap. The expression then sets the variable hV with a handle to that object.

Nightmares

Since types are defined recursively in C++, there are few limitations on the types of nightmarish expressions you can create beyond the limitations of the CLR.

For example, the following valid expression declares the variable p to be a pointer to a function taking int and char and returning a pointer to an array of pointers of pointers to functions taking int and returning handles to R:

```
R ^ (**(*(*p)(int, char))[])(int);
```

In general, this is how you read complex declarations: Start at the name of the variable in the center. In this case, the variable name is p. From there, look to the right. If you see an opening parenthesis, it's a function. If you see an opening square bracket, it is an array. If you see a semicolon, a closing parenthesis, or nothing at all, look to the left. If you see a ^, it's a handle. If you see a *, it's a pointer. From there, continue to telescope your way outward, respecting parentheses and skipping over tokens you've already used. Clearly, this is an algorithm that is easier said than done.

The nice thing about complex declarations is that the only limits are those of your imagination.

Summary

In this chapter, I introduced you to pointers and unsafe code, hopefully without scaring you so much that you'll give up programming and move to Antarctica. If I've failed, be sure to send me a postcard—preferably one with penguins or dogs.

You may not be an expert on pointers now, but given the run-through and examples in this chapter, you'll know, at least, how to recognize them as well as apply them in simple cases. In the next chapter, we'll look at properties and events in C++/CLI.

Properties and Events

Annual income twenty pounds, annual expenditure nineteen nineteen six, result happiness. Annual income twenty pounds, annual expenditure twenty pound ought and six, result misery.

—Charles Dickens, *David Copperfield*

Properties were created to provide field-like functionality for data in a context that allows the programmer to either access the data or abstract the data in an entirely different fashion than is provided by the type system.

Normal fields are simple type declarations within a class. A property contains a method for retrieving data called a *getter*, a method for storing data called a *setter*, or both wrapped in a single, consistent syntax that allows a property to look and act like a field. The getter and setter are also commonly known as the get accessor and the set accessor, respectively.

Properties are common elements of both C# and C++/CLI, although their syntax is quite different. Properties are not currently an element of standard C++, although there is no reason why they may not be added to the language and standardized at some future date.

A Basic Example Using Properties in C#

Suppose we want to write a Clock class in which we store the hour as a number between 0 and 11, but we still want the caller to be able to use the hour as a number between 1 and 12. We could use a property in C# to store the data any way we want and use getters and setters to convert the data between formats. I won't dwell on the merits of this sort of representation here; suffice it to say that it is useful for performing various calculations.

Here is this example in C#:

```
using System;
class Clock
{
    public int Hour
    {
        get
        {
            if(hour == 0)
            {
                return 12;
```

```
                }
                else
                {
                    return hour;
                }
            }
        set
        {
            hour = value % 12;
        }
    }
    private int hour;
    public static void Main()
    {
        DateTime t = DateTime.Now;
        Clock c = new Clock();
        c.Hour = t.Hour;
        Console.WriteLine("The little hand is on the {0}", c.Hour);
        c.Hour = 12;
        Console.WriteLine("at midnight it will be {0} o'clock", c.Hour);
    }
}
```

In this example, Hour is a property. Let's have a look at the setter:

```
set
{
    hour = value % 12;
}
```

In this case, the variable value is the implied input to the setter. Our private variable hour is then set to value modulo 12, which converts it into a number between 0 and 11.

The getter handles the interaction in the other direction. If hour is 0, it returns 12, and returns the clock hour for any other value:

```
get
{
    if(hour == 0)
    {
        return 12;
    }
    else
    {
        return hour;
    }
}
```

Here are the results:

```
C:\>csc /nologo test.cs
C:\>test
The little hand is on the 7
at midnight it will be 12 o'clock
```

A Basic Example Using Properties in C++/CLI

A similar program in C++/CLI follows:

```
using namespace System;
private ref class Clock
{
public:
    property int Hour
    {
        int get()
        {
            if(hour == 0)
            {
                return 12;
            }
            else
            {
                return hour;
            }
        }
        void set(int value)
        {
            hour = value % 12;
        }
    }
private:
    int hour;
public:
    static void Main()
    {
        DateTime t = DateTime::Now;
        Clock ^c = gcnew Clock();
        c->Hour = t.Hour;
        Console::WriteLine("The little hand is on the {0}", c->Hour);
        c->Hour = 12;
        Console::WriteLine("at midnight it will be {0} o'clock", c->Hour);
    }
};
void main() { Clock::Main();}
```

Let's look at the results in C++/CLI:

```
C:\>cl /clr:pure /nologo test.cpp
C:\>test
The little hand is on the 7
at midnight it will be 12 o'clock
```

Although this example produces the same results, the syntax is completely different. The setter is written as follows:

```
void set(int value)
{
    hour = value % 12;
}
```

Rather than having a distinct syntax, C++/CLI accessors are written just like methods. In this case, the C# implicit parameter value is declared explicitly as a function parameter. In fact, it could be named anything in C++/CLI, not just value. Note that the set accessor returns void; a void return is required by the standard.

The getter has similar distinctions:

```
int get()
{
    if(hour == 0)
    {
        return 12;
    }
    else
    {
        return hour;
    }
}
```

It has method-style syntax and has a return value, int, identical to the type of the property. Although the C++/CLI syntax is completely different than the C# syntax, it is also quite intuitive, because it reflects the fact that the getter and setter are methods in actuality.

A Look Inside the Grammar

When properties are parsed in C++/CLI, the accesses are converted to either set() or get() method calls depending on whether the property is being read or written, for example:

```
c->Hour = t.Hour
```

This expression would be converted to the following:

```
c->Hour::set(t.Hour);
```

Now take the following line for example:

```
int i = c->Hour;
```

This expression would be converted to

```
int i = c->Hour::get();
```

In fact, the language itself accepts this explicit syntax as well as the implicit syntax. We can rewrite the previous `Main()` method as follows and see the same results:

```
static void Main()
{
    DateTime t = DateTime::Now;
    Clock ^c = gcnew Clock();
    c->Hour::set(t.Hour);
    Console::WriteLine("The little hand is on the {0}", c->Hour::get());
    c->Hour::set(12);
    Console::WriteLine("at midnight it will be {0} o'clock",c->Hour::get());
}
```

Of course, this defeats some of the purpose of properties in the first place. Still, knowledge of this conversion helps in understanding some tricky diagnostics we will encounter later in the chapter. It is also important to note that the property name scopes the `get` and `set` methods. In other words, it can be viewed as a namespace that contains the methods inside the class, which makes the syntax used to explicitly access the methods intuitive.

Trivial Properties

A *trivial property* is one in which there is no explicit getter or setter; it is the compiler that creates a default getter and setter from the property declaration as well as a data placeholder to hold the information. The property is just another field inside the class and is called the *backing store* in compiler terminology. This is clearly the most basic kind of property and differs only slightly from a field declaration, but there are advantages. A trivial property is useful as a placeholder during the development stage for items that will eventually be rewritten as full properties. In the meantime, their existence as properties prevents you from inadvertently writing expressions that work for fields but not for properties; see the section titled "Caveats" below.

Syntax

To declare a trivial property, you declare a property without the curly bracketed getter or setter, as follows:

```
property int Hour;
```

This creates a property called `Hour`, with implicitly created methods `Hour::get()` and `Hour::set()` and a backing store of type `int` to store the property data. The compiler-generated getter and setter methods have the following declarations:

```
int get();
void set(int);
```

In other words, the basic syntax for a trivial property is

```
property-type property identifier;
```

You may be asking yourself, "If this is called a trivial property, what do we call the property we defined explicitly in the previous example?" Well, you guessed it. We intuitively call it a *nontrivial property*.

Example

A simple example of the use of a trivial property follows:

```
using namespace System;
ref struct Test
{
    property int Item;
    int UseItem()
    {
        Item = 3;
        return Item;
    }
};
```

The method UseItem() both reads and writes the trivial property item.

Indexed Properties

An *indexed property* is like a property array. An indexed property uses other parameters, called *indices*, to determine the result of a get or set operation. These parameters need not be integers; in fact, property indices may be of any type.

Syntax

To declare an indexed property, you surround the list of comma-separated parameters in square brackets. You also need to copy this list to the declaration of the getter and the setter, starting with the indices from left to right and ending with the property type, in the case of the setter. This syntax makes declaration of properties of certain complex pointer types (those similar to the nightmares encountered in Chapter 9) problematic. You can get around that with a typedef, a C++ language feature that will be covered in Chapter 20. In addition, indexed properties cannot be trivial, because the compiler would be at a loss to figure out what kind of implicit accessors to create.

Example

An example using an indexed property follows:

```
using namespace System;
ref struct R
{
    String ^m_Key;
    int m_Value;
    property int Hash[String ^]
    {
```

```
        int get(String^Key)
        {
            if(Key == m_Key)
            {
                return m_Value;
            }
            else
            {
                return -1;
            }
        }
        void set(String^Key, int Value)
        {
            m_Key = Key;
            m_Value = Value;
        }
    }
    R()
    {
        Hash["dog"]=3;
    }
    static void Main()
    {
        R ^ r = gcnew R();
        r->Hash["first"]=42;
        Console::WriteLine(r->Hash["first"]);
        Console::WriteLine(r->Hash["second"]);
    }
};
void main() { R::Main(); }
```

In this example, we create a very simple hash. It is only capable of storing a single value; trying to read any other value returns -1. A string is used to index this hash. In main(), we first prime the hash by setting the Hash property with index "first" to be 42. All subsequent reads of the hash return 42 if the index first is used, or else -1 for errors. Ignore the constructor for now; it will be used to demonstrate differences between C# and C++/CLI later in the chapter.

Let's examine the results:

```
C:\>cl /clr:pure /nologo test.cpp
C:\>test
42
-1
```

Default Indexed Properties

For indexed properties, the keyword default may be substituted instead of the property identifier. This is not allowed for *scalar*, or nonindexed, properties. Using default allows you to
think of the class itself as the container for a property, because the property has no unique
identifier. This concept might be easier to understand using an example.

We can translate the previous example into a default-indexed property as follows:

```
using namespace System;
ref struct R
{
    String ^m_Key;
    int m_Value;
    property int default[String ^]
    {
        int get(String^Key)
        {
            if(Key == m_Key)
            {
                return m_Value;
            }
            else
            {
                return -1;
            }
        }
        void set(String^Key, int Value)
        {
            m_Key = Key;
            m_Value = Value;
        }
    }
    R()
    {
        default["dog"]=3;
    }
    static void Main()
    {
        R ^ r = gcnew R();
        r["first"]=42;
        Console::WriteLine(r["first"]);
        Console::WriteLine(r["second"]);    }
};
void main() { R::Main(); }
```

As you can see, the only difference between these code examples is that the identifier Hash
is not used for default-indexed properties.

C# Properties

Because of the way properties are implemented transparently as methods in C++/CLI, I felt it instructive to explain C++/CLI indexed properties directly rather than basing the discussion on a translation from C#. Personally, I consider the C# property syntax somewhat ad hoc.

There remain, however, some interesting C# idiosyncrasies that still deserve a place in this section.

Scalar Properties in C#

An example of a scalar, or nonindexed, property in C# follows:

```
class R
{
    int savedValue;
    public int BasicProperty
    {
        get
        {
            return savedValue;
        }
        set
        {
            savedValue = value;
        }
    }
}
```

In C#, the value parameter to the set accessor is implicitly declared and has an identifier of value. Using .NET Reflector, we can see that these accessors translate to the following methods:

```
public int get_BasicProperty()
{
    return this.savedValue;
}
public void set_BasicProperty(int value)
{
    this.savedValue = value;
}
```

As you can see, the C# syntax generates code similar to the C++/CLI syntax.

Indexed Properties in C#

The main difference between indexed properties in C# and indexed properties in C++/CLI is that all indexed properties are default-indexed properties in C#. In C++/CLI, you can have more than one indexed property in a class, whereas you are limited to exactly one in a C#

class. Because of this limitation, both C++/CLI and C# allow you to avoid using a keyword like default to access the property. Since there is at most one default property in a class, the identifier is implicit. Here is our default-indexed property example converted to C#:

```csharp
using System;
class R
{
    string m_Key;
    int m_Value;
    public int this[string Key]
    {
        get
        {
            if (Key == this.m_Key)
            {
                return this.m_Value;
            }
            return -1;
        }
        set
        {
            this.m_Key = Key;
            this.m_Value = value;
        }
    }
    R()
    {
        this["dog"]=3;
    }
    public static void Main()
    {
        R r = new R();
        r["first"]=42;
        Console.WriteLine(r["first"]);
        Console.WriteLine(r["second"]);
    }
}
```

In the Main() function, you access the property using the following syntax:

```csharp
r["first"]=42;
```

In C++/CLI, the equivalent syntax is the same:

```csharp
r["first"]=42;
```

The C# constructor uses the following syntax, using the keyword this to access the property:

```csharp
this["dog"]=3;
```

In C++/CLI, the equivalent syntax is

```
default["dog"]=3;
```

The C++/CLI version uses the keyword `default`, although for reference types, you can also use keyword `this`.[1]

Advanced Properties of Properties

There are many benefits to choosing properties over fields when implementing object-oriented paradigms and abstractions, because you can do just about everything with a property that you can do with a method. Since they are supported within the framework, you can pretty much have the best of both worlds.

Read-Only and Write-Only Properties

It is quite simple to make a property read-only or write-only. To do this, merely do not provide a setter or a getter, respectively.

Read-Only Property

A read-only property follows; a *read-only property* is one that lacks a `set` accessor:

```
using namespace System;
ref struct R
{
    property DateTime Time
    {
        DateTime get()
        {
            return DateTime::Now;
        }
    }
    static void Main()
    {
        R ^ r = gcnew R();
        Console::WriteLine(r->Time);
    }
};
void main() { R::Main(); }
```

---

1. Something interesting happens when the class is of `value` type. In value types, `this` is considered an interior pointer to the value type instead of a tracking handle. Therefore, when the compiler sees `this["dog"]`, it tries to dereference the pointer like it would a native array and complains that `"dog"` is not a valid array subscript. Remember that in C++ native arrays behave exactly like pointers, except they are bound to a specific length.

This property allows us to read the current time. Here is what I got when I ran this:

```
C:\>cl /clr:pure /nologo test.cpp
C:\>test
2/18/2006 12:16:12 PM
```

Your results may vary.

Write-Only Property

Creating a write-only property is similar to creating a read-only property, except that, in this case, the getter is missing. I am including the following example anyway to show you how write-only can be useful; using a property is not the only way to access the data:

```
using namespace System;
ref struct R
{
    int SavedValue;
    property int SetOptions
    {
        void set(int Value)
        {
            SavedValue = Value;
        }
    }
    static void Main()
    {
        R ^ r = gcnew R();
        r->SetOptions = 3;
        Console::WriteLine(r->SavedValue);
    }
};
void main() { R::Main(); }
```

And the results are as follows:

```
C:\>cl /clr:pure /nologo test.cpp
C:\>test
3
```

Static Properties

Just like fields and methods, properties can also be made static, so that they do not require instantiation for use. In fact, let's rewrite our time example using a static property, which makes more sense when you think about it:

```
using namespace System;
ref struct R
{
    static property DateTime Time
    {
        DateTime get()
        {
            return DateTime::Now;
        }
    }
};
void main()
{
    Console::WriteLine(R::Time);
}
```

In fact, if you use .NET Reflector to look at System::DateTime::Now, you find that it is also a static read-only property (see Figure 10-1).

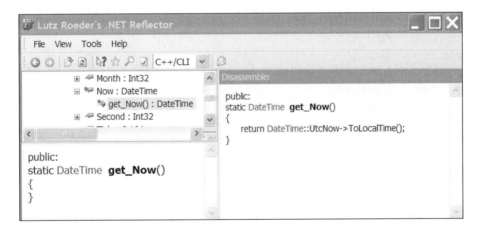

Figure 10-1. *System::DateTime::Now in .NET Reflector*

Virtual Properties

Not only can properties be virtual but they can also be used to override other methods, just like regular methods. Consider the following example, where the get accessor is overridden in a base class, just like the examples in Chapter 8:

```
using namespace System;
ref struct Base
{
    property int Prop
    {
```

```
        virtual int get()
        {
            return 1;
        }
    }
    void Test()
    {
        Console::WriteLine(Prop);
    }
};
ref struct Derived : Base
{
    int value;
    property int Prop
    {
        virtual int get() override
        {
            return 3;
        }
    }
};
void main()
{
    Derived ^d = gcnew Derived();
    Base ^b = gcnew Base();
    b->Test();
    Console::WriteLine(d->Prop);
    d->Test();
}
```

The results follow:

```
C:\>cl /clr:pure /nologo test.cpp
C:\>test
1
3
3
```

In this example, the get() method from the base class returns 1, whereas the overridden method returns 3. As you can see from the output, Derived::Prop::get() not only returns 3 but also affects Base::Prop::get() when called on an instance of the derived class.

Abstract and Sealed Properties

Property accessors may also be declared abstract and sealed. The following example shows an abstract getter in a base class implemented and sealed in a derived class:

```
using namespace System;
ref struct Base abstract
{
    property int Prop
    {
        virtual int get() abstract;
    }
};
ref struct Derived : Base
{
    property int Prop
    {
        virtual int get() override sealed
        {
            return 1;
        }
    }
};
void main()  {}
```

Properties declared in an interface are also abstract by definition. It is not necessary to state this explicitly.

Named Overriding

Explicit overriding of a virtual function by a property is also possible. Consider the following example:

```
using namespace System;
ref struct Base
{
    virtual String ^GetProp()
    {
        return "Base";
    }
};
ref struct Derived : Base
{
    property String ^ Prop
    {
        virtual String ^ get() = Base::GetProp
        {
            return "Derived";
        }
    }
};
void main()
{
```

```
    Derived ^d = gcnew Derived();
    Base ^b = d;
    Console::WriteLine(b->GetProp());
}
```

Here are the results:

```
C:\>cl /clr:pure /nologo test.cpp
C:\>test
Derived
```

In Chapter 8, you saw an example where a third-party library release forced you to explicitly override a virtual function of a different name. This is the same situation. In this case, you have an existing function, GetProp(), in the base class that you would like to override by a property get accessor in the derived class. This allows you to replace an obsolete paradigm with a more-abstracted paradigm with minimal impact on preexisting code.

Though not as common, it is also possible to make a named override in the opposite direction, for example:

```
using namespace System;
ref struct Base
{
    property String^ Prop
    {
        virtual String^ get()
        {
            return "Base";
        }
    }
};
ref struct Derived : Base
{
    virtual String ^ GetProp() = Base::Prop::get
    {
        return "Derived";
    }
};
void main()
{
    Derived ^d = gcnew Derived();
    Base ^b = d;
    Console::WriteLine(b->Prop);
}
```

In this example, the derived method overrides the get accessor in the base class. Here are the results when overriding in this direction:

```
C:\>cl /clr:pure /nologo test.cpp
C:\>test
Derived
```

As you can see, either way, we are always displaying the results from the Derived class that has the overriding method.

Property Protection Mechanisms

You can restrict the accessibility of a property, its getter, its setter, or both its getter and setter. Accessibility applied to the property carries over to the accessibility of the getter and setter unless you specify otherwise. The only restriction is that the accessibility of the getter and setter cannot be less restrictive than that of the property itself.

For example, consider the following code:

```
using namespace System;
ref struct R
{
private:
    static property DateTime Time
    {
public:
        DateTime get()
        {
            return DateTime::Now;
        }
    }
};
void main()
{
    Console::WriteLine(R::Time);
}
```

When we try to compile this, we encounter the following diagnostic:

```
C:\>cl /clr:pure /nologo test.cpp
test.cpp(7) : error C3908: access level less restrictive than that of 'R::Time'
        test.cpp(5) : see declaration of 'R::Time'
```

This diagnostic is issued, because the property access level is private, which limits the getter and setter to, at most, private.

On the other hand, consider the following code:

```
using namespace System;
ref struct R
{
public:
    static property DateTime Time
```

```
    {
        DateTime get()
        {
            return DateTime::Now;
        }
private:
        void set(DateTime t)
        {
        }
    }
};
void main()
{
    Console::WriteLine(R::Time);
}
```

In this case, the protection level of the setter is more restrictive than that of the property, and this program compiles fine. All that is left to do is fill in the set accessor!

Property Caveats

Since properties follow field syntax, it is tempting to use them in complex expressions as you might use a regular field. This does not always work because of the restriction that the set accessor returns void rather than the type of the property.[2] Consider the following example:

```
ref struct Test
{
    property int PropInt;
    int RealInt;
};
void main()
{
    Test ^a = gcnew Test();
    Test ^b = gcnew Test();
    Test ^c = gcnew Test();
    a->RealInt = b->RealInt = c->RealInt;
    a->PropInt = b->PropInt = c->PropInt;
}
```

---

2. There was a huge discussion about setters needing to return void on the C++ Language Designers distribution list before the current version of the language was finalized. Both this book's technical reviewer and I were among those advocating for allowing users to be flexible on set method return codes; we lost.

Let's try to compile this:

```
C:\>cl /clr:pure /nologo test.cpp
test.cpp(12) : error C2664: 'Test::PropInt::set' : cannot convert parameter 1 from
void' to 'int'
        Expressions of type void cannot be converted to other types
```

The first construction, a->RealInt = b->RealInt = c->RealInt, works fine and is resolved from right to left using C++/CLI's order of evaluation rules. The second example, using a property of type int, does not compile because of the fact that setters return void.

The property expression is converted to the following by the compiler:

```
a->PropInt::set(b->PropInt::set(c->PropInt::get()));
```

In fact, if you replace the property expression with this expression, you get the exact same error code. As you can see, a->PropInt::set() is attempting to act on an item of type void, which is what is returned by b->PropInt::set().

It was designed this way because of optimization and design concerns. Requiring the return of a value from the set() method would cause a quandary for programmers. What if the property mimics or accesses a hardware device in which the set() method indicates device-programming information and the get() method returns the status? Should the compiler always automatically insert an additional call to get() each time this kind of syntax arises? There are well-defined rules dealing with programming languages that define acceptable optimizations. These rules govern whether the compiler may attempt spurious reads of addresses and so on, as often these sorts of operations have real results, though of course the CLR is an emulated environment, or at least it is right now. Someday there may be hardware that implements the CLR directly.

I think these sorts of concerns influenced the design of properties, though there is no guarantee that future revisions of the compiler may support set() functions that return values other than void.

Miscellaneous Property Details

Property types cannot be const, volatile, or mutable. You can add the const keyword to a variable to make it read-only. Classes can be constant, which makes the class instance read-only; only const methods can be called with const classes. The mutable keyword attached to a variable of a const class exempts that variable from being const. The volatile keyword indicates that optimizations that assume that the variable never changes should not be performed. This is useful for memory-mapped variables. We will revisit these keywords in context as the book unfolds.

Events and Delegates

C++/CLI events and delegates are similar in form and function to the corresponding C# forms. This section focuses primarily on the syntactic differences, but it still provides some illustrative examples.

Delegates

A *delegate* is a type-safe version of a pointer to a function. In .NET, a single delegate can embody calls to several methods, and it is the ideal way to encapsulate callbacks from external or asynchronous occurrences or events.

Sorting

In this section, I present an example of a simple sort and guide its evolution using delegates. Suppose you have an array of classes, named MyObject, each of which has a field named Value, and you want to sort them by this Value. A simple implementation of a bubble sort might look something like this:

```
using namespace System;
ref struct MyObject
{
    int Value;
    MyObject(int Value)
    {
        this->Value = Value;
    }
    virtual String ^ToString() override
    {
        return Value.ToString();
    }
};
void main()
{
    array<MyObject^> ^myObjectArray = gcnew array<MyObject^>
    {
        gcnew MyObject(5),
        gcnew MyObject(3),
        gcnew MyObject(1),
        gcnew MyObject(4),
        gcnew MyObject(2),
    };
    for(int i=1; i<myObjectArray->Length; i++)
    {
        for (int j=0; j<i; j++)
        {
            if(myObjectArray[i]->Value < myObjectArray[j]->Value)
            {
                MyObject ^tempObject;
                tempObject = myObjectArray[i];
                myObjectArray[i]=myObjectArray[j];
                myObjectArray[j]=tempObject;
            }
        }
    }
```

```
    }
    for each(MyObject^ o in myObjectArray)
    {
        Console::Write(o);
    }
    Console::WriteLine();
}
```

This is all pretty standard: you take several passes over the array, swapping neighbors if they're in the wrong order, and the larger objects bubble up to the top.

There are a couple of interesting things to note about the code. I am sometimes a bit lazy, and I like to use ToString() to print the type. In this case, I do that as follows:

```
int Value;
return Value.ToString();
```

This allocates a string on the managed heap that has the Unicode representation of the value of the integer Value.

Another interesting piece from the constructor follows:

```
int Value;
MyObject(int Value)
{
    this->Value = Value;
}
```

In this case, there are two distinct integers named Value; it is true that I did not have to give both of them the same name. In fact, people usually don't, using something like m_Value for the member variable. In this case, I wanted to show how you can distinguish them using this; the variable pointed to by this is the instance variable, and the variable lacking this is the input parameter.

We can make this code more versatile using delegates in the following ways:

- Decouple the sorting procedure from the type of the array. Create a generic sort class, which sorts objects of an arbitrary type.

- Decouple the sorting algorithm from the sorting procedure. Sorting algorithms perform differently depending on the order of the array. Some algorithms excel at sorting random arrays; others excel when the array has just a few elements out of order. It would be nice to allow the user to select the algorithm based on the data.

We will do both of these using delegates.

- We will first cast so that the sort procedure can sort an array of Object^ and use a class-specific comparison procedure to sort the actual objects. A delegate will be used to access the comparison procedure.

- Next, we will implement a delegate for the sorting algorithm itself. In this case, the delegate will point to an implementation of the bubble sort algorithm.

Determining Delegates

To create a delegate, we first have to decide what kind of method we want to call. There are a couple of fundamental ways of dealing with objects of arbitrary types. One way is to perform polymorphism of parameters, discussed in Chapter 14 and beyond, when I cover generics and templates. Another is to perform polymorphism of types, cast the arbitrary types to a common base class, and perform operations on the base class. Let's adopt the latter strategy and cast the arbitrary objects to Object^.

This strategy decouples the type of the object from the sorting procedure. Our invoking algorithm passes the address of a method that can compare two items for the sorting program. We use a delegate to represent this. The model for our method follows:

```
bool Compare(Object ^, Object ^);
```

The Compare() method returns true if the first Object is smaller than the second. A delegate is a type, so it appears at class-level scope and has visibility specifiers. It is created by prepending a similar method declaration with the keyword delegate. To enforce type safety, the input parameters and return type must match the target method exactly:

```
public delegate bool DelCompare(Object ^o1, Object^ o2);
```

The grammar is a little delicate here. Suppose you forget the return type:

```
public delegate dog();
```

If so, you may see a somewhat misleading diagnostic:

```
test.cpp(1) : error C2059: syntax error : 'public'
```

If you ever get a misleading diagnostic, do not assume that it is caused by a compiler bug. Rather double- and triple-check your code to make sure it is valid C++.

The new MyObject class with the comparison method and delegate declaration follows:

```
using namespace System;
public delegate bool DelCompare(Object^, Object^);
ref struct MyObject
{
    int Value;
    static DelCompare ^dCompare = gcnew DelCompare(Compare);
    MyObject(int Value)
    {
        this->Value = Value;
    }
    static bool Compare(Object ^o1, Object ^o2)
    {
        MyObject ^m1 = (MyObject^) o1;
        MyObject ^m2 = (MyObject^) o2;
        return (m1->Value < m2->Value);
    }
    virtual String ^ToString() override
```

```
    {
        return Value.ToString();
    }
};
```

Now we need to create a sorting class for an arbitrary type. This gives us an opportunity to see a delegate type's method taking a delegate as a parameter. We want to have a delegate for our sort algorithm that provides it with the exact information it needs to sort the array—in this case, a delegate for the comparison procedure and a reference to the array. Therefore, in this case, we have the following:

```
public delegate void DelAlgorithm(DelCompare ^dCompare, array<Object^> ^a);
```

Next we add the sorting class and the bubble sort algorithm itself:

```
ref struct Sorter abstract sealed
{
    static DelAlgorithm ^dAlgorithm = gcnew DelAlgorithm(Bubble);
    static void Bubble(DelCompare ^dCompare, array<Object^> ^a)
    {
        for(int i=1; i<a->Length; i++)
        {
            for (int j=0; j<i; j++)
            {
                if(dCompare(a[i], a[j]))
                {
                    Object ^tempObject;
                    tempObject = a[i];
                    a[i]=a[j];
                    a[j]=tempObject;
                }
            }
        }
    }
    static void Sort(array<Object^> ^a, DelCompare ^dCompare)
    {
        dAlgorithm(dCompare, a);
    }
};
```

Note that this class is abstract sealed. We want to make sure that no one ever instantiates this class, either as itself or as a derived class. It is designed to be a container for the Sort() method, just as System::Console is a container for Write().

And finally, here is the modified main() procedure:

```
void main()
{
    array<MyObject^> ^myObjectArray = gcnew array<MyObject^>
    {
        gcnew MyObject(5),
```

```
        gcnew MyObject(3),
        gcnew MyObject(1),
        gcnew MyObject(4),
        gcnew MyObject(2),
    };
    Sorter::Sort(myObjectArray, MyObject::dCompare);
    for(int i=0; i< myObjectArray->Length; i++)
    {
        Console::Write(myObjectArray[i]);
    }
    Console::WriteLine();
}
```

Is that all? Perhaps we can kick it up a notch.

The Next Level

This implementation is fairly slick, but there is still one bit of unnecessary tedium. We are required to pass the dCompare delegate to the Sort() routine. Perhaps we have smoothed over MyObject too much; it is nice to still remember that MyObject is a class that has the needed delegate. Interfaces can help us out here. We create an interface, ICompare, that tells the compiler that our special object has the ability to return a delegate that directs ordering of the elements in the array. The completed routine follows for you to study on your own:

```
using namespace System;
public delegate bool DelCompare(Object^, Object^);
interface class ICompare
{
    virtual DelCompare ^getCompareDelegate();
};
ref struct MyObject : ICompare
{
    int Value;
    static DelCompare ^dCompare = gcnew DelCompare(Compare);
    MyObject(int Value)
    {
        this->Value = Value;
    }
    static bool Compare(Object ^o1, Object ^o2)
    {
        MyObject ^m1 = (MyObject^) o1;
        MyObject ^m2 = (MyObject^) o2;
        return (m1->Value < m2->Value);
    }
    virtual String ^ToString() override
    {
        return Value.ToString();
    }
    virtual DelCompare ^getCompareDelegate()
```

```
    {
        return dCompare;
    }
};
public delegate void DelAlgorithm(DelCompare ^dCompare, array<Object^> ^a);
ref struct Sorter abstract sealed
{
    static DelAlgorithm ^dAlgorithm = gcnew DelAlgorithm(Bubble);
    static void Bubble(DelCompare ^dCompare, array<Object^> ^a)
    {
        for(int i=1; i<a->Length; i++)
        {
            for (int j=0; j<i; j++)
            {
                if(dCompare(a[i], a[j]))
                {
                    Object ^tempObject;
                    tempObject = a[i];
                    a[i]=a[j];
                    a[j]=tempObject;
                }
            }
        }
    }
    static void Sort(array<Object^> ^a)
    {
        ICompare ^ic = (ICompare^)a[0];
        dAlgorithm(ic->getCompareDelegate(), a);
    }
};
void main()
{
    array<MyObject^> ^myObjectArray = gcnew array<MyObject^>
    {
        gcnew MyObject(5),
        gcnew MyObject(3),
        gcnew MyObject(1),
        gcnew MyObject(4),
        gcnew MyObject(2),
    };
    Sorter::Sort(myObjectArray);
    for(int i=0; i< myObjectArray->Length; i++)
    {
        Console::Write(myObjectArray[i]);
    }
    Console::WriteLine();
}
```

When we run the routine, we get the following results:

```
C:\>cl /clr:pure /nologo test.cpp
C:\>test
12345
```

Multicast Delegates

Multicast delegates are delegates that call more than one method. To create a multicast delegate, add more methods to the delegate itself; there is no difference in the declaration. Methods may be added to a delegate using the += operator, and likewise subtracted using -=. To make this work, we need to use the gcnew operator with each method, as follows:

```
using namespace System;
public delegate void Handler(String^);
ref struct Class1
{
    static void News(String^s)
    {
        Console::WriteLine("Class1 : {0}",s);
    }
};
ref struct Class2
{
    static void News(String^s)
    {
        Console::WriteLine("Class2 : {0}",s);
    }
};
ref struct Class3
{
    static void News(String^s)
    {
        Console::WriteLine("Class3 : {0}",s);
    }
};
void main()
{
    Handler ^dNews1 = gcnew Handler(Class1::News);
    Handler ^dNews2 = gcnew Handler(Class2::News);
    Handler ^dNews3 = gcnew Handler(Class3::News);
    Handler ^dNews;
    dNews = dNews1 + dNews2 + dNews3;
    dNews("News has arrived!");
    dNews -= (dNews2+dNews3);
    dNews("We lost subscribers");
```

```
dNews += dNews3;
dNews("A subscriber has returned");
}
```

In this example, we have three classes, Class1, Class2, and Class3, each of which is interested in receiving news. They each have a static method, News(), which should be called when we have news to broadcast. In main(), we create a delegate dNews, which is allocated to send news to all three classes using the + operator. We then use the += and -= operators to change who receives news. In this way, many classes can subscribe to the same news feed using a delegate.

Instance Delegates

All of the examples of delegates so far have used a static method within a class to receive notifications. Unfortunately, static methods cannot be virtual, which restricts how we can override them. We can pass an instance method to a delegate. Rather than writing the following:

```
Handler ^dNews1 = gcnew Handler(Class1::News);
```

write

```
Handler ^dNews1 = gcnew Handler(gcnew(Class1),&Class1::News);
```

In this way, we pass a handle to the instance of the class as well as the address of the method, as denoted by the & operator. We don't have to write this on one line; the following also works:

```
Class1 ^ pClass1 = gcnew(Class1);
Handler ^dNews1 = gcnew Handler(pClass1,&Class1::News);
```

Now that we are using instances, we can refactor the previous example:

```
using namespace System;
public delegate void Handler(String^);
ref struct Base
{
    virtual void News(String^s)
    {
        Console::WriteLine("{0} : {1}",ToString(),s);
    }
};
ref struct Class1 : Base {};
ref struct Class2 : Base {};
ref struct Class3 : Base {};
void main()
{
    Handler ^dNews1 = gcnew Handler(gcnew(Class1),&Class1::News);
    Handler ^dNews2 = gcnew Handler(gcnew(Class2),&Class2::News);
    Handler ^dNews3 = gcnew Handler(gcnew(Class3),&Class3::News);
    Handler ^dNews;
```

```
    dNews = dNews1 + dNews2 + dNews3;
    dNews("News has arrived!");
    dNews -= (dNews2+dNews3);
    dNews("We lost subscribers");
    dNews += dNews3;
    dNews("A subscriber has returned");
}
```

This version is much cleaner. The base class now has the common message, and the derived classes are free to change it if that's desired.

Events

Events are the .NET mechanism for notification. Events provide protection for delegates and allow customization through adding and removing subscribers, as well as activating another event, such as sending the news in the previous example.

Events contain three methods: add, remove, and raise. Each of these methods has it own accessibility. Like properties, these methods can be declared and implemented explicitly or implicitly by the compiler. Events with implicit add, remove, and raise methods are called trivial events.

Trivial Events

Here is the previous example modified to use a trivial event:

```
using namespace System;
public delegate void Handler(String^);
ref struct Base
{
    virtual void News(String^s)
    {
        Console::WriteLine("{0} : {1}",ToString(),s);
    }
};
ref struct Class1 : Base {};
ref struct Class2 : Base {};
ref struct Class3 : Base {};
ref struct Holder
{
    void Deliver(String ^s)
    {
        News(s);
    }
    event Handler ^News;
};
void main()
{
```

```
    Holder ^h = gcnew Holder();
    h->News += gcnew Handler(gcnew(Class1),&Class1::News);
    h->Deliver("News has arrived!");
}
```

We can compile and run this:

```
C:\>cl /clr:pure /nologo test.cpp
C:\>test
Class1 : News has arrived!
```

This is a simple example with just one news delivery.

Nontrivial Events

In the previous example, we used the following construction:

```
event Handler ^News;
```

to declare a trivial event. We could have declared an explicit event and implemented the add, remove, and raise methods. The following code is the previous trivial event code translated to the nontrivial event equivalent; note the different protection levels for add, remove, and raise:

```
using namespace System;
public delegate void Handler(String^);
ref struct Base
{
    virtual void News(String^s)
    {
        Console::WriteLine("{0} : {1}",ToString(),s);
    }
};
ref struct Class1 : Base {};
ref struct Class2 : Base {};
ref struct Class3 : Base {};
ref struct Holder
{
    void Deliver(String ^s)
    {
        News(s);
    }
    event Handler ^News
    {
    public:
        void add( Handler^ d )
        {
            this->_News += d;
```

```
        }
    protected:
        void remove( Handler^ d )
        {
            this->_News -= d;
        }
    private:
        void raise( String ^s)
        {
            this->_News(s);
        }
    }
private:
    Handler ^_News;
};
void main()
{
    Holder ^h = gcnew Holder();
    h->News += gcnew Handler(gcnew(Class1),&Class1::News);
    h->Deliver("News has arrived!");
}
```

If we compile and run this, we get the same results:

```
C:\>cl /clr:pure /nologo test.cpp
C:\>test
Class1 : News has arrived!
```

Summary

The examples in this chapter should provide you with a base for using properties, delegates, and events. Don't worry if it feels overwhelming at first. Even though this is an area that takes a bit of getting used to, it certainly adds a few powerful tools to your coding arsenal.

In the next chapter, we'll have a look at expressions and operators in both C# and C++.

■ ■ ■

Expressions and Operators

Argue for your limitations, and sure enough, they're yours.

—Richard Bach, *Illusions*

In this chapter, we'll cover expressions and operators in the context of how they differ from C#. We'll start with a caveat: don't assume that expression evaluation is the same in C# and C++. C# and C++/CLI have different rules that control the evaluation of expressions, and this can surprise you if you're writing overly complex expressions.

Here is an old C++ trick that often shows up on interview questions. It is not guaranteed to work according to the C++ standard, but it works on all of the major C++ compilers for the x86. It is called the XOR swap, and it allows you to swap the values of two integers without declaring an explicit temporary. The code follows:

```
using namespace System;
void main()
{
    int i=3, j=6;
    Console::WriteLine("{0}, {1}", i, j);
    i ^= j ^= i ^= j;
    Console::WriteLine("{0}, {1}", i, j);
}
```

Let's run it:

```
C:\>cl /clr:pure /nologo test.cpp
C:\>test
3, 6
6, 3
```

Look at the following line:

```
i ^= j ^= i ^= j;
```

As you can see, it swaps the values of i and j, because it evaluates the same as the following:

```
i ^= j;
j ^= i;
i ^= j;
```

The first XOR swap stores the bitwise difference between i and j in i. The next line changes j by this difference, turning it into i. The last line, in turn, changes what's left of i into j by changing what was originally i (currently j) by the difference (currently i) too. This relies on the following identities for exclusive OR:

```
x == y ^ (x^y)
```

It more or less breaks up x and y into two parts: the part they have in common, and the part that differs, like taking two numbers and knowing they are equidistant from their average.

Now let's try to do this in C#:

```
using System;
class R
{
    public static void Main()
    {
        int i=3, j=6;
        Console.WriteLine("{0}, {1}", i, j);
        i ^= j ^= i ^= j;
        Console.WriteLine("{0}, {1}", i, j);
    }
}
```

The results follow:

```
C:\>csc /nologo test.cs
C:\>test
3, 6
0, 3
```

As you can see, this just does not work. It's probably just a lack of parentheses, right? What if we try this?

```
i ^= (j ^= (i ^= j));
```

That won't work either; we get the same results. The answer here is that C# and C++ evaluate expressions differently. The rules are pretty complicated, and you don't really need to know them that well unless your chosen vocation is rules lawyer.

■**Note** In this case, the C# code evaluates differently, because C# separates the evaluation of an expression with the evaluation of a variable, in order to help optimizers. C++ evaluates expressions as parenthesized; C# is free to scan the entire statement, preevaluate variables, and use those values to evaluate the expression. This code relies on the interim values of i and j being updated in the middle of the expression in order to work correctly.

It's good programming practice simply to avoid these esoteric constructs. The easy and safe way to write code that works correctly with both languages is to subdivide the expression:

```
i ^= j;
j ^= i;
i ^= j;
```

This sequence works correctly in both C# and C++. Ten years ago, weaving these expressions together might have produced faster code; today's optimizing compilers are sophisticated enough to figure out what you're trying to do and compensate for the expansion.

Operator Overloading

One of the most important aspects of C# and C++/CLI is the support that they offer for elevating user-defined types to the level of built-in types; one important aspect of this is the ability to define operators to work with new types. The examples most commonly encountered in the published literature define types for complex variables or fractions, but that is really just the tip of the iceberg. It is also common practice to define operators to perform operations that have absolutely nothing to do with their mathematical definitions, pushing the boundaries of our limited paradigms and often redefining new ones.

Of course, there are limitations, which include the following:

- Unary operators must remain unary; binary operators must remain binary. In other words, you cannot redefine the plus sign (+) to take three arguments instead of two.

- You cannot make up operators that do not exist. You cannot define a /% operator, even though it could logically be disambiguated by the grammar. You are limited to the language's built-in operators.

- You cannot control the predefined order of evaluation, and you can't expect complicated expressions to evaluate the same way across C++/CLI and C#. As mentioned before, C# and C++/CLI have different rules that control the evaluation of expressions.

Complex Numbers, a Basic Example

Recall that we can consider a simple complex number class in C++/CLI and that complex numbers are numbers of the form:

$a + bi$

where

$i = \sqrt{-1}$

This helps us to lay a foundation for Chapter 15, when we revisit complex numbers using templates in the context of numbers of the form:

$(a + b\sqrt{5})$

This form is very useful when working with the golden ratio:

$$\phi = \frac{1}{2}(1 + \sqrt{5})$$

Using the golden ratio, we can calculate the Fibonacci numbers with a nonrecursive, simple, closed form.[1]

A Review of Complex Numbers

A review of the fundamental mathematical operations using complex numbers follows:[2]

Addition:

$$(a + bi) + (c + di) = (a + c) + (b + d)i$$

Subtraction:

$$(a + bi) - (c + di) = (a - c) + (b - d)i$$

Complex conjugation:

$$\overline{(a + bi)} = (a - bi)$$

Multiplication:

$$(a + bi) \times (c + di) = (ac - bd) + (ad + bc)i$$

---

1. Knuth, Donald E. *Art of Computer Programming, vol. 1: Fundamental Algorithms*, 3rd ed. (Boston: Addison-Wesley, 1997).

2. These are derived from the associative, commutative, and distributive laws of the field of complex numbers, along with the definition of i.

Division by a scalar (real) number:

$$\frac{(a+bi)}{m}=\frac{a}{m}+\frac{b}{m}i$$

Division between complex numbers: Using complex conjugation, multiplication, division by a scalar, and the following identity,

$$(c+di)\overline{(c+di)}=(c^2+d^2)$$

we can derive division between complex numbers:

$$\frac{(a+bi)}{(c+di)}=\frac{(a+bi)\times\overline{(c+di)}}{(c+di)\times\overline{(c+di)}}$$

Note how this divide operation defers to complex conjugation as well as multiplication for calculation of the quotient.

Simple Implementation

We implement this class by defining class data as well as the operators that act on the data. The class data is, very simply, two doubles that correspond to the real part and the imaginary part, which is multiplied by the following:

$$i=\sqrt{-1}$$

The data structure follows:

```
value struct Complex
{
    double re;
    double im;
}
```

As for the operators themselves, there are several ways to define them, depending on whether we want our code to be Common Language Specification (CLS) compliant (we'll revisit this later in the chapter). Essentially, our operators are static member functions, and they return objects rather than references.

Unary Operators

CLI unary operations have the following format:

```
static type operator op (type a)
```

We'll use the following operator in our class:

Complex conjugation:

```
static Complex operator ~ (Complex a);
```

Binary Operators

CLI binary operations have the following format:

```
static type operator op (type a, type b)
```

We'll use these operators in our class:

Addition:

```
static Complex operator + (Complex a, Complex b);
```

Subtraction:

```
static Complex operator - (Complex a, Complex b);
```

Multiplication:

```
static Complex operator * (Complex a, Complex b);
```

Division by double:

```
static Complex operator / (Complex a, double b);
```

Division by complex:

```
static Complex operator / (Complex a, Complex b);
```

Order Matters

Note that the code makes no assumption of commutativity; it is perfectly reasonable to define a/b to be different from b/a, so it is also possible to implement the following line:

```
static Complex operator / (Complex a, double b)
```

in a different method from this line:

```
static Complex operator / (double a, Complex b)
```

The Product of Our Efforts

The completed program follows:

```
using namespace System;
value struct Complex
{
    double re;
    double im;
    Complex(double re, double im)
    {
        this->re = re;
        this->im = im;
    }
```

```
    static Complex operator + (Complex a, Complex b)
    {
        return Complex(a.re+b.re, a.im+b.im);
    }
    static Complex operator - (Complex a, Complex b)
    {
        return Complex(a.re-b.re, a.im-b.im);
    }
    static Complex operator ~ (Complex a)
    {
        return Complex(a.re, - a.im);
    }
    static Complex operator * (Complex a, Complex b)
    {
        return Complex(a.re*b.re - a.im*b.im, a.re*b.im + a.im*b.re);
    }
    static Complex operator / (Complex a, Complex b)
    {
        return a / (b.re*b.re+b.im*b.im) * ~b;
    }
    virtual String ^ ToString() override
    {
        String ^s = re.ToString();
        if(im != 0)
        {
            return s += " + " + im.ToString() + "i";
        }
        return s;
    }
private:
    static Complex operator / (Complex a, double f)
    {
        return Complex(a.re/f, a.im/f);
    }
};
void main()
{
    Complex a(-5,10), b(3,4);
    Console::WriteLine("({0}) / ({1}) = {2}",a,b,a/b);
}
```

As you can see, the basic operators +, -, *, and / have been overloaded to operate on
Complex types rather than the subtypes they are based on, which in this case is double.

The unary complement operator ~ from Boolean logic doesn't intuitively correspond to
any operation that you would perform on a complex number over the real numbers. It is,
therefore, an ideal candidate for satisfying our need for a unary operator for complex conjugation, which we need to implement operator/. The compiler does not enforce any logical

paradigm beyond number of arguments and argument type. You are free to define `operator*` as division and `operator/` as multiplication. This, of course, is bad form unless obfuscation is your goal.

The results from a quick compile and run follow:

```
C:\>cl /clr:pure /nologo test.cpp
C:\>test
(-5 + 10i) / (3 + 4i) = 1 + 2i
```

Resolution of Overloads

You might also have noticed that there are two different `operator/` methods for division. Both C# and C++ have built-in rules for choosing which method to call, but these differ in surprising ways. Two methods that share the same name yet have different parameters are called *overloads*. The process of determining the closest match for a given set of parameters is called *overload resolution*, and I introduce it here in the context of `operator/`, though it will continue to be a topic we cover in passing.

Suppose we replace the previous `main()` function with the following one:

```
void main()
{
    Complex a(-5,10);
    float b = 5.0f;
    Console::WriteLine("({0}) / ({1}) = {2}",a,b,a/b);
}
```

Let's run this example:

```
C:\>cl /clr:pure /nologo test.cpp
C:\>test
(-5 + 10i) / (5) = -1 + 2i
```

When this example is executed, the compiler needs to look up how to calculate a/b, where the variable a is of type `Complex`, and the variable b is of type `float`.

The compiler parses a/b and begins to look for a compatible method of the form

```
operator/(Complex a,float b)
```

In the source of the program, there is no method that has this exact signature, so the compiler gathers up a list of possible candidate methods and tries to determine the best match. In this case, the possible choices are as follows:

```
operator/(Complex a,double b)
operator/(Complex a,Complex b)
```

Neither of these is an exact match. There are well-defined rules within the C++ standard governing the resolution of overloads, and these rules apply not only to operators but to functions in general. I don't want to dwell too much on this; for now, know that the intuitive choice in this case is the winner. A permitted operation is to promote (extend) the float to a double and choose the following:

```
operator/(Complex a,double b)
```

The rules for overload resolution provide a multitiered approach to dealing with implicit and explicit conversions. Certain conversions are favored over other conversions, and this is anything but arbitrary. At first glance, it does not seem to be a topic fraught with danger, but consider the following: Suppose we added an implicit conversion from double to Complex to our code. If the compiler could perform this conversion automatically, would we have to worry about creating an infinite recursion? Since operator/(Complex, Complex) calls operator/(Complex, double), adding an implicit conversion from double to Complex might result in either an ambiguity or an infinite loop. In this case, it does not because of the prioritization rules in the C++ specification, which assign a rank to each type of conversion and prioritize them by rank. We'll discuss implicit and explicit conversions later on in the chapter.

Just when you thought that the subject of complex numbers was getting too mathematical, brace yourself—I am pleased to present the following mathematical diversion.

A Mathematical Diversion: Numbers Modulo Primes

Both C# and C++/CLI use the percent sign as an operator for the calculation of one number modulo a different number. Recall that (number%p) is equal to the remainder when number is divided by p. It is easy to define a class of numbers modulo a number p. The following is simply the set of numbers:

$$\left\{0,1,\cdots(p-1)\right\}$$

Now we just need to figure out how to perform operations on them.

We can easily redefine the basic operators of addition, multiplication, and subtraction by calculating the result modulo p. Division would normally cause us to run into the use of fractions, but a result from elementary number theory tells us that division can be defined without fractions when the modulus p is prime. For example, let's consider the numbers modulo 13, and suppose we're trying to figure out what a quarter, 1 divided by 4, is. In other words, what is the inverse of 4?

A simple calculation shows that (4 * 10) % 13 = 1, since 4*10=40=39+1, thus 1 is the remainder when 40 is divided by 13.

Let's use the compiler to prove this:

```
using namespace System;
void main()
{
    Console::WriteLine("4 * 10 = {0} (13)", 4*10%13);
}
```

When we compile and execute this, we have the following:

```
C:\>cl /nologo /clr:pure test.cpp
C:\>test
4 * 10 = 1 (13)
```

10 is the inverse of 4. If we divide both sides by 4, we get the following:

$$\frac{1}{4} \equiv 10 \text{ modulo } 13$$

because

$$4 \times 10 = 1 + 13 \times 3 \equiv 1$$

Likewise, all nonzero numbers modulo 13 have an inverse in the same way. To find it, we have to use another result from number theory. It turns out, that for every two numbers a and b, there exist numbers x and y such that

$$ax + by = \gcd(a,b)$$

If one of the numbers is a prime, and the other is not a multiple of this prime, then the greatest common divisor (gcd) of these two numbers is 1, and we have the following:

$$ax + py = 1$$

Since any multiple of p is 0 by definition, we get

$$py \equiv 0 \text{ modulo } p$$

Read the preceding expression as follows: py is congruent to 0 modulo p, since py has remainder 0 when divided by p. Combining these facts, we conclude that there exists a number x such that

$$ax \equiv 1 \text{ modulo } p$$

In other words, we just need to find the number x, and we have our inverse! I won't bore you with any more details or derivations, but there is an extended version of the Euclidean algorithm that will do this for you.[3] It's in the following code; note that ExtendedEuclid() is implemented as a global function, not a class method, and it takes references to integers as some of its parameters:

```
using namespace System;
void ExtendedEuclid(int a, int b, int %d, int %x, int %y)
{
    if(b==0)
    {
        d=a;
        x=1;
        y=0;
    }
    else
    {
        ExtendedEuclid(b,a%b, d, y, x);
        y-= (a/b)*x;
```

---

3. Cormen, Thomas H. *Introduction to Algorithms*, 2nd ed. (Cambridge, MA: MIT Press, 2001).

```
    }
}
value struct F13
{
    unsigned Value;
    initonly static unsigned P = 13;
    F13(unsigned Val)
    {
        Value = Val % P;
    }
    static F13 operator * (F13 arg1, F13 arg2)
    {
        return F13((arg1.Value * arg2.Value) % P);
    }
    static F13 operator + (F13 arg1, F13 arg2)
    {
        return F13((arg1.Value + arg2.Value) % P);
    }
    static F13 operator - (F13 arg1, F13 arg2)
    {
        return F13((arg1.Value - arg2.Value) % P);
    }
    static F13 operator - (F13 arg1)
    {
        return F13((P - arg1.Value) % P );
    }
    static F13 operator / (F13 arg1, F13 arg2)
    {
        int d, x, y;
        ExtendedEuclid(arg2.Value,P,d,x,y);
        return arg1*F13(x*d);
    }
    virtual String ^ ToString() override
    {
        Value = (Value+P) % P;
        String ^s = Value.ToString();
        return s;
    }
};
void main()
{
    F13 a(6), b(9), c(4), d(10);
    Console::WriteLine("{0} * {1} is {2}", a, b, a*b);
    Console::WriteLine("{0} / {1} is {2}", a, b, a/b);
    Console::WriteLine("{0} * {1} is {2}", c, d, c*d);
}
```

And here are the results:

```
C:\>cl /clr:pure /nologo test.cpp
C:\>test
6 * 9 is 2
6 / 9 is 5
4 * 10 is 1
```

Implicit and Explicit Conversions of Built-in Types

Both C# and C++/CLI support defining implicit and explicit conversions between types. This is the user-defined type equivalent of promoting a float to a double or a short to an int. Implicit conversions are the conversions that the compiler can apply automatically, where explicit conversions require a cast operator. Let's talk a little bit about conversions between built-in types.

Conversion Differences Between C# and C++

Unfortunately, the implicit conversions over the built-in types differ between C++ and C#. C++ is historically notoriously lax in preventing conversions that risk data loss. Consider the following example:

```
using namespace System;
void main()
{
    long l=65537;
    short s=0;
    s=l;
    l=s;
    Console::WriteLine(l);
}
```

Now let's give this a try:

```
C:\>cl /clr:pure /nologo test.cpp
C:\>test
1
```

In this case, the compiler implicitly converted between short and long, and vice versa, without a warning as to the possible loss of data. If we raise the warning level to 3, we get the following output:

```
C:\>cl /clr:pure /nologo /W3 test.cpp
test.cpp(6) : warning C4244: '=' : conversion from 'long' to 'short', possible loss
of data
```

Now that's more like it!

Suppose we change the `long` to an `int` and compile at warning level 3. The data loss remains:

```
C:\>cl /clr:pure /nologo /W3 test.cpp
C:\>test
1
```

At best, that's an annoyance. At worst, it's a recall-class bug. Luckily, if we boost the warning level to level 4, we get the following:

```
C:\>cl /clr:pure /nologo /W4 test.cpp
test.cpp
test.cpp(6) : warning C4244: '=' : conversion from 'int' to 'short', possible loss
of data
```

The only problem with level-4 warnings is that they are considered more advisory than diagnostic, and sometimes come up as spurious or noisy warnings. The lesson learned is that you need to be careful. The C++ compiler isn't watching your back as much as the C# compiler in this area, and as I've recommended before, when you're developing your code, turn on /W4 warnings every now and then.

Signed/Unsigned Mismatches

The C++/CLI compiler does have the ability to warn if you attempt to assign a signed value to an unsigned variable and vice versa. It is disabled by default, but can be enabled using the /Wall compiler option, which enables all warnings that are disabled by default in the compilation.

For example, consider the following:

```
void main()
{
    unsigned u=0;
    int i=0;
    i=u;
}
```

After compiling, we get

```
C:\>cl /Wall /nologo test.cpp
test.cpp(5) : warning C4365: '=' : conversion from 'unsigned int' to 'int',
signed/unsigned mismatch
```

Integer Conversion Tables

Let's go over some of the built-in conversions in C++ and C#. Use the following list of abbreviations as a key to interpret the integer conversion tables (Table 11-1 to Table 11-5):

ex: Explicit

im: Implicit, no warning

i2: Implicit, warning level 2

i3: Implicit, warning level 3

i4: Implicit, warning level 4

ia: Implicit, warning /Wall only (to indicate signed/unsigned mismatch)

X: No conversion needed

Let's first look at the integer types in Table 11-1.

Table 11-1. *C++/CLI Conversion Table for a Sampling of Built-in Integer Types*

C++	From					
To		**From** short	**From** int	**From** long	**From** long long	**From** unsigned int	**From** unsigned long long
To short	X	i4	i3	i3	i4	i3
To int	im	X	im	i3	ia	i3
To long	im	im	X	i3	ia	i3
To long long	im	im	im	X	im	ia
To unsigned int	ia	ia	ia	i3	X	i3
To unsigned long long	ia	ia	ia	ia	ia	X

Let's look at the C# table for the integer types in Table 11-2.

Table 11-2. *C# Conversion Table for a Sampling of Built-in Integer Types*

C++	From				
To		**From** short	**From** int	**From** long	**From** uint	**From** ulong
To short	X	ex	ex	ex	ex
To int	im	X	ex	ex	ex
To long	im	im	X	im	ex
To uint	ex	ex	ex	X	im
To ulong	ex	ex	ex	im	X

Remember when you read these tables that you must take into account that long means a different thing in C# than in C++. In C++/CLI, both long and int are aliases for System::Int32, and long long is used for System::Int64, whereas C# achieves it by using long. Table 11-3 is an excerpt from the type table included in Chapter 6.

Table 11-3. *A Partial Type Table*

C#	C++/CLI	Size	Type	Signed	Marshal	Example
short	short	2	Int16	Yes	No	-1
ushort	unsigned short	2	UInt16	No	No	3u
int	int	4	Int32	Yes	No	-1l
uint	unsigned int	4	UInt32	No	No	3ul
long	long long	8	Int64	Yes	No	3ll
ulong	unsigned long long	8	UInt64	No	No	3ull
float	float	4	Single	Yes	No	4.0f
double	double	8	Double	Yes	No	3.0

Now let's look at the conversion tables. You may notice in the C# table that there is no possible loss of data. I'm a C++ advocate, but I must admit that I prefer the C# implementation in this area. Notice also that C++/CLI also considers implicit every conversion that C# considers implicit but still reports a signed/unsigned mismatch when extending from unsigned int to long.

The good news is that, when we look at these tables, we discover that C++/CLI has a way to get the same warning levels you've come to expect in C#. It's unintuitive but simple—don't use int.

In C++/CLI, int and long both map to System::Int32, and unsigned int and unsigned long both map to System::UInt32, but they are treated differently for warning purposes by the C++ compiler. Much of the reason for this is historical; short and long were initially defined as the minimum and maximum integer sizes supported by the target architecture. The type int was defined as the most efficient size for the target architecture. Over time, implementations found that this sort of floating definition made porting programs between platforms problematic. This led to the current implementation on .NET which fixes short at 16 bits, and int and long at 32 bits. The type long long was added to the language for 64 bits for .NET.

For other target architectures, int is either implemented as a short or a long, making the issuance of warnings problematic. The unofficial programming practice was to use int when you didn't really care about conversion problems and needed fast, efficient code; if the data itself called for it, you'd use short or long. This practice still applies today in .NET: use short and long over int, and the compiler will do its part and issue warnings.

Now let's have a look at floating point conversions.

Floating Point Conversion Tables

Let's examine some cross conversions in C++ in Table 11-4.

Table 11-4. *C++ Conversion Table for Floating Point Types and for a Sampling of Integer Types*

C++	From			
To		**From** int	**From** float	**From** double
	To int	X	i2	i2
	To float	i2	X	i3
	To double	im	im	X

Let's examine some cross conversions in C# in Table 11-5.

Table 11-5. *C# Conversion Table for Floating Point Types and for a Sampling of Integer Types*

C++	From			
To		**From** int	**From** float	**From** double
	To int	X	ex	ex
	To float	im	X	ex
	To double	im	im	X

One interesting thing to note about the floating point conversion tables is that C++ issues a level 2 warning when promoting an int to a float but not when promoting an int to a double. Consider the following snippet:

```
using namespace System;
void main()
{
    int i0 = int::MaxValue;
    int i;
    float f;
    double d;
    f = i0;
    i = f;
    Console::WriteLine("int {0}, to float {1}, back to int {2}", i0, f, i);
    d = i0;
    i = d;
    Console::WriteLine("int {0}, to double {1}, back to int {2}", i0, d, i);
}
```

In this example, we take the maximum positive integer and convert it to a float and back, with loss of data. Even though int and float are both 4 bytes long, float uses some of those bits to store exponent and sign information, so it is not able to store the integer information with full precision. If you take a similar round-trip using double, there is no data loss. Thus, the warning is correct:

```
C:\>cl /clr:pure /nologo /W4 test.cpp
test.cpp(8) : warning C4244: '=' : conversion from 'int' to 'float', possible loss
of data
test.cpp(9) : warning C4244: '=' : conversion from 'float' to 'int', possible loss
of data
test.cpp(12) : warning C4244: '=' : conversion from 'double' to 'int', possible loss
of data
C:\>test
int 2147483647, to float 2.147484E+09, back to int -2147483648
int 2147483647, to double 2147483647, back to int 2147483647
```

You might think there is a problem with the C# compiler, as it allows the conversion from int to float without warning about possible loss of data. However, C# requires the conversion back to int from float to have an explicit conversion or cast, so you can argue that a warning on the outbound direction is extraneous. The C# code follows:

```
using System;
class R
{
    public static void Main()
    {
        int i0 = int.MaxValue;
        int i;
        float f;
        double d;
        f = i0;
        i = (int)f;
        Console.WriteLine("int {0}, to float {1}, back to int {2}", i0, f, i);
        d = i0;
        i = (int)d;
        Console.WriteLine("int {0}, to double {1}, back to int {2}", i0, d, i);
    }
}
```

The results for the C# version follow:

```
C:\>csc /nologo test.cs
C:\>test
int 2147483647, to float 2.147484E+09, back to int -2147483648
int 2147483647, to double 2147483647, back to int 2147483647
```

Note that the C# version required explicit conversions in order to compile.

User-Defined Conversions

In the same way that the compiler defines implicit and explicit conversions between built-in types, users can define implicit and explicit conversions between user-defined types. In C#, you use the implicit and explicit keywords. In C++/CLI, conversions are implicit by default, and you use the explicit keyword to specify an explicit conversion.

Implicit Conversions

In our Complex class, we used a private helper function to define division of a complex number by a double. Why not expose this? Beyond that, why not allow users to multiply a complex number by a double or a double by a complex number?

We could write specific overloads for each of these operations, or we could define an implicit operator that converts a double to a Complex. Here it is, in C++/CLI syntax; it is a static member function that takes a double parameter:

```
static operator Complex(double re)
{
    return Complex(re,0);
}
```

Now users can perform all of the basic mathematical operations on complex numbers and doubles. Here is a new version of main() that uses this implicit operator:

```
void main()
{
    Complex a(-5,10), b(3,4);
    double c(3.5);
    Console::WriteLine("({0}) / ({1}) = {2}",a,b,a/b);
    Console::WriteLine("({0}) * ({1}) = {2}",a,c,a*c);
    Console::WriteLine("({0}) / ({1}) = {2}",c,a,c/a);
}
```

After compiling and running, we get the following:

```
C:\>cl /clr:pure /nologo test.cpp
C:\>test
(-5 + 10i) / (3 + 4i) = 1 + 2i
(-5 + 10i) * (3.5) = -17.5 + 35i
(3.5) / (-5 + 10i) = -0.14 + -0.28i
```

That's a lot of power for a little bit of work. What about going the other direction, from a Complex to a double?

Explicit Conversions

Going from a Complex to a double is going to involve some data loss, so this should not be an implicit conversion. What might this mean? Should we project the complex number onto the real line, and just return the real part of the complex number? Should we return the magnitude of the complex number? Should a conversion to double even exist? It's really up to us to decide which way to go.

Personally, I am drawn to the idea of using magnitude:

$$|a+bi| = \sqrt{a^2 + b^2}$$

The explicit conversion looks the same as the implicit conversion, except for the explicit keyword:

```
static explicit operator double(Complex c)
{
    return Math::Sqrt(c.re*c.re + c.im * c.im);
}
```

Just for neatness, we can replace the following code:

```
static Complex operator / (Complex a, Complex b)
{
    return a / (b.re*b.re+b.im*b.im) * ~b;
}
```

with

```
static Complex operator / (Complex a, Complex b)
{
    return a / ((double)b * (double)b) * ~b;
}
```

This gives us the following finished program; note that operator/(Complex, double) is no longer private:

```
using namespace System;
value struct Complex
{
    double re;
    double im;
    Complex(double re, double im)
    {
        this->re = re;
        this->im = im;
    }
    static Complex operator + (Complex a, Complex b)
    {
        return Complex(a.re+b.re, a.im+b.im);
    }
    static Complex operator - (Complex a, Complex b)
    {
        return Complex(a.re-b.re, a.im-b.im);
    }
    static Complex operator ~ (Complex a)
    {
```

```
        return Complex(a.re, - a.im);
    }
    static Complex operator * (Complex a, Complex b)
    {
        return Complex(a.re*b.re - a.im*b.im, a.re*b.im + a.im*b.re);
    }
    virtual String ^ ToString() override
    {
        String ^s = re.ToString();
        if(im != 0)
        {
            return s += " + " + im.ToString() + "i";
        }
        return s;
    }
    static Complex operator / (Complex a, Complex b)
    {
        return a / ((double)b * (double)b) * ~b;
    }
    static operator Complex(double re)
    {
        return Complex(re,0);
    }
    static explicit operator double(Complex c)
    {
        return Math::Sqrt(c.re*c.re + c.im * c.im);
    }
    static Complex operator / (Complex a, double f)
    {
        return Complex(a.re/f, a.im/f);
    }
};
void main()
{
    Complex a(-5,10), b(3,4);
    double c(3.5);
    Console::WriteLine("({0}) / ({1}) = {2}",a,b,a/b);
    Console::WriteLine("({0}) * ({1}) = {2}",a,c,a*c);
    Console::WriteLine("({0}) / ({1}) = {2}",c,a,c/a);
}
```

CLS-Compliant Operators

There are several ways to define the operators in C++, depending on your intentions and goals. In this case, the goal is to create a CLS-compliant application. The Common Language Specification (CLS) defines how code may be made compatible with multiple CLI languages. Therefore, it is best to adopt this paradigm when writing programs that link with C# or other

.NET languages. An operator is said to be CLS-compliant when all of the following criteria are met:

- The operator is listed in the CLS-compliant tables, as stated in the CLS.

- The operator is a static member of a reference or value class.

- Parameters and return values of the operator function are not passed or returned by any pointer, reference, or handle.

Let's examine the CLS-compliant unary operators in Table 11-6. [4]

Table 11-6. *CLS-Compliant Unary Operators*

Operator Name	Function Name	C#	C++
operator&	AddressOf	No	Yes
operator!	LogicalNot	Yes	Yes
operator~	OnesComplement	Yes	Yes
operator*	PointerDereference	No	Yes
operator-	UnaryNegation	Yes	Yes
operator+	UnaryPlus	Yes	Yes
operator true	true	Yes	No
operator false	false	Yes	No

Let's examine the CLS-compliant binary operators in Table 11-7.

Table 11-7. *CLS-Compliant Binary Operators*

Operator Name	Function Name	C#	C++
operator+	Addition	Yes	Yes
operator&	BitwiseAnd	Yes	Yes
operator|	BitwiseOr	Yes	Yes
operator,	Comma	Yes	Yes
operator--	Decrement	Yes	Yes
operator/	Division	Yes	Yes
operator==	Equality	Yes	Yes
operator^	ExclusiveOr	Yes	Yes
operator>	GreaterThan	Yes	Yes
operator>=	GreaterThanOrEqual	Yes	Yes
operator++	Increment	Yes	Yes
operator!=	Inequality	Yes	Yes

Continued

---

4. These tables are from the C++/CLI Language Specification.

Table 11-7. *Continued*

Operator Name	Function Name	C#	C++
operator<<	LeftShift	Yes	Yes
operator<	LessThan	Yes	Yes
operator<=	LessThanOrEqual	Yes	Yes
operator&&	LogicalAnd	No	Yes
operator||	LogicalOr	No	Yes
operator%	Modulus	Yes	Yes
operator*	Multiply	Yes	Yes
operator>>	RightShift	Yes	Yes
operator-	Subtraction	Yes	Yes

Most of these operators are fairly self-explanatory. Only a few merit special mention:

- operator* can either be Multiply or PointerDereference, depending on whether it is a binary or unary operator.

- operator& can either be BitwiseAnd or AddressOf, depending on whether it is a binary or unary operator.

- Both operator&& and operator|| can be overloaded in C++/CLI. These cannot be overloaded in C#.

- operator true and operator false are not implemented in C++.

operator true and operator false

operator true and operator false are used in the following C# code, which cannot be written similarly in C++/CLI:

```
using System;
class R
{
    int value;
    R(int V)
    {
        value = V;
    }
    public static bool operator true (R r)
    {
        return r.value!=0;
    }
    public static bool operator false ( R r)
    {
        return r.value==0;
    }
```

```
    public void Test(String name)
    {
        if(this)
        {
            Console.WriteLine("{0} is true", name);
        }
        else
        {
            Console.WriteLine("{0} is false", name);
        }
    }
    public static void Main()
    {
        R r3 = new R(3);
        r3.Test("r3");
        R r0 = new R(0);
        r0.Test("r0");
    }
}
```

If you compile and run this in C#, you get the following results:

```
C:\>csc /nologo test.cs
C:\>test
r3 is true
r0 is false
```

There is a nice workaround in C++ using an implicit conversion to bool:

```
using namespace System;
ref class R
{
private:
    int value;
    R(int V)
    {
        value = V;
    }
public:
    static operator bool(R^ r)
    {
        return r->value != 0;
    }
    void Test(String^ name)
    {
        if(this)
        {
            Console::WriteLine("{0} is true", name);
```

```
        }
        else
        {
            Console::WriteLine("{0} is false", name);
        }
    }
    static void Main()
    {
        R ^r3 = gcnew R(3);
        r3->Test("r3");
        R ^r0 = gcnew R(0);
        r0->Test("r0");
    }
};
void main()
{
    R::Main();
}
```

Other Operators

C++ allows you to overload the assignment operators, function calls (operator()), and indices (operator[]) in a manner that is not CLS compliant.

Summary

Having a good feel for expressions and operators is essential in object-oriented programming. They allow you to extend your classes and work with them as if they were built-in types.

In the next chapter, we'll complete our tour of basic C++ by filling in some of the details that have not been covered in any of the broad categories of previous chapters. After that, you will be well prepared to go into greater depth and detail in the chapters that follow.

CHAPTER 12

■ ■ ■

The End of the Beginning

Yu, shall I teach you what knowledge is? When you know a thing, to realize that you know it; and when you do not know a thing, to allow that you do not know it: this is knowledge.

—Confucius

In this chapter, we'll fill in the gaps and complete our introduction to basic C++. We'll talk about include files, scope resolution, miscellaneous operator details, and exceptions.

Include Files

One major difference between C# and C++/CLI is the multipass nature of C#. C++ was designed as a wrapper around C, which was designed to function on computers far less powerful than the contemporary home PC relegated to the den as too slow to be good for anything other than checking e-mail. Therefore, C was essentially a one-pass language in that the compiler could compile the entire program, digesting and translating C into assembly language, statement by statement. This required either the programmer to arrange the code so that basic subroutines came first, followed by subroutines that called the basic subroutines, finally followed by the main() procedure, which could call any of the preceding subroutines.

This requirement works for simple code, but it does not work when subroutines or classes are cross-referential, which is quite common in everyday coding. One common data structure that is typically cross referential is a type-safe function *callback*: a method of one class calls a second class to register a callback to the first class.

Forward Declarations

To get around this, C added the concept of forward declarations. A *forward declaration* is a prototype of a function or class that tells the compiler that a certain identifier is a class or function or provides details the class structure itself. When C++ added methods to classes, it also expanded the design of classes, so that classes themselves are not single-pass but two-pass elements. In case you are wondering, in C, a class is declared using the struct keyword.

C++ is a one-pass language, but classes themselves are resolved in two passes. Therefore, forward declarations are required when you access a function or variable before its definition, except when they are members of the same class. In addition, C++ compiles files into object files first and requires declarations to bind these object files into a single module or executable using a program called a *linker*.

In contrast, C# is not only essentially a two-pass language, but it also considers all the files of a single module at the same time when compiling. Compilation of C# becomes more and more inefficient when more and more source files are added without subdividing them into modules. On the other hand, C++ scales well, since each source file generates a new object file. Also, declarations describe what is external to the file, so a new file can be added and recompiled without requiring a complete rebuild of the entire module.

The Problem

The advantages and disadvantages of C++'s approach are fairly clear. Since C++ requires accurate declarations to compile correctly and bind object files together, what happens if the declarations are inaccurate? What happens if you change the definition of a function without changing the corresponding declaration of the function? If these become out of sync, the program does not compile correctly. Even worse, you could make a mistake in the order of compilation and it could compile, thus the linker would end up binding usage of a particular function with the function definition for another function.

The Solution

To keep all of the forward declarations and prototypes in sync, both C and C++ make use of include files to keep track of prototypes. *Include files* are files containing declarations and prototypes that are included into the source of the program when it is compiled. In this way, one include file can be shared by multiple source files, so everyone is always working with the most up-to-date version of the prototypes and declarations. If an include file changes, a *make program* can be used to force recompilation of all the source files that include it. If a declaration of an item in an include file ever becomes out of sync with the corresponding definition in a source file, the compiler issues an error, and the declaration can be corrected. Include files typically have an extension of .h, for header files that contain declarations, class definitions, and preprocessor definitions, and .hxx and .hpp for header files that also contain instantiations and variable definitions.

Include File Caveats

Note that this paradigm is user-defined. The compiler does not compile code differently if it originates in an included file versus a top-level source file—to the compiler, C++ is C++. You can, therefore, get into trouble if you place definitions in included files. If a definition is included into multiple source files, it is defined in each one, and you end up with a multiply defined symbol error. For example, consider the following three files:

```
// test1.cpp
#include "a.h"
```

```
// test2.cpp
#include "a.h"
```

```
// a.h
void hello()
{
}
```

Compile test1.cpp and test2.cpp with the following command line:

```
C:\>cl /nologo test1.cpp test2.cpp
test1.cpp
test2.cpp
Generating Code...
test2.obj : error LNK2005: "void __cdecl hello(void)" (?hello@@YAXXZ) already
defined in test1.obj
LINK : fatal error LNK1561: entry point must be defined
```

Note that we also get a linker error, because the global function main() is nowhere to be found in any of our source files.

Types of Declarations

Declarations come in all shapes and sizes. They can define classes or global objects, and class declarations may occur with anything from no definition to a complete definition.

Class Declaration Without Definition

When the knowledge of the internal structure of a class is not needed to compile a file, it suffices to declare that an identifier is a class, as in the following example:

```
class A;
class B
{
    A *pA;
};
```

Since we only have a pointer to type A, class B does not need to know the definition of A in order to allocate space for a pointer, pA—the simple declaration suffices.

Class Declaration With Definition

The following code does not compile:

```
class A;
class B
{
    A a;
};
```

The compiler is being asked to create an instance of A with every instance of B. In this example, the compiler needs to know the size and structure of A before it can complete the definition of B. Define A to fix the code.

The compiler output follows:

```
C:\>cl /nologo test.cpp
test.cpp(4) : error C2079: 'B::a' uses undefined class 'A'
```

Declaration of Global Variables

Global variables may or may not be declared using the extern keyword, as follows:

```
class A;
extern int i;
extern A * pA;
```

Variables declared at global scope are extern by default, which means that they are visible outside the compilation unit in which they are declared. This is also known as *external linkage*. The opposite of external linkage is *internal linkage*, which is achieved with the static keyword.

Separation of the Declaration and Definition of a class

The declaration of a class may be separated from the definition as follows:

```
//include file (a.h)
class A
{
    A();
    void Method();
};

//source file (a.cpp)
A::A()
{
}
void A::Method()
{
}
```

In this example, the declaration of class A can appear in an include file, which is included into several source files, and the definition of the individual methods, using the fully qualified name, appears in a single source file. Recall that partial classes are not supported in C++; partial classes are incompatible with the C++ paradigm. In C#, the compiler can search all source files for the partial class definitions and gather them together before defining the class. In C++, this is not possible.

Implicit Forward Reference to the Multipass Nature of Class Parsing

The following code works fine in C++, even without a forward declaration. The real question is which version of Hello() does the compiler use?

```
using namespace System;
void Hello()
{
    Console::WriteLine("::Hello");
}
ref class R
{
public:
    R()
    {
        Hello();
    }
    void Hello()
    {
        Console::WriteLine("R::Hello");
    }
};
void main()
{
    R ^r = gcnew R();
}
```

Let's try it and see:

```
C:\>cl /nologo /clr test.cpp
C:\>test
R::Hello
```

As you can see, the class version of Hello() is preferred over the global version, even though R::Hello() has not yet appeared in the code when Hello() is called from the constructor. A class version will always be preferred over a global version, because it is closer in scope, and the class version will be a candidate, because the entire class is parsed for declarations before any of the definitions are parsed. This is an example of the two-pass nature of C++ class parsing. This implementation is on par with the scoping rules of C++, which specify that the class scope has preference over the global scope while inside the class scope.

Scope Resolution Operator

What if we wanted, in the previous example, to invoke the global version of the Hello() function rather than the class version? In C++, you specify the global namespace by preceding the name with colon-colon. For example, let's change the constructor to the following:

```
R()
{
    ::Hello();
    Hello();
}
```

Now let's see what happens:

```
C:\>cl /nologo /clr test.cpp
C:\>test
::Hello
R::Hello
```

As you can see, the first call, ::Hello(), invoked the global function, and the second Hello() call invoked the member function. Preceding an identifier with the colon-colon scope resolution operator begins the search for the identifier at the global namespace.

In the following example the identifier in question is not a global function but a member function of another class:

```
using namespace System;
ref struct Outer
{
    ref struct Inner
    {
        Inner()
        {
            Console::WriteLine(__FUNCSIG__);
        }
        ref struct Outer
        {
            ref struct Inner
            {
                Inner()
                {
                    Console::WriteLine(__FUNCSIG__);
                }
            }
        public:
            static void Test()
            {
                Outer::Inner ^m0 = gcnew Outer::Inner();
                ::Outer::Inner ^m1 = gcnew ::Outer::Inner();
            }
        };
        };
    };
};
void main()
{
    Outer::Inner::Outer::Inner::Test();
}
```

In this code, we use the __FUNCSIG__ macro to print the signature of each Inner() method. If we compile and run this, we get the following:

```
C:\>cl /nologo /clr:pure test.cpp
test.cpp

C:\>test
__clrcall Outer::Inner::Outer::Inner::Inner(void)
__clrcall Outer::Inner::Inner(void)
```

This output shows that the colon-colon scope resolution operator at the beginning of the second allocation referenced Outer::Inner from the global context rather than the local context.

Nullable Types

Version 2.0 of the .NET Framework added nullable data types. A *nullable data type* is an extension of an underlying type that adds the null value to the set of legal values of the underlying type. Nullable types are supported in C++/CLI as well as C#.

Examples in C# and C++/CLI

In C#, the construction of a nullable type is indicated by appending a question mark to the type name. For example, consider the following C# code for a nullable instance of bool:

```
class R
{
    static void Main()
    {
        bool? b = null;
        if(b != null)
        {
            System.Console.WriteLine(b);
        }
        else
        {
            System.Console.WriteLine("null");
        }
    }
}
```

The expression

```
bool? b = null;
```

declares a nullable type based on a bool and sets it to null. The next line contains the following expression:

```
(b != null)
```

This expression, in turn, determines whether b has been set to null. C++/CLI also supports nullable types, but the syntax is not as simple. The C++/CLI syntax more closely reflects the generated IL, whereas the C# syntax is at a higher level of abstraction.

In order to use nullable types in C++/CLI, you need to do the following:

- Use pseudo-template syntax for the nullable type based on the keyword Nullable.

- Use the System namespace; Nullable<> is defined in this namespace.

- Use Nullable<type>() instead of null when you assign to an instance of a nullable type.

- Use the property HasValue rather than comparing to null when you use the instance in a comparison expression.

The C# declaration and initialization line that follows

```
bool? b = null;
```

becomes the following one in C++/CLI:

```
Nullable<bool> b = Nullable<bool>();
```

This C# expression

```
(b != null)
```

becomes the following one in C++/CLI:

```
(!b.HasValue)
```

Taking these guidelines and conversions into account, we discover C++/CLI code that accomplishes the same thing:

```
using namespace System;
ref struct R
{
    static void Main()
    {
        Nullable<bool> b = Nullable<bool>();
        if(!b.HasValue)
        {
            System::Console::WriteLine("null");
        }
        else
        {
            System::Console::WriteLine(b);
        }
    }
};
void main() {R::Main();}
```

Executing either version gives the following result:

```
null
```

Note that nullable data types may be created from user-defined types as well as built-in types. Consider the following example based on the user-defined type V, which also displays null:

```
using namespace System;
value struct V {};
ref struct R
{
    static void Main()
    {
        Nullable<V> b = Nullable<V>();
        if(!b.HasValue)
        {
            System::Console::WriteLine("null");
        }
    }
};
void main() {R::Main();}
```

The ?? Operator in C#

In C#, the ?? is a binary operator that works on nullable types. It evaluates to the first argument if it is not equal to null, or else it evaluates to the second. Although this syntax is not supported in C++/CLI, crafting code to perform an identical operation is straightforward.

Consider the following C# code:

```
using System;
class R
{
    static void Main()
    {
        bool? b;
        bool? c = true;
        b = null;
        Console.WriteLine(b ?? c);
        b = false;
        Console.WriteLine(b ?? c);
    }
}
```

After compiling and executing, we find the following:

```
C:\>csc /nologo test.cs

C:\>test
True
False
```

The first time (b??c) is evaluated (b==null), so the result of the expression is the value of c. The second time (b!=null), so the result of the expression is the value of b.

In C++/CLI, you can accomplish the same thing using the ?: ternary operator by changing the following:

```
(b??c)
```

to

```
Nullable<bool>( b.HasValue ? b : c );
```

This statement checks to see if b has a value and, if so, uses that value. Otherwise, the value of c is used. It's not as succinct as the C# version, but it accomplishes the same thing. Here is the entire snippet redone:

```
using namespace System;
ref struct R
{
    static void Main()
    {
        Nullable<bool> b;
        Nullable<bool> c = Nullable<bool>(true);
        b = Nullable<bool>();
        Console::WriteLine(Nullable<bool>( b.HasValue ? b : c ));
        b = Nullable<bool>(false);
        Console::WriteLine(Nullable<bool>( b.HasValue ? b : c ));
    }
};
void main() {R::Main();}
```

Under the Hood

Interestingly enough, if you load .NET Reflector and examine the IL for nullable types, you do not see anything remotely resembling the slick C# syntaxes of type? or ??. What you see instead is something much more akin to the C++/CLI code, which shows Nullable implemented as a generic class. Generics will be explained in more detail in Chapter 14. In fact, the C# version of the method Main() follows, decompiled to C++/CLI from .NET Reflector. Similar to the C++/CLI version, isn't it?

```
private:
static void  Main()
{
      Nullable<Boolean> nullable2 = Nullable<Boolean>(1) ;
      Nullable<Boolean> nullable1 = Nullable<Boolean>();
      Nullable<Boolean> nullable3 = nullable1;
      Console::WriteLine((nullable3.HasValue ? nullable3 : nullable2));
      nullable1 = Nullable<Boolean>(0) ;
      nullable3 = nullable1;
      Console::WriteLine((nullable3.HasValue ? nullable3 : nullable2));
}
```

Checked Expressions

In a previous example, we used the following expression:

```
int i0 = int::MaxValue;
```

This expression allows us to determine the maximum value of an integer. There is a highly questionable, and unfortunately somewhat common, way of doing the same sort of thing in C++. It takes advantage of the fact that integers are stored in two's complement on most target architectures, and a conversion between integers and unsigned integers is a conversion between data types of the same size. In this case, the int "–1" corresponds to the highest possible unsigned int, and this number, divided by 2, allows us to calculate the highest possible integer. Here is the expression in C++:

```
int i0=(int)(((unsigned)(int)-1)/2);
```

The preceding code does not compile in C#, even after you change the keyword unsigned to uint. The C# compiler knows you're doing a scary thing with this expression, and it requires you to embed this into an unchecked expression block to compile it, as follows:

```
class R
{
    public static void Main()
    {
        unchecked
        {
            int i0 = (int)(((uint)(int)-1)/2);
            System.Console.WriteLine(i0);
        }
    }
}
```

After compiling and executing this code in C#, we get the following:

```
C:\>csc /nologo test.cs
C:\>test
2147483647
```

In C#, there are two ways to control the checking of expressions:

- Embed the code in a checked or unchecked block; these are blocks preceded by the checked or unchecked keyword.

- Specify /checked+ or /checked- on the command line to enable or disable expression checking globally for code not embedded in checked or unchecked blocks.

C++ has no analogue to this type of checked expression.

Anonymous Methods

C# has a nifty syntax for creating nested methods using delegates called *anonymous methods*. It was added for C# 2.0, and C++ has no analogue yet. Anonymous methods allow you to create a method on the fly within the context of another method; they save time and can lead to greater code clarity. Anonymous methods are allowed to access local variables in the containing methods, as demonstrated in the following example:

```
using System;
class R
{
    public delegate void SayHello(string Message);
    SayHello dSayHello;
    public static void Main()
    {
        int Count = 0;
        R r = new R();
        r.dSayHello += delegate(string Message)
        {
            Console.WriteLine("{0} : {1} ", ++Count, Message);
        };
        r.dSayHello("call");
        r.dSayHello("call");
    }
}
```

Context-Sensitive Keywords

A *context-sensitive keyword* is an identifier that is interpreted as a keyword in specific grammatical contexts. Most of the new C++/CLI keywords were added as context-sensitive keywords, so that that the majority of legacy code would compile under C++/CLI unchanged.

For example, consider the following snippet:

```
void main()
{
    int property = 3;
    int event = 2;
}
```

This code was valid C++ before the new C++/CLI syntax was developed, and the compiler needs to compile it correctly. It uses the identifiers property and event, but they are not considered keywords in this context, so this code can be compiled for the CLR without error.

Context-sensitive keywords can lead to some entertaining examples, where identifiers are sometimes keywords and sometimes not. Consider the following valid C++/CLI code:

```
value struct property {};
ref struct Test
{
    property property property;
};
void main() {}
```

In this case, we have a trivial property named property that is of type property.

Method Group Conversion

C# has an abbreviated syntax for registering event handlers called *method group conversion*. This provides a simpler syntax for using events and delegates, as in the following example:

```
using System;
class R
{
    public delegate void SayHello(string Message);
    SayHello dSayHello;
    int Count = 0;
    public void DisplayMessage(string Message)
    {
        Console.WriteLine("{0} : {1} ", ++Count, Message);
    }
    public static void Main()
    {
        R r = new R();
//      r.dSayHello = new SayHello(r.DisplayMessage);
        r.dSayHello = r.DisplayMessage;
        r.dSayHello("call");
        r.dSayHello("call");
    }
}
```

The commented out line may be replaced by the bold line following it. C++ has no equivalent syntax.

This sort of syntactic sugar is very common in the C# language. The language offers a lot of these little shortcuts that save the user a few lines of code here and there, thus making developing applications with C# faster.

■**Note** Delegate and event code is always tricky to translate, as diagnostics can be misleading. We can lay most of the blame at the doorstep of the compiler's ability to interpret context-sensitive keywords. These keywords are determined in a disambiguation grammar, and if this grammar concludes that either `delegate` or `event` is not a keyword in this context, they are interpreted as regular identifiers, and the diagnostics are less than helpful.

Here is the previous example converted to C++/CLI, without using method group conversion:

```
using namespace System;
ref struct R
{
    delegate void SayHello(String^ Message);
    SayHello ^dSayHello;
    int Count;
    R() : Count(0) {}
    void DisplayMessage(String^ Message)
    {
        Console::WriteLine("{0} : {1} ", ++Count, Message);
    }
    static void Main()
    {
        R^ r = gcnew R();
        r->dSayHello = gcnew SayHello(r, &R::DisplayMessage);
        r->dSayHello("call");
        r->dSayHello("call");
    }
};
void main() {R::Main();}
```

Constructor-Initialized Variables

In C#, variables that can only be initialized within the constructor, the constructor member initializer list, or the class declaration are defined by marking them readonly. In C++/CLI, these variables are marked using the initonly keyword.

In C++, only static variables may be initialized within the class declaration, whether or not they are marked `initonly`. C# is able to create an implicit instance and static constructors that initialize class variables, whereas C++/CLI only creates implicit static constructors.

For example consider the following C# code:

```
using System;
class R
{
    readonly int i0=3;
    static readonly int i1=4;
    static void Main() {}
}
```

Here is the C++/CLI equivalent:

```
using namespace System;
ref class R
{
    initonly int i0;
    static initonly int i1=4;
    R()
    {
        i0=3;
    }
public:
    static void Main() {}
};
void main() {R::Main();}
```

The compiler creates a static constructor implicitly; initialization of nonstatic `initonly` variables must be explicitly performed within the instance constructor.

Expression Statements with No Effect

C# disallows most expression statements that have no effect. These are allowed in C++, because they are often useful for debugging or used as a remnant of a conditional preprocessor statement.

Consider the following C# code:

```
using System;
class R
{
    static void Main()
    {
        int i=3;
        (i==2);    // invalid in C#
    }
}
```

The results follow:

```
C:\>csc /nologo test.cs
test.cs(7,9): error CS0201: Only assignment, call, increment, decrement, and new
object expressions can be used as a statement
```

An expression statement like (i==2); is valid syntax in C++ and compiles with neither error nor warning.

Exceptions

For the most part, exception handling is quite similar in C# and C++/CLI.[1] C++ supports exceptions in the same contexts as C# with the addition of a special construct called function-try blocks, which we will cover later in this section.

Let's start with the basics.

Basic Exception Handling

Here is a short yet comprehensive example of basic exception handling in C#:

```
using System;
class MyException : Exception
{
    public MyException(string message) : base(message)
    {
    }
}
class R
{
    static void Main()
    {
        try
        {
            throw new MyException("exception");
        }
        catch (MyException e)
        {
            Console.WriteLine("caught : {0}", e);
            return;
        }
        catch
```

----

1. Native C++ exception handling can get complicated, as several variants are supported by the compiler. Consult the Visual C++ documentation for further details.

```
    {
    }
    finally
    {
        Console.WriteLine("in the finally block");
    }
}
}
```

In this example, we start by defining a custom exception called MyException derived from System::Exception. The constructor takes a string as a parameter and forwards it to the base class. In order to convert this to C++, we have to take the following steps:

1. Change class to ref class.

2. Change string to String^. string is an alias that does not exist in C++; C++ invokes the reference type System::String explicitly.

3. Change base to Exception, as C++ refers to the base class constructor explicitly by name.

4. Add a semicolon to the end of the class definition.

5. Add a colon to the public keyword.

We then have the following:

```
ref class MyException : Exception
{
public:
    MyException(String ^message) : Exception(message)
    {
    }
};
```

Next, we make similar changes to the body.

Since MyException is a reference type, we need to treat it as such, and change

```
MyException e
```

to

```
MyException ^e
```

In addition, we need to take these steps:

1. Change class to ref class.

2. Change new to gcnew.

3. Change Console.WriteLine to Console::WriteLine.

4. Add a semicolon to the end of the class definition.

5. Change the generic catch handler from `catch` to `catch(. . .)`. The generic catch handler is the last handler that catches all exceptions previously uncaught. The C++ syntax requires the ellipsis.

6. Insert the `public:` keyword before the `Main()` function, and add a global `main()` function to invoke it.

The resulting code follows:

```
using namespace System;
ref class MyException : Exception
{
public:
    MyException(String ^message) : Exception(message)
    {
    }
};
class R
{
public:
    static void Main()
    {
        try
        {
            throw gcnew MyException("exception");
        }
        catch (MyException ^e)
        {
            Console::WriteLine("caught : {0}", e);
            return;
        }
        catch(...)
        {
        }
        finally
        {
            Console::WriteLine("in the finally block");
        }
    }
};
void main() {R::Main();}
```

Let's compile and execute this:

```
C:\>cl /nologo /clr:pure test.cpp
C:\>test
caught : MyException: exception
   at R.Main()
in the finally block
```

Note that the finally block is always executed at the end of the try block, whether or not there is an exception. This is true even if there is a return or break statement that might ostensibly circumvent this mechanism. In fact, the finally is always executed.

You might be tempted to use the finally statement to control the deallocation of unmanaged resources or other similar applications, but there are better ways to do this, ranging from the using statement in C# to the destructor, finalizer, or dispose paradigms in .NET and C++. We will cover this in detail in Chapter 20.

Function-Try Blocks

Function-try blocks are features unique to C++ that allow you to catch any exception that occurs within the entire body of a function. This feature may seem insignificant until you realize that it allows you to catch exceptions within the base class constructor during construction of a derived class.

The Problem

Let's look at an example in order to elucidate. In C#, it is very difficult to catch an exception generated in the base class in the context of the derived class. It needs to be caught within the method that created the derived class object, which is not local to the exception. As such, it makes exception handling problematic. A C# example with a base class and a derived class follows:

```
using System;
class Base
{
    public Base(int i)
    {
        throw new Exception("throwing in Base's constructor");
    }
}
class Derived : Base
{
    Derived(int i) : base(i)
    {
    }
    static void Main()
    {
        Derived r = new Derived(3);
    }
}
```

Let's try to compile and run this:

```
C:\>csc /nologo test.cs
C:\>test
Unhandled Exception: System.Exception: throwing in Base's constructor
    at Base..ctor(Int32 i)
    at Derived.Main()
```

Enter the Function-Try Block

In C++, you can catch this exception using a function-try block. A function-try block catches exceptions that occur anywhere in the function body and, as applied to constructors, also catches exceptions thrown in the base class constructor. Here is the syntax for a function-try block on a constructor:

```
Derived(int i)
try
: Base(i)
{
}
catch(Exception ^e)
{
}
```

It's a little different, but it works.

Since we're throwing an exception in construction, there is an implicit rethrow at the end of this sequence to notify the method that attempted to create an instance of Derived, just as in C#. We can either let this rethrow happen and catch it at the top level, or we can change the type of exception to signal that it was caught earlier. Here is a complete example, with a rethrow of a different type of exception:

```
using namespace System;
ref class MyException : Exception
{
public:
    MyException(String ^message) : Exception(message)
    {
    }
};
ref class Base
{
public:
    Base(int i)
    {
        throw gcnew Exception("throwing in Base's constructor");
    }
};
ref class Derived : Base
{
    Derived(int i)
    try
    : Base(i)
    {
    }
    catch(Exception ^e)
    {
        Console::WriteLine("caught {0}", e);
```

```
            throw gcnew MyException("caught");
    }
public:
    static void Main()
    {
        try
        {
            Derived ^r = gcnew Derived(3);
        }
        catch(Exception ^e)
        {
            Console::WriteLine("caught {0}", e);
        }
    }
};
void main() {Derived::Main();}
```

In this sequence, we use the function-try block to catch the exception thrown in base-class construction and then throw an exception of a different type within the catch clause.

Here are the results when the code compiled and executed:

```
C:\>cl /nologo /clr:pure test.cpp
test.cpp
C:\>test
caught System.Exception: throwing in Base's constructor
   at Base..ctor(Int32 i)
   at Derived..ctor(Int32 i)
caught MyException: caught
   at Derived..ctor(Int32 i)
   at Derived.Main()
```

Exercise

The complexity of exception handling tends to befuddle decompilers. Compile this example, and inspect it using .NET Reflector. How does the IL look? How does it decompile into C# and C++/CLI?

Summary

In this chapter, we finished our tour of basic C++. We talked about include files, scope resolution, miscellaneous operator details, and exceptions. In the chapters that follow, we will explore both C++/CLI and native C++ in greater depth and learn practical examples as well as more-advanced constructs.

I think it would be fun to postpone that exploration for one chapter and take a quick break in Chapter 13 to play with a few common interview questions.

CHAPTER 13

∎∎∎

Fun, Fun, and More Fun

How does a project get to be a year late? One day at a time.

—Frederick P. Brooks, Jr., *The Mythical Man-Month*

As we conclude the basic introduction to C++ and prepare to tackle more-advanced topics, perhaps it might be fitting to reward our efforts with a slight diversion. We'll look at some fun interview questions with programmatic C++ solutions.

Dropping Light Bulbs

There's an interview question floating around on the Internet[1] that asks you to determine how far a superstrong light bulb can drop without breaking. We'll break down this program mathematically and implement a nice recursive algorithm to show the solution.

Light Bulbs

You have two nearly unbreakable light bulbs and a 100-floor building. Using the fewest possible drops, determine how much of an impact this type of light bulb can withstand (e.g., it can withstand a drop from the 17th floor, but it breaks when dropped from the 18th). Note that the ever-popular binary search gives you a worst case of 50 drops. You should be able to do it in less than 20.

Initial Thoughts

The first thing to notice about this problem is that you only have two light bulbs. Once the first is broken, you can't take chances anymore. You need to follow the most conservative strategy you can to nurse your bulb until you are sure you have found the correct floor when it breaks.

---

1. You can find the questions in this chapter and others like them at http://www.techinterview.org. This site, in turn, cites *How Would You Move Mount Fuji*, by William Poundstone, as a source. Poundstone lays no claim to having invented these problems, but he has gathered them together in a single interesting text.

This means you have to go up a single floor at a time, starting just above the first floor you are sure the bulb can survive a drop from. You can't risk the second bulb breaking unless this tells you for sure what the maximum allowable impact is.

In other words, if the second bulb breaks in falling from floor n, you should have already determined that the bulb would survive a fall from floor $n-1$.

Our initial instinct is to divide the number of floors by two and go from there, so let's work out what happens when we drop the bulb from the 50th floor.

Well, what happens if it breaks on that very first drop? Since there is only one bulb left, we can't take a chance on skipping a single floor. The only strategy left is to be ultra conservative and start at the lowest possible floor and go up one at a time. We are then forced to drop the second bulb from the first floor, then the second, and so on. The worst case is then that we are forced to climb all the way up to the 49th floor, one floor at a time. This would mean a total of 50 drops (1+49 drops).

So dividing the number of floors by two for our initial drop is very inefficient. What would happen if we divided the number of floors by a larger number for our initial drop, and go from there?

A Rough Approximation

Suppose we divided the number of floors by five. Then our first drop would be from the 20th floor. If the initial bulb does not break, we could attempt drops from the 40th floor, the 60th floor, and so on up to 100. If the bulb breaks, we are left with, at most, the number of floors between the drops to determine a bulb break. In this case, that makes for 19 drops (20–1 drops). Now we can calculate the worst case. The first bulb will be dropped at most once for each floor that is a multiple of 20, or {20, 40, 60, 80, 100}. This makes five possible drops, which is also equal to 100 divided by 20, or 100/20. After any break, the second bulb will be, at most, dropped the difference between these multiples of 20, or 20-1 times. So we see that the worst case number of drops is as follows:

$(100 / 20) + 20 - 1 = 24$

Certainly 24 drops is a lot better than our previous algorithm's worst case of 50.

A Little Algebra

Perhaps, with a little bit of algebra, we can see how far we can we can push this idea. Suppose we drop our first bulb from the nth floor, for all possible values of n. By following the pattern derived previously, we get

$[100 / n] + n - 1$

There is a slight inaccuracy caused by the facts that 100 may not be exactly divisible by n, and dropping the bulb from floor 100 after a previous drop from 80 does not give you as much new information as the drop from 80 after a previous drop from 60. Still, the formula easily allows us to calculate an upper bound for an optimal algorithm.

Suppose k is the worst case for the algorithm given n. Then we have the following formula:

$[100 / n] + n - 1 = k$

and essentially,

$n^2 - (k+1)n + 100 = 0$

Now we have a quadratic equation in n, and we can use a little bit of elementary algebra to make a rough calculation. We would like to minimize k over all possible values of n and that will give us the best worst case.

A quadratic factors as follows:

$$n^2 - (a+b)n + ab = 0$$

Since the arithmetic mean is always at least as large as the geometric mean,

$$\frac{a+b}{2} \geq \sqrt{ab}$$

this achieves equality when $a=b$, and we get the following:

$$a = b = 10$$

$$a + b = 20$$

and here

$$k + 1 = 20$$

$$k = 19$$

$$n^2 - 20n + 100 = 0$$

and here.

$$(n-10)^2 \geq 0$$

We should drop the first bulb every ten floors to get the best results from this algorithm. In this case, that is k=19 drops.[2]

The goal of the interview question is to see if you can discover the 19-drop algorithm, even if you don't use algebra to reveal it.

Don't be mistaken—I am not asserting that this is the best possible algorithm. It seems to make sense to drop the first bulb the first time from the tenth floor, but if the bulb does not break, can we not use this information to reevaluate the problem? Isn't it a new problem now? It is now the problem of two bulbs and the 90-story building. For this reason, it seems a clear optimization to decrease the distance between drops if the first bulb survives the fall. This could then continue to be reevaluated with every drop. We should not be tied to dropping the bulb every ten floors simply because the tenth floor was the best place for the first drop.

Discovering a Recursive Algorithm

In this way, the recursive nature of this problem arises. Rather than thinking about this problem in terms of 100 stories, we should think of the problem in terms of N stories and consider it recursively. Then perhaps we can divine a more efficient algorithm.

---

2. This method can be generalized. For a building N stories tall, we can perform the same factoring if we choose:

$$n = \sqrt{N}$$

Then we can see that

$$k \leq 2\sqrt{N} - 1$$

In order to do this we need to define a function:

```
int Drop(int floors);
```

The function Drop() returns the minimal number of drops for a given number of floors. Of course, this doesn't tell us the floor to drop from as such, but we could adapt the program to do just that if we desired.

Suppose we are in a building where the number of floors equals floors. If we drop the first bulb from floor i, and the bulb breaks, we need to use the other bulb to determine whether it would break when falling from floors 1, 2, 3. . .(i-1) inclusive. This could take at most (i-1) drops. If the bulb does not break, then Drop(floors-i) calculates the best we can do with a building of height floors-i. As long as floors-i is always strictly less than floors, and we make note of the fact that Drop(1)==1, we will not be locked in an infinite loop.[3]

The worst case number of drops in this case is:

```
max(i, Drop(floors-i)+1)
```

If we loop on reasonable values of i, we can find the smallest worst case. What is a reasonable value for i? Trying all possible values of i, from 1 to floors is overkill. An easy optimization is to realize that we should never drop higher than the halfway from the binary example shown previously. It seems intuitive that trying values of i from 1 to the square root of floors would suffice by the argument presented previously. In the following code, I use a range of [1, floors/2]:

```
using namespace System;
ref struct Drops
{
    array<int>^floordata;
    Drops()
    {
        floordata = gcnew array<int>(300);
        floordata[1] = 1;
    }
    int Drop(int floors)
    {
        if(floordata[floors])
        {
            return floordata[floors];
        }
        int best = Int32::MaxValue;
        if(floors == 1)
        {
            best = 1;
        }
        else
        {
```

---

3. Do you notice any similarities between the implementation of a recursive algorithm and a proof by mathematical induction?

```
            int i;
            for(i=1;i<floors/2+1;i++)
            {
                int drops = Drop(floors-i) + 1;
                int thisone = (drops>i) ? drops : i;
                best = thisone<best ? thisone : best;
            }
        }
        floordata[floors]=best;
        return best;
    }
};
void main()
{
    Drops ^d = gcnew Drops();
    Console::WriteLine("For {0} floors, the minimum is {1}", 100, d->Drop(100));
}
```

The output follows:

```
For 100 floors, the minimum is 14
```

Implementation

The code itself is pretty straightforward, though one optimization is needed.

The initial version I wrote ran so slowly I thought about grabbing a cup of coffee while waiting for it to finish. Since the code is recursive, Drop(n) called Drop(n-1), Drop(n-2), and so on and caused all of those to be recalculated. Drop(n+1) does more of the same thing, in addition to invoking Drop(n), so there is so much repetition of calculation that we have to very be careful how we spend our cycles.

We need to insure that Drop(floors) is only calculated, at most, once for each value of floors, or we end up doing the same work again and again and again. To do this, we create the floordata array to save the results of previous calls to Drop(). This array is a member of the Drops class and is allocated by the constructor Drops(). For each value of floors, we check the array to see if a value has been calculated. If not, we go ahead and do the work in the Drop() function and save the result in the floordata array upon exit.

The program does make use of the ?: ternary conditional operator:

```
expression ? value1 : value2
```

This operator evaluates to value1 if expression is true, or else it evaluates to value2. It allows us to avoid if else statements for simple constructs and write in a more compact form.

Show the Way: Part 1

The program calculated that our algorithm will require at least 14 drops. Discover the bulb strength, and display the sequence of drops that leads to the worst case of 14 drops for a 100-story building.

First Drop

This program doesn't tell you the best place to drop the bulb, although it can be modified to do exactly that. It turns out that which floor you should drop the bulb from depends very strongly on how many floors are left because of the discrete nature of the problem. It is not possible, therefore, to print out a short list of instructions on how to drop the bulbs; rather, the solution is a graph. If the bulb breaks at this floor, do this, or else do that. For any given bulb strength, however, printing the sequence of drops that this optimal algorithm would follow is straightforward.

One thing you might notice, though, is that you would do well to make the first drop from the 14th floor. The rationale for this is simple: we want to make the first drop from as high a floor as possible, so we reduce the problem the most quickly. If the bulb breaks, we have at most 13 second bulb drops to determine the bulb strength, so we do no worse than our optimal worst case of 14 drops. Using a program, you can determine that an initial drop anywhere from the 11th to the 14th floor still allows you to achieve the optimal sequence of at most 14 drops.

Bridge Crossing

Another common question going around the Internet that sometimes pops up in technical interviews is that of four men crossing a dark bridge with a single flashlight.

Four Men on a Bridge

Four men have to cross a bridge at night. The bridge is old, dilapidated, and can hold, at most, two people at a time. There are no railings, and the men have only one flashlight. Anytime someone crosses, whether one or two men go, the flashlight must be carried. The flashlight must be walked back and forth; it cannot be thrown. Each man walks at a different speed. One takes 1 minute to cross, another 2 minutes, another 5, and the last 10 minutes. If two men cross together, they must walk at the slower man's pace. What is the minimum amount of time required for all four men to cross?

Background

Now the reason that this question is so popular is that there is an obvious and logical incorrect conclusion that everyone jumps to. It is only after deeper thought and a bit of insight that you can arrive at the correct answer.[4]

Think about this a moment before you read on. There you are on the bridge, walking back and forth. A couple of fast people, one extremely fast, and a couple of slower people, are sitting there on the bridge. You can even indulge yourself; imagine you're the walker who can cross in 1 minute.

---

4. Or shall we say with a bit of luck, as you're sitting there sweating in an interviewer's office with your mind frozen with fear?

The initial incorrect conclusion is that the faster walker should shepherd everyone back and forth. The 1-minute walker walks over with the 10-minute walker, which takes 10 minutes. She returns, which takes 1 minute. She fetches the next guy, and so on. This solution gives you a best case of 19 minutes for all to cross the bridge. You proudly announce this to the interviewer, who smugly says that there is a better solution. Horrified, you stumble back to the whiteboard and try to write something intelligent.

A better solution relies on a classic scheduling algorithm. You try to balance your tasks, so tasks are accomplished simultaneously. In the 19-minute solution, the 10- and 5-minute walkers go across separately, which gives you a base time of 15 minutes, no matter who is traveling with them. That's a tough thing to optimize. If you send the 5- and 10-minute walkers together, then your slow people get across in only 10 minutes, and with a bit of a flashlight handoff, you calculate that you can get everyone across in 17 minutes total. I'll leave figuring out how that works to you.

This of course, brings us to another question: Is this the best possible algorithm?

We would also love to know what kind of results we might get if we varied the speeds of the crossers. What would be the best possible traveling time then?

We can answer these questions by writing a short computer program. In order to implement it, we make the following assumptions:

- Every crossing from the start to the end contains exactly two walkers.

- Every crossing from the end to the start contains exactly one walker.

These are fairly reasonable assumptions given the nature of the problem. I am sure that it is possible to prove that no optimal solution will violate these assumptions, but proof is not the goal here, so we'll push on.

Algorithm and Implementation

One obvious algorithm is to try all possible traversals of walkers across the bridge given these assumptions. In order to do this, we have to keep track of who is on which side of the bridge as well as the location of the flashlight. Because of the assumptions, we know that every trip across the bridge with two walkers is followed by a return trip with a single walker, until we're done. Then the location of the flashlight is implicit.

We could then write a function crossover(State, Direction) that we could use for crossing the bridge in either direction. I initially wrote the program this way, and it does work, but it turns out that splitting the crossing into an outbound start(State) function, and an inbound end(State) function is cleaner.

There are several possibilities for how we keep track of the State of the crossing, but a simple bit field that indicates who is on the starting side of the bridge is sufficient and clean. We use an unsigned int to indicate who is on the starting side of the bridge. For the start(unsigned here) function, this data indicates who is on the starting side of the bridge, or "here." For the end(unsigned there) function, this data indicates who is on the other side, or "there." In either case, the data always indicates who is on the starting side of the bridge. We could always pass who is on the side where the flashlight is, by continually applying the exclusive OR on the data with a bit field, but I find that always passing the state on the starting side is the simplest way for debugging purposes.

The Code

We use a ref struct named Crossing that contains constant information that we'd prefer not to keep passing recursively. In this case, we have the traversal speed for the walkers, stored in the times array, and a Mask that allows us to calculate who is on the opposite of the bridge via a simple exclusive OR. We do not initialize these in the constructor; rather, we save times from an input parameter and recalculate Mask each time a crossing is initiated. This was more a matter of taste and style than an aspiration for accuracy. The code itself is interesting and instructive; take the time to pick through it, and continue to familiarize yourself with C++/CLI:

```
using namespace System;
ref struct Crossing
{
    array<unsigned>^ times;
    unsigned int Mask;
    int cross(...array<unsigned>^ times)
    {
        this->times = times;
        Mask = (1u<<times->Length)-1;
        return start(Mask);
    }
    int end(unsigned there)
    {
        if(there==0)
        {
            return 0;
        }
        unsigned here = Mask^there;
        unsigned best = 0xffff;
        for(int i=0;i<times->Length; i++)
        {
            if(here & (1<<i))
            {
                unsigned thistrip;
                thistrip = times[i] + start(there^(1<<i));
                if(thistrip<best)
                {
                    best = thistrip;
                }
            }
        }
        return best;
    }
    int start(unsigned here)
    {
```

```
        if(here==0)
        {
            return 0;
        }
        unsigned best = 0xffff;
        for(int i=0;i<times->Length; i++)
        {
            if(here & (1<<i))
            {
                unsigned thistrip;
                for(int j=i+1;j<times->Length; j++)
                {
                    if(here & (1<<j))
                    {
                        thistrip =
                            (times[i]>times[j]? times[i] : times[j])
                            + end(here^((1<<i)|(1<<j)));
                        if(thistrip<best)
                        {
                            best = thistrip;
                        }
                    }
                }
            }
        }
        return best;
    }
};
void main()
{
    Crossing ^c = gcnew Crossing();
    int time = c->cross(1,2,5,10);
    Console::WriteLine("It takes at least {0} minutes", time);
}
```

If you execute this program, you get the expected result:

```
It takes at least 17 minutes
```

Show the Way: Part 2

Enhance the program so that the actual minimum order of crossings is displayed. This requires passing more data recursively.

Taking the Algorithm for a Spin

Of course, since we implemented this with a `param` array that accepts a variable number of arguments, it is easy to try a different case, with a different number of walkers. If we change the following line:

```
int time = c->cross(1,2,5,10);
```

to

```
int time = c->cross(1,2,5,10,7);
```

then intuitively, we expect this to take an additional 7 minutes perhaps. The truth is out there:

It takes at least 23 minutes

That's a bit of a surprise. Adding a 7-minute walker only slows the entire process by 6 more minutes. It turns out that the 7-minute walker ends up crossing with the 10-minute walker, which leaves the 5-minute walker to deal with. The 5-minute walker does a round-trip with the 1-minute walker, which takes a total of 6 additional minutes. OK, that makes sense.

What if we add another 7-minute walker?

```
int time = c->cross(1,2,5,10,7,7);
```

Well, since he can't cross with the 10-minute walker, he's got to cross with the 5-minute walker, so that adds another 7 minutes. Let's try it out:

It takes at least 29 minutes

Wait, that's only 6 minutes more—that's another counter-intuitive answer. I'm sure there's a simple explanation; perhaps the 1-minute walker's return trip can be avoided?

This is definitely a program that is fun to play with.

Dealing with Cannibals

This question does not seem to come up in interviews as often as the other two, but it has an interesting and instructive twist.

River Crossing

Three cannibals and three anthropologists have to cross a river. Their boat is only big enough for two people. If at any point in time there are more cannibals on one side of the river than anthropologists, the cannibals will eat them. What plan can the anthropologists use for crossing the river, so they don't get eaten?

Assumptions

This problem does not seem, at first glance, to be as difficult as the bridge problem. We have a discrete number of cannibals and anthropologists, with no attached concept of traversal time (or eating time, shall we say?).

We were able to approach the previous problem by making a couple of clear assumptions about who is crossing the river. We would love to make similar assumptions here, for example:

- Two people always cross from the launching side to the landing side.

- One person always returns.

Unfortunately, these assumptions are invalid. There are very clear reasons why you might want to send two people on the return journey to maintain a safe combination of people on each side of the river. In fact, the optimal solution of 11 crossings does just this.

How can we come up with an algorithm that is guaranteed to terminate in all cases? If we try a path in which we are sending exactly two people back and forth, our recursive algorithm does not work.

The trick here is to think of this algorithm in terms of a depth-first traversal of possibilities. Rather than letting the algorithm go deeper and deeper down a potentially infinite path searching for a solution, we structure the algorithm so it asks, iteratively, "Is there a solution with iteration crossings?" We start iteration at 1, and go up until this is answered in the affirmative. This algorithm is guaranteed to succeed if a solution exists. If no solution exists, this loop continues until resources exhaust themselves; in this case, the resource is the stack.

The Code

In this program, I created a single subroutine for crossing in either direction, since these operations are completely symmetric because of the lack of assumptions. The variable dir is in the set {1,-1} and determines which way we are crossing.

Since there are only five possible combinations of people in the boat, I list them discretely using a logical OR to separate the possibilities. Just as in C#, short-circuit evaluation prevents further calls to crossover() once a call returns true.

The rest of the code is fairly simple and might be just what you need to produce on a whiteboard someday:

```
using namespace System;
ref struct Crossing
{
    int MaxA;
    int MaxC;
    int cross(int MaxA, int MaxC)
    {
        this->MaxA=MaxA;
        this->MaxC=MaxC;
        int iterations;
        for(iterations=1;  ;iterations++)
        {
```

```
            if(crossover(MaxA, MaxC, iterations, -1))
            {
                break;
            }
        }
        return iterations;
    }
    bool crossover(int A, int C, int iterations, int dir)
    {
        if(iterations--<0)
        {
            return false;
        }
        if(A==0 && C==0)
        {
            return true;
        }
        if(A<0 || C<0)
        {
            return false;
        }
        if(A>0 && C>A)
        {
            return false;
        }
        int Ap = MaxA-A;
        int Cp = MaxC-C;
        if(Ap>0 && Cp>Ap)
        {
            return false;
        }
        return (
            crossover(A+dir,C,iterations,-dir) ||
            crossover(A,C+dir,iterations,-dir) ||
            crossover(A+dir,C+dir,iterations,-dir) ||
            crossover(A+dir+dir,C,iterations,-dir) ||
            crossover(A,C+dir+dir,iterations,-dir)
        );
    }
};
void main()
{
    Crossing ^c = gcnew Crossing();
    int Count = c->cross(3,3);
    Console::WriteLine("It takes at least {0} crossings", Count);
}
```

After we run this program with three cannibals and three anthropologists, we get the expected result:

```
It takes at least 11 crossings
```

What happens if we try more or less? If there are only two cannibals and two anthropologists, we get the following result:

```
It takes at least 5 crossings
```

What if there are 4 of each? It turns out that there is no solution. The program runs until it overflows its storage capacity.

Summary

All of these examples show elegant recursive solutions to tricky problems. It's a great exercise to challenge your assumptions with these types of problems and look for not only logical solutions but also programmatic ones.

In the next chapter, we will begin to gain a deeper understanding of C++ by learning about parametric polymorphism in the context of basic generics.

PART 3

■■■

Advanced Concepts

■ ■ ■

Generics

A common mistake that people make when trying to design something completely fool-proof is to underestimate the ingenuity of complete fools.

—Douglas Adams

In this chapter, I introduce generics. This feature was introduced in version 2.0 of the .NET Framework and is supported by all of the Microsoft Visual Studio 2005 languages. You will learn how generics can help us solve a variety of problems that arise when we wish to build classes that act on different types of data without sacrificing type safety. In this chapter, we will also begin using a variety of .NET Framework classes to create more interesting and instructive examples.

A Queue of Tasks

Let's start with a simple example. We have a queue of custom classes called Task. We add Task items to the end of the queue with the main thread and read them off the beginning of the queue with a second thread. We then execute our classes in a First-In, First-Out (FIFO) fashion.

C# Implementation Under .NET 1.0

In .NET version 1.0, we would implement this in C# using the System.Collections.Queue class. Let's have a look at this using the Object Browser in the Visual Studio 2005 IDE.

Select Object Browser from the View menu, and an Object Browser tab is added to the main frame. We can expand the plus signs on mscorlib, System.Collections, and Queue, and then we can view the methods, fields, properties, and events of the System.Collections.Queue class. The Enqueue(object o) and Dequeue() methods provide the functionality we need.

Enqueue

`System.Void Enqueue(System.Object obj)`

Membership: Member of `System.Collections.Queue`.
Description: Adds an object to the end of the `System.Collections.Queue`.
Argument:

- `obj`: The object to add to the `System.Collections.Queue`. The value can be `null`.

Dequeue

`System.Object Dequeue()`

Membership: Member of `System.Collections.Queue`.
Description: Removes and returns the object at the beginning of the
`System.Collections.Queue`.
Return Value:

- The object that is removed from the beginning of the `System.Collections.Queue`.

Exception:

- `System.InvalidOperationException`: The `System.Collections.Queue` queue is empty.

Implementation

To implement our queue of instances of `Task`, we need to convert the `Task` object to a `System.Object` or `object`, since we're using C#, so that it can be used by the `Enqueue()` routine. This is performed automatically by the compiler, since `object` is a base class. Dequeuing presents more of a problem though. Dequeuing returns an `object` that must be recast to an instance of `Task`. This recasting opens up the possibility that someone somewhere down the line may `Enqueue()` an object of a type other than `Task`, thus generating an exception and making this implementation not type safe.

The core of our application looks like this:

```
using System.Collections;
namespace Task
{
    class Task
    {
        public void Execute()
        {
        }
    }
    class Program
    {
        static Queue q = new Queue();
        static void ExecutionThread()
```

```
    {
        Task t = (Task)q.Dequeue();
        t.Execute();
    }
    static void Main(string[] args)
    {
        q.Enqueue((object) new Program());
        ExecutionThread();
    }
  }
}
```

Note that the compiler automatically converts an instance of Task to an object for Enqueue(), since object is a base class for Task. The recast from Dequeue(), however, requires an explicit cast since, on its face, the compiler has no way of knowing that the queue contains a Task object. In fact, you can change the Enqueue() line to the following:

q.Enqueue(new Program());

The snippet compiles without error. Try to execute it now:

```
Unhandled Exception: System.InvalidCastException: Unable to cast
 object of type 'Task.Program' to type 'Task.Task'.
   at Task.Program.ExecutionThread()
   at Task.Program.Main(String[] args)
```

Your program compiles without any errors but generates an error on execution. You would certainly catch this upon testing if it were in one of your main code paths, but what would happen if it only existed in some seldom-used routine that would only be called under certain circumstances? This could get ugly. We'll get back to fixing this later, when we switch to generics. Meanwhile, let's get back to the sample.

Threads

To make our sample more meaningful, we want to Enqueue() and Dequeue() tasks on separate threads. For this, we take advantage of the System.Threading namespace.

The Thread Class

Let's turn to the Visual Studio Object Browser. Expand the Thread class under [mscorlib] System.Threading to find the Thread class. We are interested in this constructor overload.

Constructor

public Thread(System.Threading.ThreadStart start)

Membership: Member of System.Threading.Thread.
Description: Initializes a new instance of the System.Threading.Thread class.

Argument:

- start: A System.Threading.ThreadStart delegate that represents the methods to be invoked when this thread begins executing.

Exception:

- System.ArgumentNullException: The start argument is null.

Methods

We will use the Start() and Sleep() methods.

Start

public void Start()

Membership: Member of System.Threading.Thread.
Description: Causes the operating system to change the state of the current instance to System.Threading.ThreadState.Running.
Exceptions:

- System.Threading.ThreadStateException: The thread has already been started.

- System.Security.SecurityException: The caller does not have the appropriate System.Security.Permissions.SecurityPermission.

- System.OutOfMemoryException: There is not enough memory available to start this thread.

Sleep

public static void Sleep(int millisecondsTimeout)

Membership: Member of System.Threading.Thread.
Description: Suspends the current thread for a specified time.
Argument:

- millisecondsTimeout: The number of milliseconds for which the thread is blocked. Specify zero (0) to indicate that this thread should be suspended to allow other waiting threads to execute. Specify System.Threading.Timeout.Infinite to block the thread indefinitely.

Exception:

- System.ArgumentOutOfRangeException: The time-out value is negative and is not equal to System.Threading.Timeout.Infinite.

The ThreadStart class

In .NET, threads are initialized through the use of a delegate that contains the main method of the new thread. As you can see, the Thread class accepts a ThreadStart delegate.

Let's look at the description.

ThreadStart

```
public delegate void ThreadStart()
```

Membership: Member of System.Threading.
Description: Represents the method that executes on a System.Threading.Thread.

Making Threading Work

In order to use a second thread, we declare a method that takes no arguments and returns void, so that it matches the signature of the ThreadStart delegate. Next, we create an instance of ThreadStart and pass it to the Thread constructor in order to create a new thread. We can then start this thread using the Start() method of the Thread class.

Putting It Together

We now have two threads operating on our queue: the main thread adds tasks, and the background thread executes them. Since they are both accessing the same data object, the queue, we need to take pains to ensure that they take turns with this object. If we don't, the thread-switch mechanism may suspend one thread right in the middle of updating the state of the queue, and the resuming thread could be passed a queue in an invalid state. To make sure the threads take turns, we use the lock keyword in C#:

```
static Queue q = new Queue();
lock(q)
{
//exclusive access to q here
}
```

Using .NET Reflector in IL view, we can see that the lock keyword calls System.Threading.Monitor.Enter(object) at the beginning of the lock block and System.Threading.Monitor.Exit(object) at the end. In this way, we can assure that access to the q object is reserved until the block completes, even if the thread is switched in the middle of the lock block.

Therefore, we end up with the following:

```
using System;
using System.Collections;
using System.Threading;
namespace Task
{
    class Task
    {
        private string taskname;
        public Task(string s)
        {
```

```
            taskname = s;
        }
        public void Execute()
        {
            Console.WriteLine(taskname);
        }
    }
    class Program
    {
        static Queue q = new Queue();
        static Thread executionThread =
            new Thread(new ThreadStart(ExecutionThread));
        static void ExecutionThread()
        {
            while (true)
            {
                Task t;
                lock (q)
                {
                    if (q.Count == 0)
                    {
                        continue;
                    }
                    t = (Task)q.Dequeue();
                }
                if (t == null)
                {
                    return;
                }
                t.Execute();
            }
        }
        static void Main(string[] args)
        {
            executionThread.Start();
            lock(q)
            {
                q.Enqueue(new Task("task #1"));
                q.Enqueue(new Task("task #2"));
                q.Enqueue(null);
            }
            while (true)
            {
                Thread.Sleep(10);
                lock (q)
                {
                    if (q.Count == 0)
```

```
                        {
                            break;
                        }
                    }
                }
            }
        }
}
```

In this sample, we spawn and start the execution thread. Next, we use the `Enqueue()` method for various tasks, enqueuing a final `null` to indicate that all of the work is done. We then enter a loop and wait for the tasks to be complete.

One important thing to note is that we minimize the amount of time we hold the lock on the queue so as not to interfere with the other task. In the execution thread, this takes the form of postponing the execution of a task until after the lock is released.

Executing this program gives the following output:

```
C:\>csc /nologo task.cs
C:\>task
task #1
task #2
```

Moving to Generics

Let's move to C++/CLI and .NET 2.0 using a more-sophisticated sample. We will go over it first in C# to ease the transition.

Workin' at the Car Wash

Suppose we are simulating a car wash. First, each car is vacuumed and has its interior cleaned. Next, it is moved onto the conveyor belt that drags it through a machine that cleans its exterior. We can take advantage of pipelining: cars can have their interiors cleaned at the same time other cars are having their exteriors washed. To implement this, we maintain a separate queue as well as dedicated execution threads for each of the interior and exterior stations. Pipelining the cars allows us to increase the throughput of the car wash without affecting latency.

Let's have a look at the code in C#:

```csharp
using System;
using System.Collections.Generic;
using System.Threading;
namespace CarWash
{
    class Car
    {
        private string CarName;
        public override string ToString()
```

```
        {
            return CarName;
        }
        public Car(string s)
        {
            CarName = s;
        }
    }
    class Program
    {
        static Queue<Car> washQueue = new Queue<Car>();
        static Queue<Car> vacuumQueue = new Queue<Car>();
        static Thread WashThread = new Thread(new ThreadStart(Wash));
        static Thread VacuumThread = new Thread(new ThreadStart(Vacuum));
        static void Wash()
        {
            for (; true; Thread.Sleep(10))
            {
                Car c;
                lock (washQueue)
                {
                    if (washQueue.Count == 0)
                    {
                        continue;
                    }
                    c = washQueue.Dequeue();
                }
                if (c == null)
                {
                    break;
                }
                Console.WriteLine("-Starting Wash of {0}", c);
                Thread.Sleep(1300);
                Console.WriteLine("-Completing Wash of {0}", c);
            }
        }
        static void Vacuum()
        {
            for(;true;Thread.Sleep(10))
            {
                Car c;
                lock(vacuumQueue)
                {
                    if(vacuumQueue.Count == 0)
                    {
                        continue;
                    }
```

```
                c = vacuumQueue.Dequeue();
            }
            if (c != null)
            {
                Console.WriteLine("+Starting Vacuum of {0}", c);
                Thread.Sleep(1000);
                Console.WriteLine("+Completing Vacuum of {0}", c);
            }
            lock (washQueue)
            {
                washQueue.Enqueue(c);
            }
            if (c == null)
            {
                break;
            }
        }
    }
    static void Main(string[] args)
    {
        VacuumThread.Start();
        WashThread.Start();
        lock (vacuumQueue)
        {
            vacuumQueue.Enqueue(new Car("Volvo"));
            vacuumQueue.Enqueue(new Car("VW"));
            vacuumQueue.Enqueue(new Car("Jeep"));
            vacuumQueue.Enqueue(null);
        }
        while (VacuumThread.IsAlive || WashThread.IsAlive)
        {
            Thread.Sleep(10);
        }
    }
}
}
```

Now let's run it:

```
C:\>csc /nologo carwash.cs
C:\>carwash
+Starting Vacuum of Volvo
+Completing Vacuum of Volvo
-Starting Wash of Volvo
+Starting Vacuum of VW
+Completing Vacuum of VW
+Starting Vacuum of Jeep
```

```
-Completing Wash of Volvo
-Starting Wash of VW
+Completing Vacuum of Jeep
-Completing Wash of VW
-Starting Wash of Jeep
-Completing Wash of Jeep
```

Note that you can see the overlapping of task as well as dependency delays just from the order in which the tasks started and completed in the output.

A Review of the C# Code

This code has more or less the same elements as the previous sample, but there are some major differences.

In the first example, we used the Queue class from System.Collections to manage a queue of tasks. Since the Queue class operates on elements of type System.Object, we had to cast Task to a base class, System.Object, in order to enqueue it. This was done automatically by the compiler. When we wanted to dequeue it, we had to explicitly recast it back to Task. Recasting to the wrong type would not be caught by the compiler at compile time and could potentially cause a runtime error.

The Generic Version of Queue

In this example, we use the generic version of Queue, called Queue<T>. Using the Object Browser, we can find that this class is part of System.dll instead of mscorlib and exists in the System.Collections.Generic namespace. Now, do not be misled by the fact that these classes have similar names. Queue and Queue<T> are completely different classes. They each represent different types. Queue<T> has a more complex type, as it relies on the type parameter T. Since these types are completely different, the compiler defines no conversions, either implicit or explicit, between them. In addition, Queue<T> is an inchoate type until the type parameter T is specified. When the code, which uses Queue<T> with a defined type parameter, is executed, the runtime specializes Queue<T> using intermediate language appropriate to the type parameter T. This may vary depending on whether T is a reference type or a value type.

Let's examine the methods.

Enqueue

```
public void Enqueue(T item)
```

> *Membership*: Member of System.Collections.Generic.Queue<T>.
> *Description*: Adds an object to the end of the System.Collections.Generic.Queue<T>.
> *Argument*:
>
> - item: The object to add to the System.Collections.Generic.Queue<T>. The value can be null for reference types.

Dequeue

```
public T Dequeue()
```

> *Membership*: Member of System.Collections.Generic.Queue<T>.
> *Description*: Removes and returns the object at the beginning of the System.Collections.
> Generic.Queue<T>.
> *Return value*:
>
> - The object that is removed from the beginning of the
>   System.Collections.Generic.Queue<T>.
>
> *Exception*:
>
> - System.InvalidOperationException: The System.Collections.Generic.Queue<T> is
>   empty.

Analysis

As you can see, the methods for Enqueue() and Dequeue() in Queue<T> are similar to the ones in Queue. In this case, "vive la différence" seems an appropriate phrase. The Enqueue() method takes an item of type T, and Dequeue() returns an item of type T. In our example code, we are moving instances of class Car through the pipeline. Since we want a queue of Cars, we start by creating an instance of Queue<T>, where T is Car:

```
static Queue<Car> washQueue = new Queue<Car>();
```

If we think of Queue<Car> as a single identifier, we find this is a simple call to the constructor. Next, we can enqueue and dequeue instances of class Car, and the compiler does all of the type checking for us:

```
Car c;
washQueue.Enqueue(c);
//
c = washQueue.Dequeue();
```

And that's all there is to it. For what it's worth, Queue is a class that acts very similarly to Queue<object>, though, of course, they are not identical. They accomplish the same things though—they each manage a queue of elements of type object or System.Object.

We also use the IsAlive property to manage our threads in the car wash. We use this property to wait for the vacuuming and washing threads to complete.

IsAlive

```
public bool IsAlive { get; }
```

> *Membership*: Member of System.Threading.Thread.
> *Description*: Gets a value indicating the execution status of the current thread.

Return values:

- `true` if this thread has been started and has not terminated normally or aborted.

- `false` otherwise. As you can see, `IsAlive` is a read-only property. It has a `get` accessor but no `set` accessor.

Moving to C++/CLI

In this section, we are going to go over the C++ syntax for generics. I will also switch to C++ syntax when describing namespaces and such.

The syntax for creating and defining generic classes in C# is very different from C++. However, the syntax for using and consuming them is almost identical. This is similar to the way that managed arrays differ in the way they are declared in C# and C++, yet they are used similarly in both languages.

Because of the differences in syntax, we will first convert the CarWash program to C++/CLI and examine the definition and usage of generics in C++/CLI. Next, we will begin creating generic classes of our own.

Now let's translate the CarWash program sample into C++/CLI:

```cpp
#using <System.dll>
#include <msclr\lock.h>
using namespace msclr;
using namespace System;
using namespace System::Collections::Generic;
using namespace System::Threading;
namespace CarWash
{
    ref class Car
    {
    private:
        String ^CarName;
    public:
        virtual String ^ ToString() override
        {
            return CarName;
        }
        Car(String ^s)
        {
            CarName = s;
        }
    };
    ref class Program
    {
        static Queue<Car^> ^washQueue = gcnew Queue<Car^>();
        static Queue<Car^> ^vacuumQueue = gcnew Queue<Car^>();
        static Thread ^washThread =
            gcnew Thread(gcnew ThreadStart(wash));
```

```
static Thread ^vacuumThread =
    gcnew Thread(gcnew ThreadStart(vacuum));
static void wash()
{
    for (; true; Thread::Sleep(10))
    {
        Car ^c;
        {
            lock l(washQueue);
            if (washQueue->Count == 0)
            {
                continue;
            }
            c = washQueue->Dequeue();
        }
        if (c == nullptr)
        {
            break;
        }
        Console::WriteLine("-Starting wash of {0}", c);
        Thread::Sleep(1300);
        Console::WriteLine("-Completing wash of {0}", c);
    }
}
static void vacuum()
{
    for(;true;Thread::Sleep(10))
    {
        Car ^c;
        {
            lock l(vacuumQueue);
            if(vacuumQueue->Count == 0)
            {
                continue;
            }
            c = vacuumQueue->Dequeue();
        }
        if (c != nullptr)
        {
            Console::WriteLine("+Starting vacuum of {0}", c);
            Thread::Sleep(1000);
            Console::WriteLine(
                "+Completing vacuum of {0}", c);
        }
        {
            lock l(washQueue);
            washQueue->Enqueue(c);
```

```
                    }
                    if (c == nullptr)
                    {
                        break;
                    }
                }
            }
    public:
        static void Main(...array<String^> ^ args)
        {
            vacuumThread->Start();
            washThread->Start();
            {
                lock l(vacuumQueue);
                vacuumQueue->Enqueue(gcnew Car("Volvo"));
                vacuumQueue->Enqueue(gcnew Car("VW"));
                vacuumQueue->Enqueue(gcnew Car("Jeep"));
                vacuumQueue->Enqueue(nullptr);
            }
            while (vacuumThread->IsAlive || washThread->IsAlive)
            {
                Thread::Sleep(10);
            }
        }

    };
}
void main()
{
    CarWash::Program::Main();
}
```

It turns out that this sample is somewhat difficult to translate to C++/CLI. In addition to the run-of-the-mill translations, I'd like to point out a few in the following sections.

Override

To override a virtual method, we need to use both the `virtual` and `override` keywords in C++/CLI. Also, the order of keywords is different.

In C#, we can use the following line to override a virtual method:

```
public override string ToString()
```

In C++/CLI, we need this one:

```
public:
    virtual String ^ ToString() override
```

Add a Reference to System.dll

When we use Queue<T>, we need to tell the compiler not only which namespace contains the class but which assembly DLL. This can be done from the C# or C++/CLI command line or by an explicit #using reference within the code. You can also specify a reference to this DLL using the IDE. Specify the reference within the code as follows:

```
#using <System.dll>
```

If you neglect to add this line, the compiler issues a syntax error, as it does not find that the identifier Queue is defined, or it confuses it with the System::Collections::Queue class defined in mscorlib.dll, which is not a generic.

Translate the lock Keyword

The lock keyword in C# generates a set of blocks using the System::Threading::Monitor class. In C#, the following code:

```
class Program
{
    public static void Main()
    {
        string s = "hello";
        lock(s)
        {
            //inside the lock
        }
    }
}
```

is equivalent to this code:

```
using System.Threading;
class Program
{
    public static void Main()
    {
        string s = "hello";
        Monitor.Enter(s);
        try
        {
            //inside the lock
        }
        finally
        {
            Monitor.Exit(s);
        }
    }
}
```

Monitor.Enter() claims exclusive access to the object for the duration of the try block. When the try block completes, whether or not there has been an exception, the object is released using Monitor.Exit().

Enter

```
public static void Enter(object obj)
```

Membership: Member of System.Threading.Monitor.
Description: Acquires an exclusive lock on the specified object.
Argument:

- obj: The object on which to acquire the monitor lock.

Exception:

- System.ArgumentNullException: The obj argument is null.

Exit

```
public static void Exit(object obj)
```

Membership: Member of System.Threading.Monitor.
Description: Releases an exclusive lock on the specified object.
Argument:

- obj: The object on which to release the lock.

Exceptions:

- System.Threading.SynchronizationLockException: The current thread does not own the lock for the specified object.

- System.ArgumentNullException: The obj argument is null.

Lock in C++/CLI

It is possible to use the exact same construction in C++/CLI:

```
using namespace System;
using namespace System::Threading;
ref class Program
{
public:
    static void Main()
    {
        String ^s = "hello";
        Monitor::Enter(s);
        try
        {
```

```
            //inside the lock
        }
        finally
        {
            Monitor::Exit(s);
        }
    }
};
```

In addition, there are other ways to create a lock in C++, because it has deterministic destruction of objects. Where C# treats destructors as .NET finalizers, C++/CLI has explicit finalizers as well as destructors that are capable of deallocating resources as soon as an object goes out of scope. It is possible to duplicate much of the same functionality in C# using the IDisposable interface and the .NET Dispose() pattern, but it is much more tedious. In C++, it's automatic. Allocate an instance of a class, and it is destroyed when the block ends. Therefore, a constructor can be used to claim the lock, and the destructor used to release it.

A C++ implementation to do this would look like the following:

```
using namespace System;
using namespace System::Threading;
ref struct Locker
{
    Object ^o;
    Locker(Object ^s)
    {
        o = s;
        Monitor::Enter(o);
    }
    ~Locker()
    {
        Monitor::Exit(o);
    }
};
ref class Program
{
public:
    static void Main()
    {
        String ^s = "hello";
        {
            Locker lk(s);
            //inside the lock
        }
    }
};
```

We first create a class called Locker, which is the holder for the System::Threading::
Monitor class. The constructor is called when the locked section is entered, and the destructor
is called when the locked section is exited.

The following line creates an instance of Locker and calls the constructor with arguments:

```
Locker lk(s);
```

When the instance variable lk goes out of scope with the next closing curly brace, Locker's
destructor is called along with Monitor::Exit().

Note that the destructor is called even if the code inside the lock throws an exception. For
example, let's modify the previous code to display status as well as throw an exception:

```
using namespace System;
using namespace System::Threading;
ref struct Locker
{
    Object ^o;
    Locker(Object ^s)
    {
        o = s;
        Console::WriteLine("Lock acquired");
        Monitor::Enter(o);
    }
    ~Locker()
    {
        Console::WriteLine("Lock released");
        Monitor::Exit(o);
    }
};
ref class Program
{
public:
    static void Main()
    {
        String ^s = "hello";
        {
            Locker lk(s);
            Console::WriteLine("throw exception");
            throw;
        }
    }
};
void main()
{
    try
    {
        Program::Main();
    }
    catch(Exception ^e)
```

```
    {
        Console::WriteLine("catch exception");
    }
}
```

If we run this, we see the following:

```
C:\>cl /nologo /clr:pure test.cpp
C:\>test
Lock acquired
throw exception
Lock released
catch exception
```

This output shows that there is no danger of leaving locks lying around, and deterministic class construction and destruction are viable alternatives to try finally blocks in C++/CLI.

To do the same thing in C#, you would take advantage of the variant of using for limiting the scope of an instance to a block with a class that implements System::IDisposable. A prototype for this method in C# follows:

```
using System;
class Locker : IDisposable
{
    public void Dispose()
    {
    }
    public Locker()
    {
    }
    ~Locker()
    {
    }
}
class Program
{
    public static void Main()
    {
        using(Locker l = new Locker())
        {
        }
    }
}
```

The Predefined Lock Class

The include file msclr\lock.h defines a sophisticated class that is able to lock resources. It uses System::Threading::ReaderWriterLock as well as template programming.

All we have to do in order to take advantage of it is to add the following lines:

```
#include <msclr\lock.h>
using namespace msclr;
```

We can then instantiate `msclr::lock` classes the same way as the `Locker` class:

```
{
    lock l(vacuumQueue);
    // locked code
}
// destructor has been called and lock is released.
```

Compile and Run

Let's compile CarWash, and check the results:

```
C:\>cl /clr:pure /nologo carwash.cpp
C:\>carwash.exe
+Starting vacuum of Volvo
+Completing vacuum of Volvo
-Starting wash of Volvo
+Starting vacuum of VW
+Completing vacuum of VW
+Starting vacuum of Jeep
-Completing wash of Volvo
-Starting wash of VW
+Completing vacuum of Jeep
-Completing wash of VW
-Starting wash of Jeep
-Completing wash of Jeep
```

Creating Generic Classes in C++/CLI

In C++/CLI, the syntax for generic types is modeled off the syntax for templates. Templates are similar to generics in that they both accept type parameters. The primary difference between them is that templates are processed at compile time, and generics are processed at runtime. Templates are both more complex and more powerful because of this distinction, and we will cover this in detail in Chapter 15. For now, what is important is to realize that the C++/CLI syntax for generics is based on the syntax for C++ templates.

A basic, generic class with a single type parameter T is declared in C# as follows:

```
class R<T> {}
```

The same class is declared as follows in C++/CLI:

```
generic <typename T> ref class R {};
```

In C++/CLI, it is necessary to tell the compiler that T is a type parameter, whereas this is implicit in C#. The reason for this is that C++ has several different types of parameters for templates, including the following ones:

- Type template parameter

- Nontype template parameter

- Template template parameter

For generics under .NET 2.0, the only supported scenario is that T represents a type, but for syntactic consistency and ease of implementation under current C++ compiler grammars, the long form of declaration is required.

Within the definition of the class, the letter T is used freely as a substitute for the type name with a few caveats.

When you write a generic class, the compiler has no idea what kind of types you intend to use as generic arguments. For this reason, the class has to compile for all types, not just the ones you have in mind. The Queue<T> class is a good example of a class that operates on handles to items, without doing anything with the item themselves. The compiler need not know anything about the type T beyond the fact that it is derived from System::Object. All generic types are assumed to derive from System::Object. More specialized classes that can work with instances of the data themselves can be created using templates, generic constraints, or the cast operators. The next two chapters on templates and advanced generics and classes will help you to write more powerful classes.

A simple generic class follows:

```
using namespace System;
generic <typename T>
ref struct Test
{
    static void Print(T t)
    {
        Console::WriteLine(t->ToString());
    }
};
int main()
{
    Test<int>::Print(3);
}
```

After compiling and running, we get

```
C:\>cl /nologo /clr:pure test.cpp
C:\>test
3
```

In this code snippet, we are creating a generic class named Test. Inside of it, we have a static method called Print(), which calls ToString(). Our type T inherits the method ToString() from System::Object. Note that the only methods that can be used on instances of T are those from System:Object.

For example, consider the following code:

```
using namespace System;
ref struct Hello
{
    void Function()
    {
        Console::WriteLine("Hello!");
    }
};
generic <typename T>
ref struct Test
{
    static void Run(T t)
    {
        t->Function();
    }
};
void main()
{
    Hello ^ hello = gcnew Hello();
    Test<Hello^>::Run(hello);
}
```

Will this compile? The snippet we have to worry about is right here:

```
static void Run(T t)
{
    t->Function();
}
```

For this code to compile, the type T would need to have a method called Function() that it could call, right? In this case, we are passing Hello^ as our type T when calling Run(). This seems reasonable, because when Run() executes, it finds that Hello^ has a method called Function() and this code compiles, right?

Let's give it a shot:

```
C:\>cl /nologo /clr:pure test.cpp
test.cpp
test.cpp(13) : error C2039: 'Function' : is not a member of 'System::Object'
        c:\windows\microsoft.net\framework\v2.0.50727\mscorlib.dll :
 see declaration of 'System::Object'
```

Code inside a generic class (or function) only compiles if every possible type that could conceivably be inserted for T would be valid for the code. In this case, the only assumption the compiler makes is that T derives from System::Object; therefore, you get the stated error message. There are a few ways to do this sort of thing, and we will see them in detail in Chapters 15 and 16, but I'd like to introduce them here.

Use a Constraint

A *constraint* tells the compiler that the generic type always has certain characteristics. One possibility is to say that the type T has Hello as a base class. In order to declare this, we change the generic declaration of Test to the following:

```
generic <typename T>
where T : Hello
ref struct Test
{
    static void Run(T t)
    {
        t->Function();
    }
};
```

We added this line:

```
where T : Hello
```

This line instructs the compiler to assume that Hello is a base class of T. Now let's compile it:

```
C:\>cl /nologo /clr:pure test.cpp
C:\>test
Hello!
```

Of course, if we then modify main() to pass a type that is *not* derived from Hello, we get a compilation error. Try the following lines:

```
void main()
{
    Test<int>::Run(0);
}
```

And compile the code:

```
C:\>cl /nologo /clr:pure test.cpp
test.cpp
test.cpp(21) : error C3214: 'int' : invalid type argument for generic
 parameter 'T' of generic 'Test', does not meet constraint 'Hello ^'
test.cpp(12) : see declaration of 'Test'
```

For more on constraints, see Chapter 16.

Use a Template

Generics are runtime mechanisms in which the code has to work for all types. Templates are compile-time mechanisms in which the code can be specialized for a specific type. If we merely change the single word generic to template in the original sample code before my introduction to constraints, we will get the following:

```
C:\>cl /nologo /clr:pure test.cpp
C:\>test
Hello!
```

And everything works. If we use the modified main() that passes an int instead of a Hello^, we get

```
C:\>cl /nologo /clr:pure test.cpp
test.cpp(14) : error C2227: left of '->Function' must point to
 class/struct/union/generic type
        type is 'int'
        test.cpp(13) : while compiling class template member function
'void Test<T>::Run(T)'
        with
        [
            T=int
        ]
        test.cpp(20) : see reference to class template instantiation
'Test<T>' being compiled
        with
        [
            T=int
        ]
```

For more on templates, see Chapter 15.

Use a Cast

A third way to deal with this is to let the compiler assume that the generic type parameter is only derived from System::Object and cast it at runtime to the type desired. Since this is not type safe, we want to add a bit more code to do this in an intelligent manner. Using the equivalent of the C# is and as keywords, we construct code as follows, checking to see if the type really is derived from Hello^:

```
static void Run(T t)
{
    if(t->GetType() == Hello::typeid)
    {
        Hello ^hello = safe_cast<Hello^>(t);
        hello->Function();
    }
}
```

For more on the casting mechanisms, see Chapter 16.

Generic Functions

When you only need a type parameter for a specific function rather than an entire class, it is possible to use a generic function. Generic functions are simpler than generic classes and have the advantage that the compiler can often deduce the type parameter of the function automatically from its arguments. To declare a generic function, you use a similar syntax to that of a generic class.

Here is a simple generic function that just prints out the type of a type argument:

```
using namespace System;
generic <typename T>
void Function(T t)
{
    Console::WriteLine(t->GetType());
}
ref class Test {};
int main()
{
    Function(0);
    Function<short>(0);
    Test ^t = gcnew Test();
    Function(t);
}
```

The first time we call Function(), we use type deduction, and the compiler determines that 0 is of type int. In the second call, we explicitly state that we are passing a short 0. In the last call, we are back to type deduction, as the compiler determines that Function() is passed an instance of type Test^.

Now let's compile and execute it:

```
C:\>cl /nologo /clr:pure test.cpp
C:\>test
System.Int32
System.Int16
Test
```

Summary

You should now feel that you have a basic understanding of generics along with some of the support for multiple threads provided in the .NET Framework. Now let's take it to the next level. We will build on this foundation and tackle templates in Chapter 15 and advanced generics in Chapter 16.

■ ■ ■

Introduction to Templates

Even for practical purposes, theory generally turns out the most important thing in the end.

—Oliver Wendell Holmes

In the previous chapter, we saw what you could do with C++/CLI generics. In this chapter, I will introduce templates, which are similar to generics in many ways and different in many others.

Comparison with Generics

Templates and generics both allow you to create functions and classes that implement functionality for multiple types. We can approach this in one of two ways:

- Write code that is decoupled from the type of data that is being acted upon. The code only implements algorithms that do not depend on the data type, so the algorithms act on the data in a generic fashion. This is the idea behind CLI generics.

- Write generalized high-level code that the compiler adapts for each type of data. The result is a separate set of data-dependent methods and types for each type of data that is acted upon. This is the idea behind C++ templates.

Generics types are decoupled from the data types until execution, and templates are also decoupled but bound by the compiler to specific data types during the compilation. The result of a generic method is a single method specified in the IL; the result of a template method is one method generated in the IL for each combination of type arguments passed to the template during compilation.

■**Note** Generics is a feature supported by the CLR, and generics is implemented in a variety of .NET languages including C#. In Visual Studio 2005, however, *templates* are unique to C++.

Because generic methods and classes are ignorant of their type parameters, they can easily be defined in one module, be referenced in another module defining a new type, and still be used on that type. For example, the generic `Stack<T>` class in `System.Collections.Generics` can be used to manage a stack of any number of user-defined types.

Template methods and types, although defined in a general fashion, depend on their type parameters and require a level of runtime compilation that does not exist in the CLI to operate on types defined elsewhere. For this reason, templates are compilation-unit specific.

The requirement that generic methods and classes be completely ignorant of their type parameters places severe restrictions on generics. Generic constraints help a little, in that they allow the generic types to make some assumptions about the possible type parameters and to act only on type parameters that implement a given set of interfaces.

Templates have no such restriction. A template can be applied to any type, and the compiler can determine if a syntax error is generated by an invalid type parameter. Type parameters are even able to fail during the initial substitution phase, and rather than aborting the compilation, the compiler continues to look for an appropriate template candidate for substitution without generating a syntax error. Templates can also have parameters that are not types, called *nontype template parameters*, and parameters that are templates themselves, called *template template parameters*.

Where generic types represent an efficient way to reduce code by allowing the programmer to write a single method that applies to multiple types, templates emerge as a powerful C++ metaprogramming environment and allow the programmer to take advantage of the compilation process to implement sophisticated algorithms and language extensions at compile time.

Syntactic Differences

These two type-parameter mechanisms have great a deal in common and can often be used interchangeably. The similarity of templates and generics in terms of functionality is reflected in the C++/CLI syntax. Switching from one to the other is often as simple as changing the `generic` keyword to `template`, or vice versa.

Consider the following line:

```
generic <typename T> ref class TypeGeneric {};
```

`TypeGeneric <T>` is a complete generic type capable of runtime creation. Now consider this line:

```
template <typename T> ref class TypeTemplate {};
```

`TypeTemplate <T>` is not a type at all. It is a model for a type, which can be generated by the compiler when it is used or instantiated later on in the compilation process.

Summary

While templates and generics are similar in many ways, there is one major difference between the two mechanisms. Unlike generic types, which are instantiated by the Virtual Execution System (VES) at runtime, templates are fully resolved, instantiated, and compiled by the C++ compiler. Generic types can be thought of as a packaging mechanism for CLI types, whereas templates act more like smart macros that are expanded, verified, and executed at compile time.

Compilation Process

When the compiler encounters a generic function, it verifies that it makes sense for all possible types given its constraints and implementation. A single function is then generated in the IL.

Consider the following simple generic function:

```
generic <typename T>
ref class Test
{
public:
    Test()
    {
        System::Console::WriteLine(this->ToString());
    }
};
void main()
{
    Test<int> i;
    Test<float> j;
}
```

When the class Test is parsed, IL and metadata are created for a generic class. Let's compile and run it:

```
C:\>cl /nologo /clr:pure test.cpp
C:\>test
Test`1[System.Int32]
Test`1[System.Single]
```

Now let's run ildasm.exe on it. In the ILDasm main window, open the constructor (.ctor) definition. You should find IL and metadata similar to the following:

```
.method public hidebysig specialname rtspecialname
        instance void   .ctor() cil managed
{
  // Code size       18 (0x12)
  .maxstack  1
  IL_0000:  ldarg.0
  IL_0001:  call         instance void [mscorlib]System.Object::.ctor()
  IL_0006:  ldarg.0
  IL_0007:  callvirt     instance string [mscorlib]System.Object::ToString()
  IL_000c:  call         void [mscorlib]System.Console::WriteLine(string)
  IL_0011:  ret
} // end of method Test`1::.ctor
```

The compiler created a method named Test`1::.ctor, which is the constructor of a class named Test with a single generic parameter. Note that, in this case, Test<int> and Test<float> have nothing to do with the constructor. The constructor for Test<T> is independent of the type parameter.

On the other hand, take the exact same example and substitute the keyword generic for template. Compile and run it:

```
C:\>cl /nologo /clr:pure test.cpp
C:\>test
Test<int>
Test<float>
```

As you can see, two completely different classes, Test<int> and Test<float>, are created. Let's run ildasm.exe on this and have a look (see Figure 15-1). Note that Test<float> and Test<int> are distinct.

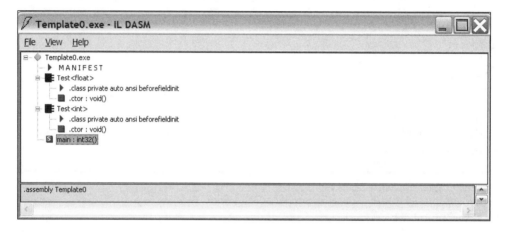

Figure 15-1. *Metadata for the different compile-time–generated template instantiations*

Now let's have a look at the code, along with a description of how the compiler parses it:

```
01: template <typename T>
02: ref class Test
03: {
04: public:
05:     Test()
06:     {
07:         System::Console::WriteLine(this->ToString());
08:     }
09: };
10: void main()
11: {
12:     Test<int> i;
13:     Test<float> j;
14: }
```

By line 9, the compiler has recognized that there is a template. It then figures out which types are determinate and indeterminate, binds any reference it can, issues any detectable syntax errors, and files the template away for future instantiation.

If a generic were used, by line 9, the compiler would have enough information to commit the class to metadata. With a template, it is just a potential class until it is instantiated. The template tells the compiler how to make a certain kind of class if you decide to make one.

Now back to parsing. On line 12, the compiler attempts to instantiate Test<int>. The template is reparsed, int is substituted for typename T, any unbound references are bound, and the class is generated. The compiler is now ready to commit Test<int> to metadata. Likewise, on line 13, the compiler is able to parse and determine whether Test<float> is valid.

Note The CLR requires that generics are designed to work for all possible types meeting any given type restraints, whereas templates only need to be designed to work with the types you actually instantiate.

Now open the Test<int> constructor (.ctor) definition. You should find metadata and IL similar to the following:

```
.method public hidebysig specialname rtspecialname
        instance void  .ctor() cil managed
{
  // Code size       18 (0x12)
  .maxstack  1
  IL_0000:  ldarg.0
  IL_0001:  call       instance void [mscorlib]System.Object::.ctor()
  IL_0006:  ldarg.0
  IL_0007:  callvirt   instance string [mscorlib]System.Object::ToString()
  IL_000c:  call       void [mscorlib]System.Console::WriteLine(string)
  IL_0011:  ret
} // end of method 'Test<int>'::.ctor
```

A quick comparison shows you that the metadata and IL for the method of the template class and the method of the generic class are identical. In this case, it seems to make more sense to use a generic, because the int and float cases are duplicates. In actuality, the performance implications are unclear, because the CLR creates duplicate instantiations for value types and creates a single, common instantiation for reference types.

Templates Don't Really Exist

Since templates are instantiated into regular CLI types and methods, from the CLI perspective, they don't exist as a special entity. The CLR supports generics explicitly, meaning that it supports IL packaging types as generic parameters. There is no specific IL for templates, and it's easy to see why.

The compiler sees a template as a set of instructions for creating a class based on type parameters. Once the types are instantiated with template arguments, the compiler knows exactly what kind of class to create, and this class is written to metadata and IL specific to the types used in the instantiation. Only instances of the template, not the template itself, make it into the module. Therefore, templates cannot be exported from an assembly like generics, and the only way for a programmer to reuse a template is to reuse the source code definition of that template.

Exercise

In theory, you could create a template generic, though this is not yet a part of the C++/CLI specification. Can you think of a compelling reason to add this feature?

Constraining Freedom Is a Good Thing

To make the generics feature somewhat useful, being able to restrict the types in some fashion became necessary. This is called *generic constraints*. Writing something using a completely arbitrary type that is in any way useful is very difficult. After all, what could you do with it? Even the previous sample routine relies on the fact that all CLR types support an interface that has the `ToString()` method. Without that implicit constraint, even the previous simple example would not compile. Therefore, constraints restrict, at compile time, the kinds of types that may be used as generic type arguments and, equivalently, tell the generic what kinds of types it needs to support. The typical paradigm is that you have a particular interface that you want to use, so you constrain your generic type to derive from that interface. I'll show an example later in the chapter.

Unlike generics, templates do not support explicit type constraints. Because generics are instantiated by the VES at runtime, they require a compile-time mechanism to prevent instantiation of a generic type with invalid type arguments, and generic type constraints are that mechanism. On the other hand, templates are resolved and instantiated by the compiler at compile time, and thus do not suffer from the invalid runtime instantiation problem. It can still be argued that some forms of explicit type constraints may be useful when used with templates, but, as a matter of design, C++ makes use of the type constraints implicitly present in the template code instead.

The Template Paradigm

Generic types are designed to work under the following paradigms:

- You only call methods from `System::Object`.

- You use a constraint to restrict the possible type parameters and only use methods enabled by the constraint (see Chapter 16).

- You use a cast operator to perform a runtime switch on the type parameter and to perform type-specific operations.

The basic idea is that generics either have to work for all possible types given the restraints, which means either `System::Object` or any constraint you define, or the types have to be forked and processed at compile time.

```
    }
};
template <typename T, typename W> ref struct R<T^,W>
{
    static R()
    {
        Console::WriteLine("T^,W: "+__FUNCTION__);
    }
};
template <typename T, typename W> ref struct R<T*,W>
{
    static R()
    {
        Console::WriteLine("T*,W: "+__FUNCTION__);
    }
};
template <typename T> ref struct R<T,T>
{
    static R()
    {
        Console::WriteLine("T,T: "+__FUNCTION__);
    }
};
void main()
{
    R<int,double> Primary;
    R<R^,int> First;
    R<int,int> Second;
    R<char*,int> Third;
}
```

We have a primary template and three partial specializations. The first specialization requires the first type parameter to be some kind of reference type, and the second specialization requires both parameters to be the same. The third specialization requires a pointer to a native type.

Let's compile and run this:

```
C:\>cl /nologo /clr:pure test.cpp
test.cpp
C:\>test
T,W: R<int,double>::R (static class constructor)
T^,W: R<struct R ^,int>::R (static class constructor)
T,T: R<int,int>::R (static class constructor)
T*,W: R<char *,int>::R (static class constructor)
```

As you can see from the results, the primary template and each of the two partial specializations are instantiated in turn.

Partial Ordering of Function Templates

What if you wanted to distinguish functions in a manner similar to partial specialization? Suppose, for example, you wanted to replace ToString() with a custom version that formats strings for your built-in variables in a certain fashion; perhaps you want to display all doubles in scientific notation:

```
using namespace System;
template <typename T> String ^MyToString(T t)
{
    return t.ToString();
}
template <typename T> String ^MyToString(T ^t)
{
    return t->ToString();
}
template <> String ^MyToString(double d)
{
    return d.ToString("0.###e+00");
}
value struct V
{
    virtual String ^ToString() override
    {
        return "it's V";
    }
};
void main()
{
    V v;
    int i = 23;
    double d=47.3;
    Console::WriteLine(MyToString<int>(i));
    Console::WriteLine(MyToString<double>(d));
    Console::WriteLine(MyToString<V>(v));
}
```

In this example, we provide a template for our most general case:

```
template <typename T> String ^MyToString(T t) {}
```

and an overload that is more specific:

```
template <typename T> String ^MyToString(T ^t) {}
```

When we invoke MyToString(), the compiler picks out the more explicit or restrictive match by a process known as *partial ordering* during overload selection. Partial ordering allows us to distinguish between a typical value type being passed by value and a typical reference type being passed by handle.

Let's compile and run this:

```
C:\>cl /nologo /clr:pure test.cpp
C:\>test
23
4.73e+01
it's V
```

In this case, we are still using ToString(), which is a method from System::Object, for our example. Unlike a generic type, the template compiles even if it does not recognize the method to be called, as long as it is not resolvable without the determination of the type parameter. For example, consider the following:

```
using namespace System;
template <typename T> String ^MyToString(T ^t)
{
    return t->MyFunction();
}
void main() {}
```

This program compiles fine even though the compiler is unable to determine whether the hypothetical handle T^t has a member method called MyFunction(). Only when the user attempts to instantiate the template using a real type parameter can the compiler determine success or failure. Generic types assume the worst; templates hope for the best.

Let's now complete this program, realizing the template's hopes:

```
using namespace System;
template <typename T> String ^MyToString(T ^t)
{
    return t->MyFunction();
}
ref struct R
{
    String ^ MyFunction()
    {
        return "Hello";
    }
};
void main()
{
    R ^r = gcnew R();
    Console::WriteLine(MyToString(r));
}
```

Now let's compile and run it:

```
C:\>cl /nologo /clr:pure test.cpp
C:\>test
Hello
```

And that is correct.

Nontype Template Parameters

One of the primary advantages of templates is the ability to have template parameters that are not types; they can be integer values, for example.

Fibonacci Number Template

Consider the following template, which generates Fibonacci numbers:

```
using namespace System;
template <int N>
struct Fibonacci
{
    enum { Value = Fibonacci<N-1>::Value + Fibonacci<N-2>::Value};
};
template <>
struct Fibonacci<0>
{
    enum {Value = 0 };
};
template <>
struct Fibonacci<1>
{
    enum {Value = 1 };
};
void main()
{
    Console::WriteLine(Fibonacci<7>::Value);
}
```

This code uses an enumeration value to set a number within a class; then it uses a recursive algorithm with two explicit specializations to calculate a Fibonacci number.

Let's compile and run it:

```
C:\>cl /nologo /clr:pure test.cpp
C:\>test
13
```

The interesting thing about this program is that it allows the value of the template to be calculated at compile time because of the way that it's written.

If we look at the program in .NET Reflector, we see the following decompiled output:

```
int main()
{
    Console::WriteLine(13);
    return 0;
}
```

The entire recursive nature of the algorithm was handled at compile time.

Square Roots Template

Let's try a more-complicated example. This example calculates the rounded square root of an integer. It uses default values in the template parameters, which is permitted in C++:

```
using namespace System;
template <int N, int low=1, int high=N>
struct Root
{
    enum { Value = Root<N, ((low+high)/2), N/((low+high)/2)>::Value};
};
template <int N, int R>
struct Root<N,R,R>
{
    enum {Value = R};
};
void main()
{
    Console::WriteLine(Root<196>::Value);
}
```

Let's compile and run it:

```
C:\>cl /nologo /clr:pure test.cpp
C:\>test
14
```

This program attempts to calculate the square root iteratively by continually averaging a guess and the number divided by the guess. The square root is always somewhere in between the two. The program is only guaranteed to work if the input is a perfect square, or else a compilation error may result.

Prime Numbers Template

In 1994, Erwin Unruh distributed a program at a C++ standards committee meeting to print out prime numbers as error messages using templates. Although the original program does not issue the same diagnostics on Visual C++ 2005, here is a version I wrote that has the same effect:

```
template <int p, int i=p-1> struct is_prime
{
    enum { value = (p%i) && is_prime<p,i-1>::value };
};
template<int p> struct is_prime<p,1>
{
    enum { value=1 };
};
template<> struct is_prime<2>
{
    enum { value=1 };
};
template <int p> ref struct Prime_print
{
    Prime_print<p-1> a;
    static void *ptr = (int)is_prime<p>::value;
};
template<> ref struct Prime_print<1> {};
void main()
{
    Prime_print<9> d;
}
```

Let's compile and run this:

```
C:\>cl  /nologo /clr:pure test.cpp
test.cpp
test.cpp(16) : error C2440: 'initializing' : cannot convert from 'int' to 'void *'
        Conversion from integral type to pointer type requires
 reinterpret_cast, C-style cast or function-style cast
        This diagnostic occurred in the compiler generated function
 'void Prime_print<p>::Prime_print(void)'
        with
        [
            p=2
        ]
test.cpp(16) : error C2440: 'initializing' : cannot convert from 'int' to 'void *'
        Conversion from integral type to pointer type requires
 reinterpret_cast, C-style cast or function-style cast
        This diagnostic occurred in the compiler generated function
 'void Prime_print<p>::Prime_print(void)'
        with
        [
            p=3
        ]
test.cpp(16) : error C2440: 'initializing' : cannot convert from 'int' to 'void *'
        Conversion from integral type to pointer type requires
```

```
reinterpret_cast, C-style cast or function-style cast
        This diagnostic occurred in the compiler generated function
'void Prime_print<p>::Prime_print(void)'
        with
        [
            p=5
        ]
test.cpp(16) : error C2440: 'initializing' : cannot convert from 'int' to 'void *'
        Conversion from integral type to pointer type requires
reinterpret_cast, C-style cast or function-style cast
        This diagnostic occurred in the compiler generated function
'void Prime_print<p>::Prime_print(void)'
        with
        [
            p=7
        ]
```

As you can see, all primes less than or equal to the nontype template parameter are displayed in the diagnostics.

Complex Numbers

In Chapter 11, we did several interesting things:

- We defined a complex number class.

- We defined a class of integers modulo 13.

- We introduced the fact that the Fibonacci numbers can be calculated using the golden ratio.

In this section, we will gather together these ostensibly different concepts into a single program that calculates Fibonacci numbers modulo any prime using the golden ratio formula. This program will use templates, type and nontype parameters, and specializations in order to create clean, modular code.

Overview

It might seem odd that to use a complex number class in association with the Fibonacci number formula, but it all depends on our definition of complex number pairs. Let's generalize what it means to be a complex number by consider pairs (a, b) where the second number is multiplied by the square root of 5 instead of the square root of –1. In fact, we can use a nontype template parameter of type integer to indicate what number is under the square root. Our complex number class will also have a type parameter to indicate the type of each number in our pair (a,b). We will use this type parameter to allow us to feed the class type of Modulo<P>, where Modulo is our class template for numbers modulo a prime P, and P is the nontype template parameter.

Mathematical Formulas

It is a mathematical fact that the sequence of Fibonacci numbers can be produced from powers of the golden ratio and its conjugate. The specific formulas follow:

$$\Phi = \frac{(1 + \sqrt{5})}{2}$$

$$\Theta = \frac{(1 - \sqrt{5})}{2}$$

$$F_n = \frac{\Phi^n - \Theta^n}{\Phi - \Theta}$$

As stated previously, our `Complex` class template is able to use pairs of arbitrary types, where the number inside the radical is an arbitrary integer, such as 5. To do this, we use a non-type template parameter whose nontype template arguments are integer constants, as well as another type parameter for the underlying type of the pair:

```
template <typename T, int N> value struct Complex;
```

In our complex number class in Chapter 11, we used two doubles as our private data members, corresponding to the real and imaginary parts of the complex number. The imaginary part was the double that was implicitly multiplied by the square root of –1 to create the complex number. In this chapter's class, we will also use a real and an imaginary part of an arbitrary type and consider the part that is multiplied by the integer under the square root of the imaginary part.

We will implement the complex number class using 5 as the radix to create the golden ratio and its complement for the Fibonacci formula. But again, why stop there? Rather than using doubles, why not use integers modulo a prime for our numbers? Having types with operators for the basic mathematical operations allows us to do just that.

So we're going to base our complex numbers on types other than `int`, such as `float` and `double`. It seems like a natural task for generics, right? In order to implement a generic complex number class, all we have to do is to be able to add, subtract, multiply, and divide these built-in types. That is an ostensibly simple thing to do but looks can be deceiving.

Generic Implementation

Generic operations are all defined in terms of virtual function calls in the IL. Therefore, when generics are parsed, the compiler has to be able to figure out which functions to call for a particular expression. If there were a common `multiply` interface that all types supported, then generic classes would be able to call a `multiply` function for the arbitrary types and resolve the expression. As it is, there is no common arithmetic interface for all types, for two reasons:

- Arithmetic doesn't always have any meaning for an arbitrary type that is descended from `Object^`. For example, what does `String^` multiplied by `String^` mean?

- Implementing extra interfaces for arbitrary types is burdensome to programmers.

Of course, it is also impossible to rewrite retroactively the built-in types to support an arithmetic interface, so we are faced with the unpleasant task of creating a wrapper class for each of the built-in types that support the kind of arithmetic interface required to implement a Complex variable based on an arbitrary built-in type. We could then constrain the types to derive from the arithmetic interface. This solution is neither elegant nor optimal.

Templates to the Rescue

Implementation using class templates is as straightforward as it is efficient. The compiler can determine at compile time that it already knows how to multiply two items of type float. When the template is instantiated, the types are not a mystery to the compiler, so it is able to produce the correct IL in each case. There is no need to create a single function that is able to handle arbitrary types. In fact, the instantiations may produce completely different code based on the definitions of the types themselves!

Without further ado, here are the Complex<typename T, int N>, Modulo<int P>, and Fibonacci<typename T> classes; it's probably the longest example in the book, but I think it's worth it:

```
using namespace System;
template <int P> String^ Radix()
{
    return " sqr("+P.ToString()+")";
}
template <> String^ Radix<-1>()
{
    return "i";
}
template <typename T, int N>
value struct Complex
{
    T re;
    T im;
    Complex(T _re, T _im)
    {
        re = _re;
        im = _im;
    }
    Complex(T _re)
    {
        re = _re;
        im = T(0);
    }
    static Complex operator* (Complex lhs, Complex rhs)
    {
        return Complex(lhs.re*rhs.re + (lhs.im*rhs.im*T(N)),
            lhs.re*rhs.im + lhs.im*rhs.re);
    }
    static Complex operator/ (Complex lhs, Complex rhs)
    {
        T bottom = rhs.re*rhs.re - rhs.im*rhs.im*T(N);
```

```
            Complex product = Complex(lhs * ~rhs);
            return Complex(product.re/bottom, product.im/bottom);
        }
    static Complex operator+ (Complex lhs, Complex rhs)
    {
            return Complex(lhs.re+rhs.re, lhs.im+rhs.im);
    }
    static Complex operator- (Complex lhs, Complex rhs)
    {
            return Complex(lhs.re-rhs.re, lhs.im-rhs.im);
    }
    static Complex operator~ (Complex lhs)
    {
            return Complex(lhs.re, -lhs.im);
    }
    virtual String^ ToString() override
    {
            return re.ToString() + (!!im ? " + " + im.ToString() +  Radix<N>() : "");
    }
};
template <int P>
value struct Modulo
{
    int Value;
    Modulo(int Val)
    {
            Value = Val % P;
    }
    static bool operator!(Modulo rhs)
    {
            return !rhs.Value;
    }
    static void ExtendedEuclid(int a, int b, int %d, int %x, int %y)
    {
            if(b==0)
            {
                d=a;
                x=1;
                y=0;
            }
            else
            {
                ExtendedEuclid(b,a%b, d, y, x);
                y-= (a/b)*x;
            }
    }
    static bool operator==(Modulo lhs, Modulo rhs)
```

```
    {
        return((rhs.Value-lhs.Value) % P == 0);
    }
    static bool operator!=(Modulo lhs, Modulo rhs)
    {
        return !(lhs == rhs);
    }
    static Modulo operator* (Modulo lhs, Modulo rhs)
    {
        return Modulo((lhs.Value * rhs.Value) % P);
    }
    static Modulo operator+ (Modulo lhs, Modulo rhs)
    {
        return Modulo((lhs.Value + rhs.Value) % P);
    }
    static Modulo operator- (Modulo lhs, Modulo rhs)
    {
        return Modulo((lhs.Value - rhs.Value) % P);
    }
    static Modulo operator- (Modulo lhs)
    {
        return Modulo((P - lhs.Value) % P);
    }
    static Modulo operator/ (Modulo lhs, Modulo rhs)
    {
        int d, x, y;
        ExtendedEuclid(rhs.Value,P,d,x,y);
        return lhs*Modulo(x*d);
    }
    virtual String ^ ToString() override
    {
        Value = (Value+P) % P;
        String ^s = Value.ToString();
        return s;
    }
};
template <typename T> ref struct Fibonacci
{
    static T half = T(1)/T(2);
    static Complex<T,5> phi = Complex<T,5>(half,half);
    static Complex<T,5> theta = Complex<T,5>(half,-half);
    static Complex<T,5> difference = phi-theta;
    template <int N>
    ref struct Result
    {
        static initonly Complex<T,5> phi_n = Result<N-1>::phi_n * phi;
        static initonly Complex<T,5> theta_n = Result<N-1>::theta_n * theta;
```

```
        static initonly Complex<T,5> Value = (phi_n-theta_n)/difference;
    };
    template <>
    ref struct Result<0>
    {
        static initonly Complex<T,5> phi_n = Complex<T,5>(T(1));
        static initonly Complex<T,5> theta_n = Complex<T,5>(T(1));
        static initonly Complex<T,5> Value = Complex<T,5>(T(0));
    };
    template <int N>
    static void Print()
    {
        Print<N-1>();
        Console::Write("{0,4} ", Result<N>::Value);
    }
    template <>
    static void Print<0>()
    {
    }
};
void main()
{
    Fibonacci<double>::Print<14>();
    Console::WriteLine();
    Fibonacci<Modulo<7>>::Print<14>();
    Console::WriteLine();
    Fibonacci<Modulo<13>>::Print<14>();
    Console::WriteLine();
}
```

```
C:\>cl /clr:safe /nologo test.cpp
C:\>test
    1    1    2    3    5    8   13   21   34   55   89  144  233  377
    1    1    2    3    5    1    6    0    6    6    5    4    2    6
    1    1    2    3    5    8    0    8    8    3   11    1   12    0
```

Note that the 7th Fibonacci number is (–1 modulo 7), and the 13th is (–1 modulo 13). In fact, for prime numbers p other than 5, the pth Fibonacci number is always equal to either 1 or –1 modulo p.

In this example, we have a generic class G, which has a single type parameter T. A type constraint on T indicates that it has to support the interface I. In this case, I^ satisfies this via the identity conversion; R^ supports I^ through the handle conversion, and the value type V may be boxed and passed to G. In addition, the nested class N is able to use T as a type argument, since T satisfies V's constraint by definition.

The gcnew Constraint

The gcnew constraint allows you to allocate instances of the type parameter by calling the default constructor. Since not all types may be freely allocated (consider sealed or abstract types), this constraint allows you to write generic functions and classes that can allocate instances. The gcnew constraint also verifies that the constrained type parameter of the generic function or class may be allocated on the managed heap via a public parameterless constructor, for example:

```
using namespace System;
generic <typename T>
where T : gcnew()
void Function()
{
    T t = gcnew T();
}
ref class R {};
int main()
{
    Function<R^>();
}
```

The value class Constraint

The value class constraint instructs the compiler that the type parameter is a value type. Recall that, when you work with value types, you are working with the data itself rather than a handle to the data. This makes functions like the following one possible:

```
using namespace System;
generic <typename T>
where T : value class
void Swap(T % a, T % b)
{
    Console::WriteLine("Swapping...");
    T temp = a;
    a = b;
    b = temp;
}
int main()
{
```

```
    int i=3, j=4;
    Console::WriteLine("i = {0}, j={1}", i, j);
    Swap<int>(i,j);
    Console::WriteLine("i = {0}, j={1}", i, j);
}
```

In this program, we constrain T to be a value type. The global function Swap() expects two references to value types and performs a simple swap. The result follows:

```
C:\>cl /nologo /clr:pure test.cpp
test.cpp

C:\>test
i = 3, j=4
Swapping...
i = 4, j=3
```

Try instantiating the generic type parameter with a ref class argument to see how the compiler enforces the constraint.

The ref class Constraint

Here is an example of a similar construct using reference types:

```
using namespace System;
interface class I
{
    virtual property int P;
};
ref struct R : I
{
    virtual property int P;
};
value struct V : I
{
    virtual property int P;
};
generic <typename T>
where T : I
void ChangePropertyData(T t)
{
    t->P = 2;
}
int main()
{
    R ^ r = gcnew R();
```

```
        Console::WriteLine("changing R...");
        ChangePropertyData(r);
        Console::WriteLine("r->P == {0}", r->P);
        V v = V();
        Console::WriteLine("changing V...");
        ChangePropertyData(v);
        Console::WriteLine("v.P == {0}", v.P);
}
```

In this code sample, we have an interface with a property P. We have a generic function constrained to accept a type parameter that has this interface. This function uses the property to modify the underlying value. If we call this function with a reference type, we get the desired behavior, since we pass a handle to the data, and this handle can be used to modify the original data. On the other hand, if we call this function with a value type, we pass a copy of the data, and the original data is unchanged.

Here are the results:

```
C:\>cl /nologo /clr:pure test.cpp
C:\>test
changing R...
r->P == 2
changing V...
v.P == 0
```

As you can see, the original value of v.P is unchanged, which is not what we wanted the function to do. To prevent this kind of behavior, we can constrain the type T to be a ref class by adding the ref class constraint:

```
where T : I, ref class
```

Now when we compile, we get the following results:

```
C:\>cl /nologo /clr:pure test.cpp
test.cpp(28) : error C3390: 'V' : invalid type argument for generic parameter 'T'
 of generic 'ChangePropertyData', must be a reference type
        test.cpp(16) : see declaration of 'ChangePropertyData'
```

Summary

Constraints are useful for creating generic functions and classes for operating on custom sets of types or types that have predefined interfaces. Oftentimes, however, you do not have control over the definitions of the type for which you wish to write a generic; for example, System::Int32. Suppose you want to write a simple generic function to add two numbers, where the numbers can be either float or double or of integer type, depending on the context. Constraints won't solve this problem; a cast will. I'll show how in the next section.

Cast Operators

In C++, there are several types of cast operators that are designed to make your code accurate and easily maintainable. Think of the standard "type inside parenthesis" operator as a sledge hammer that smashes everything. The C++ cast operators are restricted in that they only perform certain types of conversions, and in this way, you ensure that the code is not changing in an unexpected fashion. Rather than using a sledge hammer or fire-fighter's axe to open a door, first, we can try to see if one of our keys fits.

The special cast operators help you avoid problems in two primary ways:

Casts during development: When you use a cast in code development, you are effectively overriding the compiler and forcing it to attempt to convert the item in question. In doing so, you prevent the compiler from issuing diagnostics that ought to tell you that what you're doing is a bad idea. Each time you use a cast, you should be asking yourself whether it's really a good idea. When the special cast operators are used, the compiler is not taken out of the picture altogether. Rather, it is instructed to let certain kinds of conversions pass and to block others. Therefore, you are forced to think about what you are doing and make sure the contemplated cast in your mind coincides with the actual kind of cast required to create accurate code.

Casts during maintenance: Working with polymorphic classes with abstracted interfaces means that you possess a somewhat-limited knowledge of the definitions of classes. You may write code relying on the facts that the class possessed a certain defined pedigree of base classes and that the classes are defined in certain ways, but that may change as the code matures. Somewhere down the line, your analysis that an instance of one class may be converted into an instance of another without issues may be completely wrong. In addition, the standard cast operator prevents the compiler from notifying the individual who modifies the class definitions that there may be a problem downstream. Therefore, hidden bugs are introduced that may go unnoticed until after the code is shipped to the end user. The special cast operators reduce the likelihood of such an occurrence. The use of explicit and implicit conversion operators and runtime type identification further reduce the likelihood of such an occurrence.

Runtime Type Identification

Runtime type identification is the ability of the instances of the classes themselves to identify what type they are. In the .NET Framework, the method GetType() is a member of System::Object, so it is always available to obtain information about object instances of reference types and value types. C# has the typeof() operator, which allows you to get the System::Type information for a class. The C++/CLI equivalent is the ::typeid static property. You can use these functions to identify a class or object and work with it.

Consider the following generic function:

```
using namespace System;
generic <typename T>
void Function()
{
    Console::WriteLine(T::typeid);
```

```
}
ref struct R {};
generic <typename T> ref struct GenericType {};
generic <typename T> ref struct Outer
{
    generic <typename V, typename W> ref struct Inner
    {
    };
};
int main()
{
    Function<int>();
    Function<R^>();
    Function<GenericType<int>^>();
    Function<Outer<int>::Inner<R^, short> ^>();
}
```

This function prints out the typeids. If we execute it and compile it, we get the following:

```
C:\>cl /nologo /clr:pure test.cpp
C:\>test
System.Int32
R
GenericType`1[System.Int32]
Outer`1+Inner`2[System.Int32,R,System.Int16]
```

As you can see, the typeids for the generics display with decoration. The back tick (`) indicates a generic, and it indicates the number of generic parameters at that level of nesting. The plus sign (+) divides the nesting of generic types. Although it is not shown here, the signatures of generic functions are similar, except that they use two back ticks (``) between the function identifier and the number of generic parameters.

const_cast<>()

Several modifiers in both C# and C++ affect the mutability of fields and types. The const_cast<>() operator allows you to add or remove the const or volatile type qualifiers to the type of an expression. An example follows:

```
void main()
{
    const int i = 0;
    //i=2 will not compile
    *const_cast<int *>(&i) = 2;
}
```

I will return to the mutability type qualifiers in Chapter 20.

static_cast<>()

static_cast<>() is used to call user-defined conversions as well as to cast an instance of a base class back to a derived class. You should only do the latter when you are sure it will work, as this is a fast cast, and the compiler does not do any further checking.

An example using static_cast<>() follows:

```
using namespace System;
ref class Base {};
ref class Derived : Base {};
void main()
{
    Base ^ b = gcnew Derived();
    Derived ^ d = static_cast<Derived^>(b);
    Console::WriteLine("{0}, {1}", b->GetType(), d->GetType());
}
```

Here are the results:

```
C:\>cl /nologo /clr:pure test.cpp
C:\>test
Derived, Derived
```

dynamic_cast<>()

dynamic_cast<>() is also used to cast an instance of a base class back to a derived class, but dynamic_cast<>() is used only when the types involved are *polymorphic*, meaning they have a virtual function. The compiler uses this information to determine whether the cast is allowed. If the cast is not allowed, dynamic_cast<>() returns nullptr. Since reference types inherit virtually from System::Object, and value types are sealed and cannot be inherited from at all, if the cast is valid, it works; for example:

```
using namespace System;
ref class Base {};
ref class Derived : Base {};
ref class Cat {};
void main()
{
    Base ^ b = gcnew Derived();
    Derived ^ d = dynamic_cast<Derived^>(b);
    Cat ^ c = dynamic_cast<Cat^>(b);
    Console::WriteLine("Derived^d = {0}, Cat^c = {1}",
        d!=nullptr ? d->ToString() : "nullptr",
        c!=nullptr ? c->ToString() : "nullptr");
}
```

```
C:\>cl /nologo /clr:pure test.cpp
C:\>test
Derived^d = Derived, Cat^c = nullptr
```

In a previous example in Chapter 14, we used typeid or GetType() along with
safe_cast<>() rather than dynamic_cast<>(), even though dynamic_cast<>() seems like
a more accurate solution.

Consider the following code:

```
using namespace System;
ref class Base {};
ref class Derived : Base {};
generic <typename T>
void Function(T t)
{
    if(Derived ^d = dynamic_cast<Derived^>(t))
    {
        Console::WriteLine("success");
    }
}
void main()
{
    Base ^b = gcnew Derived();
    Function(b);
}
```

If you attempt to compile this, you receive the following error:

```
C:\>cl /nologo /clr:pure test.cpp
test.cpp(9) : error C2681: 'T' : invalid expression type for dynamic_cast}
```

There is one case in which dynamic_cast<>() does not return nullptr and throws an
exception—when casting to a reference (& or %). Since only pointer and handle types can be
assigned nullptr, and references are neither pointer nor handle types, the compiler needs
another way to report an unsuccessful cast. Try out the following code:

```
ref class A
{
public:
    virtual void f() {}
};

ref class B : public A
{
};
```

```
void main()
{
    A a;
    B %rb = dynamic_cast<B%>(a);
}
```

reinterpret_cast<>()

reinterpret_cast<>() is used to convert constants into instances of types and to convert between completely unrelated pointers types, for example:

```
void main()
{
    char *pVideo = reinterpret_cast<char *>(0xb8000000);
}
```

This is sometimes necessary in unsafe or low-level code. It comes in handy when you're working with native programming, inline assembly, and low-level coding. This cast is the "you must really know what you are doing" cast.

safe_cast<>()

safe_cast<>() allows you to do much the same thing as static_cast<>(), except that it raises an exception if it cannot perform the conversion. It also only attempts conversions that make sense. It works with generic types as well. It is a variant that is limited to C++/CLI as it does not exist in native C++. A safe_cast<>() example follows:

```
using namespace System;
ref class Base {};
ref class Derived : Base {};
ref class Cat {};
void main()
{
    Base ^ b = gcnew Derived();
    Cat ^ c = safe_cast<Cat^>(b);
}
```

And here are the results:

```
C:\>cl /nologo /clr:pure test.cpp
test.cpp(8) : error C2682: cannot use 'safe_cast' to convert from
 'Base ^' to 'Cat ^'
        No user-defined-conversion operator available, or
        Types pointed to are unrelated; conversion requires reinterpret_cast,
 C-style cast or function-style cast
```

The following example uses safe_cast<>() with generics:

```
using namespace System;
ref class Base {};
ref class Derived : Base {};
ref class Cat {};
generic <typename T>
void Function(T t)
{
    try
    {
        Cat ^c = safe_cast<Cat^>(t);
    }
    catch(Exception ^e)
    {
        Console::WriteLine("Exception: {0}", e);
    }
}
void main()
{
    Base ^ b = gcnew Derived();
    Function(b);
}
```

with the following results:

```
C:\>cl /nologo /clr:pure test.cpp
test.cpp

C:\>test
Exception: System.InvalidCastException: Unable to cast object of type
  'Derived' to type 'Cat'.
    at Function[T](T t)
```

An Adder

Earlier in this section, I pledged to show you how to use casts to do something you cannot do with constraints—add two integers or floats. The problem arises because there is no defined interface that states that System::Int32 has an Add() function. Of course, we can create custom types with this functionality, but it's nice to just use the built-in types—here's how:

```
using namespace System;
generic <typename T>
where T : value class
T Add(T a, T b)
{
    if(T::typeid == int::typeid)
```

```
    {
        int a0 = safe_cast<int>(a);
        int b0 = safe_cast<int>(b);
        return safe_cast<T>(a0+b0);
    }
    if(T::typeid == double::typeid)
    {
        double a0 = safe_cast<double>(a);
        double b0 = safe_cast<double>(b);
        return safe_cast<T>(a0+b0);
    }
    String ^s = String::Format("{0} is not a valid type for addition", T::typeid);
    throw gcnew Exception(s);
}
int main()
{
    try
    {
        Console::WriteLine("{0}+{1}={2}", 3, 4, Add(3,4));
        Console::WriteLine("{0}+{1}={2}", 3.1, 4.2, Add(3.1,4.2));
        Console::WriteLine("{0}+{1}={2}", 3.1, 4.2, Add(3.1f,4.2f));
    }
    catch(Exception ^e)
    {
        Console::WriteLine("Exception: {0}", e);
    }
}
```

In this snippet, we use ::typeid and safe_cast<>() to add instances of the types we know how to add. In this case, we can add integers and doubles. When we try to call Add<T>() with float values, we generate an exception:

```
C:\>cl /nologo /clr:pure test.cpp
C:\>test
3+4=7
3.1+4.2=7.3
Exception: System.Exception: System.Single is not a valid type for addition
    at Add[T](T a, T b)
    at main()
```

The following version of the code uses templates:

```
using namespace System;
template <typename T>
T Add(T a, T b)
{
    return a+b;
}
```

```
int main()
{
    try
    {
        Console::WriteLine("{0}+{1}={2}", 3, 4, Add(3,4));
        Console::WriteLine("{0}+{1}={2}", 3.1, 4.2, Add(3.1,4.2));
        Console::WriteLine("{0}+{1}={2}", 3.1, 4.2, Add(3.1f,4.2f));
    }
    catch(Exception ^e)
    {
        Console::WriteLine("Exception: {0}", e);
    }
}
```

As you can see, the version that uses templates is far shorter. We ask the compiler to perform the add operation on the two instances of the type parameters, and we get a compiler error if the operation is not possible on the types, such as when we try to add instances of System::Object.

Generic Delegates

Delegates may also be generic. A simple example follows:

```
using namespace System;
ref struct Test
{
    generic<typename T> delegate void Del(T item);
    static void Notify(int i)
    {
        Console::WriteLine("notified...");
    }
};
void main()
{
    Test::Del<int> ^m1 = gcnew Test::Del<int>(Test::Notify);
    m1(3);
}
```

In this example, we create a generic delegate and call it with an integer type. Let's compile and execute it:

```
C:\>cl /clr:pure /nologo test.cpp
C:\>test
notified...
```

Summary

In this chapter, I've gone a little deeper with generics, but you really have no idea how deep the rabbit hole goes yet. In Chapter 20, we'll revisit templates and generics to consider them separately and in combination one last time.

In the next chapter, we'll have a look at the other C++ compile-time metaprogramming sublanguage, the preprocessor.

CHAPTER 17

■ ■ ■

The Preprocessor

Power tends to corrupt; absolute power corrupts absolutely.

—Lord Acton

The preprocessor in C was historically a separate program that was able to affect code compilation based on the value of flags defined at compile time. Over time, the preprocessor was extended and integrated into the C++ compiler. The designers of C# chose to adopt a subset of the C++ preprocessor, retaining only the conditional compilation commands and rejecting the macro substitution language in order to keep C# code simple.

Preprocessor directives all begin with the # symbol. Modern compilers increase throughput by integrating the preprocessor into the compiler so that they may perform preprocessing on a line-by-line basis. The preprocessor plays a much greater role in C++ programming than it does in C# programming. It implements a rich text substitution language that allows you to completely change the face of your code.

For a while, using the C preprocessor to do complex and amazing things was in vogue. Oftentimes, the motivation for generating these esoteric constructions was to develop a foundation for object-oriented programming on a platform that did not yet support it. Unfortunately, this practice often led to obfuscation, and code became more and more difficult to debug and maintain.

The emergence and standardization of C++ obviated most of these sorts of heroic measures, but there remain several important ways in which the preprocessor can make your code cleaner and more efficient.

C# Preprocessor Commands

The C# preprocessor is fairly limited in scope and function. It defines code regions and determines compilation options at no finer granularity than the class level.

Code Regions

C# has two preprocessor commands, `#region` and `#endregion`, which allow you to tag certain areas of the code as having a function or label, so that you may hide these intelligently using the IDE. These do not yet exist in standard C++, though they exist in the Microsoft Visual C++ compiler as a `#pragma` directive (see the "#pragma" section later in this chapter).

Conditional Code Compilation

The C# directives #define, #undef, #if, #else, #elif, and #endif enable you to specify code sections that are compiled depending on the state of certain flags. Flags can be defined at the start of the file before compilation begins or on the command line. This makes it very easy to add a section of code that will only be added to the executable during a debug build. In C#, #define and #undef may only be used at the start of a file. If you violate this rule in C#, you will get the following diagnostic:

```
test.cs(5,2): error CS1032: Cannot define/undefine preprocessor symbols
 after first token in file
```

C++ Preprocessor Commands

C++ also supports the conditional code compilation directives, but without the restriction that #define and #undef must be used at the start of a file. But the C++ preprocessor is even more powerful than that.

In C++, the preprocessor is a full macro replacement language. You can use #define to create macros that allow you to make sweeping changes to both the appearance and function of your code.

For example, if we wanted to make our C++ look a tiny bit more C# like, we could do the following:

```
#define USING using namespace
USING System;
#define NEW gcnew
#define CLASS ref class
#define STRUCT value class
#define PUBLIC public:
public STRUCT Struct
{
    PUBLIC int i;
};
public CLASS Test
{
    PUBLIC static void Main()
    {
        Struct ^ s = NEW Struct();
        s->i = 42;
        Console::WriteLine(s->i);
    }
};
void main()
{
    Test::Main();
}
```

Of course, if you write code like this, you will drive other programmers nuts trying to figure out what your code really does. You might drive yourself nuts as well.

Full Text Substitution Language

Just like template metaprogramming, the collection of C++ preprocessor commands is considered a sublanguage all by itself. Not only can you assign values to flags but you can also create function-style macros that are able to perform function-like tasks in your code.

Debugging Support

Microsoft Visual C++ 2005 supports debugging preprocessor macros in a few different ways. The /E and /P compilation options can be used to restrict compiler execution to the preprocessor. The /E option sends the output to stdout, where it can be redirected to a file or piped through a process, and the /P option writes the output directly to a file.

The IDE supports the use of macros by displaying tool tips with macro definitions and graying out code that is part of an inactive, conditional compilation block. You can also see a list of the macros defined in your projects by going to Class View and expanding the Macros and Constants node.

Function Syntax

Function syntax for macros is pretty much what you'd expect it to be. Rather than defining the value of a flag or label to be a fixed value, you define it to be a text operation that works on arguments or parameters. There is no concept of type checking relative to these parameters, and whether the parameters ultimately end up being identifiers, keywords, or literals depends on the macro definition and implementation context. Here is a function-style macro to calculate the maximum of two numbers:

```
#define max(a,b) a>b?a:b
```

Here it is in action:

```
using namespace System;
#define max(a,b) a>b?a:b
void main()
{
    Console::WriteLine(max(3,4));
}
```

When we attempt to run this, we get

```
C:\>cl /nologo /clr:pure test.cpp
C:\>test
4
```

Unfortunately, there's a bug in this program. Can you see it?

Suppose we want to add 2 to the value before we printed it out, so we modify the invocation of max() as follows:

```
Console::WriteLine(2+max(3,4));
```

Let's compile and execute this:

```
C:\>cl /nologo /clr:pure test.cpp
C:\>test
3
```

We added 2 to the result and got one number less. What's going on here? We can use the /E option of the C++ compiler to help determine the problem.

```
C:\>cl /nologo /clr:pure /E test.cpp
test.cpp
#line 1 "test.cpp"
using namespace System;

void main()
{
    Console::WriteLine(2+3>4?3:4);
}
```

Using the /E option, it's clear why this program does not do what we expect. Since there are no parentheses around the calculation in the max() macro, the expansion is calculated differently than we'd like by the compiler. We can fix this by redefining the macro with parentheses as follows:

```
#define max(a,b) ((a)>(b)?(a):(b))
```

Now when we compile and execute, we get the following:

```
C:\>cl /nologo /clr:pure test.cpp
C:\>test
6
```

And that is what we expect.

■**Note** The compiler keeps track of line numbers and file names using the #line directive. This allows you to compile the results of a file that is preprocessed using the /E (preprocess to stdout) or /P (preprocess to file) command-line options and still get the same diagnostics as you would with a direct compile. This is true even if your primary file brings in several other files using #include. Many companies use these flags to insert custom passes between the preprocessor and the main compilation phase.

Concatenation Operator

C++ allows you to use the ## concatenation operator within a macro to indicate that two symbols should be concatenated to make a new symbol. An interesting variant of the "Hello, World" program follows:

```
using namespace System;
#define CONCAT_(x,y) x##y
void CONCAT_(ma, in) ()
{
    Console::WriteLine("Hello, World");
}
```

In this case, CONCAT_(ma, in) expands to main, and the program compiles. Let's compile and run it:

```
C:\>cl /nologo /clr:pure test.cpp
C:\>test
Hello, World
```

Wow, "Hello, World" yet again!

String Operator

Using the # prefix operator within a macro converts an argument into a string, for example:

```
#define STR_(x) #x
using namespace System;
void main()
{
    Console::WriteLine(STR_(Hello));
}
```

If we compile and execute this, we see the following:

```
C:\>cl /nologo /clr:pure test.cpp
C:\>test
Hello
```

Macros on Macros

Things start to get interesting when macros call other macros. In general, macro recursion is not the same as template or function recursion, since macro expansion is not infinitely recursive. For example, consider the following:

```
using namespace System;
#define CONCAT_(x,y) x##y
void main()
{
    int i = CONCAT_(1, CONCAT_(2,3));
    Console::WriteLine(i);
}
```

Preprocessing, we get

```
C:\>cl /nologo /clr:pure /E test.cpp
#line 1 "test.cpp"
using namespace System;

void main()
{
    int i = 1CONCAT_(2,3);
    Console::WriteLine(i);
}
```

As you can see, the concatenation of (2,3) was not performed. The compiler took the enclosing macro literally and concatenated the symbol "1" to the symbol "CONCAT_(2,3)", resulting in "1CONCAT_(2,3)", which is ineligible for further macro expansion. If we want a concatenation macro that can work around this problem, we need to define a second macro.

Consider the following snippet:

```
#define CONCAT_(x,y) x##y
#define CONCAT(x,y) CONCAT_(x,y)
void main()
{
    int i = CONCAT(1, CONCAT(2,3));
    System::Console::WriteLine(i);
}
```

Preprocessing, we get

```
C:\>cl /nologo /clr:pure /E test.cpp
#line 1 "test.cpp"


void main()
{
    int i = 123;
    System::Console::WriteLine(i);
}
```

Why did it work this time? To understand this, it's necessary to understand a bit more about how the preprocessor works. The preprocessor scans the parameters of the macro as either potential tokens or literals depending on the context. Only tokens are able to undergo further macro expansion. The presence of the # or ## operators classifies the arguments as literals. Lacking these, the argument is scanned for macro replacement.[1]

---

1. Section 16.3.1 of the C++ Standard of April 1, 2003, says about argument substitution ([cpp.subst]), "After the arguments for the invocation of a function-like macro have been identified, argument substitution takes place. A parameter in the replacement list, unless preceded by a # or ## preprocessing token or followed by a ## preprocessing token . . . is replaced by the corresponding argument after all macros contained therein have been expanded. Before being substituted, each argument's preprocessing tokens are completely macro replaced as if they formed the rest of the translation unit; no other preprocessing tokens are available."

Consider the following macro:

```
#define CONCAT_(x,y) x##y
```

The preprocessor treats x and y literally, and no further expansion occurs because of the ## operator. On the other hand, in

```
#define CONCAT_(x,y) x##y
#define CONCAT(x,y) CONCAT_(x,y)
```

the macro CONCAT(x,y) parses x and y for potential macro replacement because of the lack of string or concatenation operators the first time x and y are encountered.

Here's another example from basic algebra. Remember the "first, inner, outer, last" (or FOIL) rule for multiplying binomials?

```
#define FOIL(a,b,c,d) ((a)*(c) + (b)*(c) + (d)*(a) + (b)*(d))
#define STR_(x) #x
#define STR(x) STR_(x)
using namespace System;
void main()
{
    Console::WriteLine("(x+1)*(x+2)={0}", STR(FOIL(x,1,x,2)));
}
```

The preceding code generates

```
C:\>cl /nologo /clr:pure test.cpp
C:\>test
(x+1)*(x+2)=((x)*(x) + (1)*(x) + (2)*(x) + (1)*(2))
```

Of course, this result is not as pretty as the following:

$$(x+1)(x+2)=x^2+3x+2$$

But it is just as accurate.

Special Preprocessor Predefined Macros

There are several macros, wrapped in double underscores, that are predefined for use in your code:

- __LINE__: Evaluates to the current line number

- __FILE__: Evaluates to the current file name

- __DATE__: Evaluates to the date of compilation

- __TIME__: Evaluates to the time of compilation

- __FUNCTION__: Evaluates to the name of a function or method

- __FUNCSIG__: Evaluates to the complete signature of a function or method

They're fairly self explanatory; the latter two are only valid within a function. Here is a quick example that allows you to find the origin of exceptions in your code:

```
using namespace System;
#define THROWIF(condition) ThrowIf(condition, #condition, __LINE__)
void ThrowIf(bool condition, String^ message, int line)
{
    if(condition)
    {
        String ^s =
            "(" + message + ")" + " @ line " + line + "\n"
            + "in " + __FILE__
            + ", build " + __DATE__
            + " " + __TIME__;
        throw gcnew Exception(s);
    }
}
void main()
{
    int x = 1, y = 2;
    try
    {
        THROWIF(x != y);
    }
    catch(Exception ^e)
    {
        Console::WriteLine("Exception: {0}\n{1}", e->Message, e->StackTrace);
    }
}
```

Compiling and executing, we get the following:

```
C:\>cl /nologo /clr:pure test.cpp
C:\>test
Exception: (x != y) @ line 20
in macro.cpp, build Aug 13 2006 23:49:03
   at ThrowIf(Boolean condition, String message, Int32 line)
   at main()
```

#define

This command is used to define a macro, for example:

```
#define DEBUG 1
#define function(x) (x)
```

Function-style macros can not be overloaded. Once a macro is defined with a fixed number of parameters, it remains defined that way until either it is undefined or the compilation unit ends. Special kinds of function-like macros, called *variadic macros*, allow you to have an undetermined number of macro parameters. To define a variadic macro, use the ellipsis (. . .) as the final formal argument to the macro. In usage, use the __VA_ARGS__ replacement identifier to access the variable argument list. Here is a code example:

```
#include <stdio.h>
#define err_printf(...) fprintf (stderr, __VA_ARGS__)
void main()
{
    err_printf("Error number %d\n", 42);
}
```

Compiling and running this, we get the following:

```
C:\>cl  /nologo test.cpp
C:\>test
Error number 42
```

#undef

Delete a macro definition with the #undef directive.

Conditional Directives

In this section, we'll have a look at the following conditional compilation directives:

```
#ifdef <macro>
#ifndef <macro>
#if <mathematical argument>
#else
#elsif <mathematical argument>
#endif
```

These directives are similar to those found in C#. For the mathematical arguments, all of the standard operators work, including +, -, *, /, %, &, |, ^, &&, |, !, ==, !=, <, >, <=, >=, <<, and >>. There is also a special operator called defined(), which allows you to determine whether a macro is defined. This defined(macro) is true if the macro is defined. Therefore, the following two macros are equivalent:

```
#ifdef MACRO
#if defined(MACRO)
```

#include

#include is used to insert a file into the current compilation unit. There are two forms of this directive:

```
#include "file.h"
#include <file.h>
```

The angle-bracket version searches the system include directories, which includes any directories specified in the /I compiler option or in the INCLUDE environmental variable. The double–quotation mark version additionally searches the directory of the current compiland for files to include, plus any directories of any files that included the current file. The search algorithm recourses upward through the include list hierarchy, if there is one. Note that any file can be included, not just those with the extension .h. The convention is that .h files contain only macro definitions, declarations, and no instantiations of any definitions. Include files that also contain definitions are typically named with the extension .hpp.

#using

The C++/CLI #using directive instructs the compiler that certain assemblies must be referenced during the compilation process. It is the analogue to what you achieve in the C# compiler with the /reference compiler option. These files are searched for in the following order: the full path in the #using directive, the current working directory of the compilation (when deploying with the IDE, this is the folder containing your Visual C++ project file), the .NET Framework system directory, and finally, any directories added with the /AI compiler option or in the LIBPATH environmental variable. As opposed to #include, there is no difference between the quoted and angle-bracket forms of #using.

#error

The #error directive issues an immediate error. It can be used to stop a compile when compile time errors are encountered, for example:

```
#if _MSC_VER < 1400
#error "Code requires VS2005 or above."
#endif
```

#pragma

The #pragma directive encodes compiler-specific instructions. These instructions are generally not portable, as they pertain to a particular implementation. One of the more useful #pragma directives in Microsoft Visual C++ is #pragma warning. This directive allows you to enable or disable warnings in the compiler. This is especially useful if you are compiling your code with the /WX option, which treats all warnings as errors.

In C++, the function main() is defined as a global function returning int. The Microsoft Visual C++ compiler allows you to declare it as a function of type void as well, but this is not standard C++.[2] To help the porting process of converting main() entry points so they return void instead of int, the compiler allows you to skip returning a value from main() and injects a return of 0 for you. In the case of any other function, it generates warning 4716 if you forget to return a value.

---

2. Section 3.6.1 of the C++ Standard of April 1, 2003, says about the main function ([basic.start.main]), "A program shall contain a global function called main, which is the designated start of the program . . . It shall have a return type of type int, but otherwise its type is implementation-defined."

Consider this one-line program:

```
int hello() {}
```

After compiling it, we get

```
C:\>cl /nologo /clr:pure test.cpp
c:\test.cpp(1) : error C4716: 'hello' : must return a value
```

Although 4716 is a warning, it is considered an error by default by the compiler. You can still disable it with #pragma warning().

Let's add the following directive:

```
#pragma warning (disable:4716)
```

Now this compiles without warning or error.

Here's a less-contrived example:

```
#pragma warning (disable:4706)
void main()
{
    int i=3; int j;
    if(j=i)
    {
        System::Console::WriteLine(j);
    }
}
```

and the results

```
C:\>cl /nologo /clr:pure test.cpp
C:\>test
3
```

When compiling, the compiler would tell you that you have an assignment within a conditional expression with warning 4706. Usually this means that you forgot the extra = when using the conditional operator ==, but in this case, it's not a problem.

Some Useful Pragmas

As we already discussed, the following directives allow you to enable or disable one or more warnings:

```
#pragma warning (enable: <n>[,<n>, ...])
#pragma warning (disable: <n>[,<n>, ...])
```

They also work on warnings that are errors by default, such as warning 4716 (discussed previously). The diagnostics with numbers in the 4000 range are all warnings.

The following #pragma directive displays a string during the compilation process:

```
#pragma message("string")
```

If you are redirecting the compiler output, this can be useful for postprocessing:

```
#pragma message("Compiling: "__FILE__ " " __DATE__ " " __TIME__)
void main()
{
}
```

After compiling this, we get the following:

```
C:\>cl /nologo /clr:pure test.cpp
test.cpp
Compiling: test.cpp May 11 2006 20:44:13
```

One interesting thing to note about this code is that the strings used are not joined together with the + symbol, because this code uses a native array of char and not a handle to System::String. In this case, the preprocessor concatenates the strings into a single literal for you. Earlier, I showed an example of using the predefined macros in the context of a System::String. This behavior is not limited to the predefined macros, but is rather an idiosyncrasy of the implementation. There are two kinds of strings in C++: char[] and System::String^. We will revisit this in the context of #pragma managed and #pragma unmanaged:

```
#pragma managed
#pragma unmanaged
```

These directives allow you to designate particular sections of the code as unmanaged or managed, which allows you to convert your native C++ to managed code on your own schedule. Much of legacy native C++ is able to compile managed out of the box because of the compiler feature named IJW (it just works), which handles transitions to native code automatically. For example, you can compile the next native C++ code example as managed as well as unmanaged. If you compile it managed, it transitions to the native library function printf() automatically through managed-to-native and native-to-managed transitions.

Let's use the /FAsc compiler option (configure assembly listing) to see the native code generated by the compiler:

```
cl /nologo /FAsc test.cpp
```

We find the following example within the test.cod file (note that the source code for test.cpp is inline within the assembly listing):

```
_main    PROC
; 3   : {
  00000   55                    push     ebp
  00001   8b ec                 mov      ebp, esp
; 4   :    printf("Hello, World\n");
  00003   68 00 00 00 00        push     OFFSET $SG3669
```

```
  00008      e8 00 00 00 00      call     _printf
  0000d      83 c4 04            add      esp, 4
; 5    : }
  00010      33 c0               xor      eax, eax
  00012      5d                  pop      ebp
  00013      c3                  ret      0
_main      ENDP
```

This is 32-bit code generated for the x86 family of processors, and it runs fine on my Mac-Book Pro with Intel Inside.

Compiling the code managed

```
cl /nologo /clr:pure /FAsc test.cpp
```

we get the following:

```
; 4    :      printf("Hello, World\n");
  0000b      7f 00 00 00 00      ldsflda $SG6951
  00010      28 00 00 00 00      call ?printf@@$$J0YAHPBDZZ
  00015      26                  pop
; 5    : }
  00016      16                  ldc.i.0 0     ; i32 0x0
  00017      2a                  ret
```

This is CIL for the same program. It also runs on my MacBook Pro. The call to printf() has been replaced with a call to the transition code.

Using #pragma managed and #pragma unmanaged, we can merge code that will not compile managed with managed code as well as maintain certain areas as native for compatibility or performance.

Let's consider the following program:

```
#pragma managed
void Managed()
{
    System::String ^s = "Hello " + "world";
    System::Console::WriteLine(s);
}
#pragma unmanaged
#include <stdio.h>
void main()
{
    Managed();
    char t[]="Hello " "world";
    printf("%s\n", t);
}
```

Let's compile this using /clr. You cannot compile this using /clr:pure or /clr:safe because of the #pragma directives.

```
cl /nologo /FAsc /clr test.cpp
```

If you now examine the test.cod file, you will find a mixture of managed code and native code. In the managed section, "Hello " and "world" are combined via a compiler-generated call to String::Concat. In the native section, "Hello " and "world" are concatenated automatically by the compiler. We will revisit the use of these #pragma directives in Chapter 19 within the context of interoperability between native C++, C++/CLI, and C#.

The following directives implement the C++ version of #region and #endregion:

```
#pragma region any_name
#pragma endregion [any_comment]
```

Since #pragma directives are ignored by compilers that don't recognize them, avoiding adoption of the C# versions and implementing them as #pragma directives allows C++/CLI code to be preprocessed by standard C++ preprocessors.

The following directive signals to the compiler that this include file should only be processed once by the compiler:

```
#pragma once
```

In native C++ programming, since library class declarations are located in include files, interclass dependencies cause include file dependencies. Rather than requiring the programmer to unravel these dependencies by including files in the right order, the include files themselves use the #include directive for the definitions of the classes they need in order to compile. In a complex system, several classes may depend on a single class, which would cause a single include file to be brought in multiple times. This can cause performance degradation as well as compilation errors if the include file has not been designed for this scenario.

Adding #pragma once at the beginning of an include file signals to the compiler that the include file should only be processed one time per compilation. Consider Listings 17-1 and 17-2.

Listing 17-1. *File test.h*

```
#pragma once
#pragma message("compiling " __FILE__)
#include "test.h"
```

Listing 17-2. *File test.cpp*

```
#include "test.h"
#include "test.h"
void main() {}
```

In Listing 17-1, we are not only including test.h multiple times but also including it recursively:

```
C:\>cl /nologo test.cpp
test.cpp
compiling c:\test.h
```

As you can see, the body of the include file is only compiled once.

One way to accomplish the same goal while avoiding #pragma directives is to use #define. In this paradigm, you define a flag when an include file is compiled and only compile the body of the include file if the flag is not defined.

For example, consider the following self-protected header file:

```
#ifndef TEST_H
#define TEST_H
#pragma message("compiling " __FILE__)
class Class
{
public:
    void Method();
};
#endif //TEST_H
```

This is a fairly common construction.

The following #pragma directives allow you to select from the instrinsic (built-in) versions of functions and the library versions, which is especially important if you wish to create custom implementations of functions that can be generated as intrinsic functions:

```
#pragma intrinsic( function1 [, function2, ...] )
#pragma function( function1 [, function2, ...] )
```

For example, the memset() (native) library function is generated intrinsically by the compiler.

Consider the following example:

```
#include <memory.h>
#pragma intrinsic(memset)
int main()
{
    char Hello[12];
    memset(Hello, 3 ,sizeof(Hello));
    return Hello[7];
}
```

Compile this with the command line option /Oi, which enables intrinsic functions, as follows:

```
cl /nologo /Oi /FAsc test.cpp
```

Let's examine the test.cod file:

```
; 5    :      char Hello[12];
; 6    :      memset(Hello, 3 ,sizeof(Hello));
  00010 b8 03 03 03 03    mov         eax, 50529027 ; 03030303H
  00015 89 45 f0          mov         DWORD PTR _Hello$[ebp], eax
  00018 89 45 f4          mov         DWORD PTR _Hello$[ebp+4], eax
  0001b 89 45 f8          mov         DWORD PTR _Hello$[ebp+8], eax
```

In this case, we can see how the compiler has generated memset() intrinsically. Changing the #pragma directive to the following:

```
#pragma  function(memset)
```

and recompiling gives us a different test.cod file:

```
; 5    :      char Hello[12];
; 6    :      memset(Hello, 3 ,sizeof(Hello));
  00010 6a 0c            push        12    ; 0000000cH
  00012 6a 03            push        3
  00014 8d 45 f0         lea         eax, DWORD PTR _Hello$[ebp]
  00017 50               push        eax
  00018 e8 00 00 00 00   call        memset
  0001d 83 c4 0c         add         esp, 12    ; 0000000cH
```

As you can see, the function version of memset() has been generated instead. Common intrinsic functions include the following:

Absolute Value:

```
#include <math.h>
fabs()    //absolute value of a float
abs()     //absolute value of an integer
labs()    //absolute value of a long
```

String Manipulation:

```
#include <string.h>
strcmp()    //compare two strings
strcpy()     //string copy
strlen()      //string length
strcat()       //string concatenation
```

Memory Manipulation:

```
#include <memory.h>
memcmp()    //memory comparison
memcpy()     //memory copy
memset()       //set memory to a value
```

An updated list of library functions that may be generated intrinsically by the compiler can be found on the Visual C++ documentation in the MSDN site.

The following directives allow you to temporarily redefine a macro:

```
#pragma push_macro("macro_name")
#pragma pop_macro("macro_name")
```

Redefining a macro is useful in a complex system that may have multiple modules that wish to use macros in different ways.

The following #pragma directive places comments in the compiled file; these comments are used by the linker or other programs:

```
#pragma comment( lib, "emapi" )
#pragma comment( compiler )
#pragma comment( user, "Compiled on " __DATE__ " at " __TIME__ )
```

Attributes (see Chapter 20) are used to add information at the class or function level.

The following directive works with the /Gs command-line option to enable or disable stack checking:

```
#pragma check_stack(on|off)
```

This #pragma and command-line option is useful for tuning the balance of heap and stack allocation in a native program.

As C++ has evolved, library functions have been deleted or revamped to encourage programmers to use more universal and secure functions. These library functions are labeled "deprecated," and the use of these functions generates a warning at compile time:

```
#pragma deprecated(func1, func2)
__declspec(deprecated) void func1(int) {}
```

The #pragma directive is used to deprecate an entire function, whereas the __declspec() is used to deprecate a particular overload of a function. __declspec() is another source of compiler-specific extensions (see the Visual C++ documentation on MSDN for more information). In C++/CLI, the class ObsoleteAttribute indicates obsolescence, just like in C#.

A comprehensive example follows:

```
#pragma unmanaged
void test1()
{
}
void test2(int)
{
}
__declspec(deprecated) void test2(char)
{
}
void func1(int)
{
}
#pragma deprecated(test1)
#pragma managed
using namespace System;
[Obsolete] void test()
{
}
void main()
{
#line 100
    test1();
```

```
#line 200
    test2((char)0);
#line 300
    test2((int)0);
#line 400
    test();
}
```

This program uses the #line directive to make our test cases easy to find.
Compiling this, we get the following:

```
C:\>cl /nologo /clr test.cpp
test.cpp
test.cpp(100) : warning C4995: 'test1': name was marked as #pragma deprecated
test.cpp(200) : warning C4996: 'test2' was declared deprecated
        test.cpp(8) : see declaration of 'test2'
test.cpp(400) : warning C4947: 'test' : marked as obsolete
```

The overloaded call to test2(int) does not generate a warning. The remainder generates
various diagnostics depending on whether the function was declared deprecated or obsolete.

Summary

The preprocessor is one of the most powerful aspects of C++. Used properly, the possibilities
are endless. Abused, it can render your code esoteric and unmaintainable. As Niccolò Machi-
avelli wrote, "In the actions of all men . . . when there is no impartial arbiter, one must consider
the final result."

In the next chapter, we'll look deeper at native C++ and see how it differs both from
C++/CLI and C#.

CHAPTER 18

■ ■ ■

Native C++

Wise men learn by other men's mistakes, fools by their own.

—H. G. Wells

In this chapter, we'll take a survey of some of the characteristics of native C++ programming. We will look at common library functions, template libraries, and C++ features that do not work on managed types.

The iostream Library

In native C++ programming, one of the most popular libraries for file input and output is the iostream library. It is part of the C++ Standard. In it, the << and >> operators are overloaded within the include file iostream to provide easy output to the console. They are used with the types cout for output and cin for input and provide a syntax similar to operating system piping operators. The type endl is used to indicate the end of the line.

An example follows:

```
#include <iostream>
using namespace std;
int main()
{
    int i;
    cout << "enter a number" << endl;
    cin >> i;
    cout << "the number was " << i << endl;
}
```

After compiling and running, we get the following:

```
C:\>cl /nologo /EHsc test.cpp
C:\>test
enter a number
4
the number was 4
```

Since this is C++, it almost goes without saying that all of these can be overloaded again locally, for example:

```
#include <iostream>
using namespace std;
namespace R
{
    ostream&  endl ( ostream& os )
    {
        ::operator<<(os, " <END> ");
        ::endl(os);
        return os;
    }
    ostream& operator<< (ostream& os, const char* str )
    {
        ::operator<<(os, " -> ");
        ::operator<<(os, str);
        ::operator<<(os, " <- ");
        return os;
    }
    static int Test()
    {
        cout << "Hello" << endl;
        return 0;
    }
};
int main()
{
    R::Test();
}
```

Again, after compiling and executing, we get

```
C:\>cl /nologo /EHsc test.cpp
C:\>test
 -> Hello <-  <END>
```

Pointers to Members

In C++, it is possible to create a pointer to an element of a class that is not bound to a particular instance of a class. These are called *pointers to members*.

Pointers to members are not really pointers per se. Rather, they are offsets within a class definition to a particular member, and when combined with a pointer to a class instance, they can be resolved to an actual member. Pointers to members turn out to be extremely powerful in several areas. Since pointers to members are not supported by the .NET Framework, they may only be used with native classes.

Why Use Pointers to Members?

Pointers to members are extremely useful in switching control between classes, which is important in native C++ programs that use callbacks. A *callback* is a mechanism where an address of a function, named a *callback function*, is passed to a second function for later invocation. In .NET, you can use delegates to perform callbacks; native C++ lacks delegates.

Syntax

A pointer-to-member function is declared in a similar fashion to a regular pointer except that the asterisk is preceded by a class specification. They are assigned by taking the address of a class member in the same manner as a static member—without regard to any particular instance. Dereferencing uses an extra asterisk just before the pointer-to-member function.

Perhaps a few examples will clarify faster than using Backus-Naur Form (BNF)[1]:

```
struct Class
{
    int i;
    void Function(int i) {}
};
void main()
{
    Class c;
    Class *pClass = &c;
    int Class:: *pInt = &Class::i;
    void (Class::*pFunction)(int) = &Class::Function;
    c.*pInt = 3;
    (c.*pFunction)(3);
    pClass->*pInt = 4;
    (pClass->*pFunction)(4);
}
```

In this example, we have a class with an int field and a member function taking an int and returning void. We declare a couple of pointers to members, pInt and pFunction, and initialize them to point at the corresponding members of Class.

Using an instance variable c and a pointer to Class, pClass, we then observe the syntax for dereferencing each of these.

Motivation

Where would a pointer-to-member function come in handy? Suppose you have a queue of tasks that are being consumed by a background thread. As each task is performed, you would like to notify the class that requested the task (the producer) that the task is completed. Different types of tasks may have different entry points for notification within the requesting task.

---

1. BNF is the syntax definition language we all love.

One way to solve this problem is with a pointer-to-member function. You define the pro-
totypical signature of a generic notification procedure and define several notification procedures
consistent with the requesting class. Within the task itself, you can declare a holder to point at
the instance of the requesting class along with a pointer-to-member function for the proper
notification routine within the requesting class. When the task is completed, it is able to call
the proper notification routine within the requesting class using the pointer-to-member function, in the case of the following example, a pointer to a member function:

```cpp
#include <iostream>
#include <deque>
using namespace std;
enum REQUEST
{
    READ, WRITE
};
struct Task;
deque<Task*> t;
struct Requestor
{
    void ReadDone(bool success)
    {
        cout << "Read Done notification" << endl;
    }
    void WriteDone(bool success)
    {
        cout << "Write Done notification" << endl;
    }
    void SetupRequests();
};
struct Task
{
    enum REQUEST request;
    Requestor *pCallBackInstance;
    void (Requestor::*Notify)(bool);
};
void Requestor::SetupRequests()
{
    Task *readTask = new Task();
    readTask->Notify = &Requestor::ReadDone;
    readTask->pCallBackInstance = this;
    readTask->request = READ;
    t.push_front(readTask);
    Task *writeTask = new Task();
    writeTask->Notify = &Requestor::WriteDone;
    writeTask->pCallBackInstance = this;
    writeTask->request = WRITE;
    t.push_front(writeTask);
}
```

```
int main()
{
    Requestor *r = new Requestor();
    r->SetupRequests();
    while(!t.empty())
    {
        Task *pTask = t.back();
        t.pop_back();
        switch(pTask->request)
        {
        case READ:
            cout << "reading " << endl;
            break;
        case WRITE:
            cout << "writing " << endl;
            break;
        }
        ((pTask->pCallBackInstance)->*pTask->Notify)(true);
        delete pTask;
    }
    delete r;
}
```

Let's compile and run this one:

```
C:\>cl /nologo /EHsc test.cpp
C:\>test
reading
Read Done notification
writing
Write Done notification
```

The examples are definitely getting more complicated as the text progresses. In this example, we define a producer class named Requestor. Requestor allocates a READ task and a WRITE task, each with a different notification callback. These tasks are pushed onto a Standard Template Library (STL) deque for consumption (see the section on STL later in this chapter).

We then consume these tasks first-in, first-out in the main loop, call the appropriate notification callback using the pointer to the member, free the task's memory (more on this later in the chapter), and then we're finished.

Similar to standard pointers, the pointer operator, ->*, may be overloaded by defining operator->*. On the other hand, the instance operator.* is not overloadable.

Operators new and delete

C++/CLI uses gcnew to allocate memory on the managed heap and new to allocate memory on the native heap. All types—reference, value, and native—may also be allocated on the stack. Reference types are special though. Even though they behave semantically as allocated on the stack, they are still physically contained in the managed heap. Since there is no garbage collection support on the native heap, it is the programmer's responsibility to make sure that memory is freed when it is no longer required. Deterministic destruction of types makes sure that types on the stack are destroyed and deallocated when appropriate; memory allocated on the native heap must be freed explicitly using delete as observed in the previous code sample. Both new and delete can be overloaded using operator new() and operator delete().

There are two versions of the new and delete operators: one version appropriate for single instances and another appropriate for arrays.

An example of new and delete follows:

```cpp
#include <iostream>
using namespace std;
static int Count = 0;
struct N
{
    int _Count;
    N() : _Count(Count++)
    {
        cout << "constructor of " << _Count << endl;
    }
    ~N()
    {
        cout << "destructor of " << _Count << endl;
    }
};
void main()
{
    N n;
    N *pN = new N;
    N *pNs = new N[3];
    delete pN;
    delete [] pNs;
}
```

After compiling and running this, we get

```
C:\>cl /nologo /EHsc test.cpp
C:\>test
constructor of 0
constructor of 1
constructor of 2
constructor of 3
constructor of 4
destructor of 1
destructor of 4
destructor of 3
destructor of 2
destructor of 0
```

Note that each constructed instance of N is destroyed exactly once.

Confusing delete and delete[]

Always make sure that you do not confuse the single and array versions of the delete operator. If you confuse them, you will plant hidden problems in your code. For example, in the previous example case, the destructor will not be called for all three allocated instances of N.

Suppose we change the main() routine from the previous example to the following one:

```
void main()
{
    N *pNs = new N[3];
    delete pNs;
}
```

Compiling and running this, we get

```
C:\>cl /nologo /EHsc test.cpp
C:\>test
constructor of 0
constructor of 1
constructor of 2
destructor of 0
```

Now we have a memory leak caused by using the wrong version of delete.

/Zc:forScope

In standard C++, the scope of a variable declared within the initialization of a for loop is limited to the scope inside the loop itself. This standard behavior is turned on by using the /Zc:forScope compiler option, which is used by default in a compilation. The behavior can be relaxed by using /Zc:forScope- to expand the scope of this variable to the scope containing the loop declaration, for example:

```
int main()
{
    for(int i=0; i<3; i++)
    {
    }
    i = 3;
}
```

```
C:\>cl /nologo /EHsc test.cpp
test.cpp
test.cpp(6) : error C2065: 'i' : undeclared identifier
```

Using /Zc:forScope-, the program compiles without error:

```
C:\>cl /nologo /EHsc /Zc:forScope- test.cpp
```

/Zc:wchar_t

This switch controls whether wchar_t is considered a fundamental type within C++. This switch is provided for backwards compatibility with previous versions of Microsoft Visual C++, in which the type was defined in a header file using a typedef.

```
int main()
{
    wchar_t c;
}
```

In Visual C++ 2005, the preceding code compiles by default. With /Zc:wchar_t-, you get the following diagnostics:

```
C:\>cl /nologo /EHsc /Zc:wchar_t- test.cpp
test.cpp
test.cpp(3) : error C2065: 'wchar_t' : undeclared identifier
test.cpp(3) : error C2146: syntax error : missing ';' before identifier 'c'
test.cpp(3) : error C2065: 'c' : undeclared identifier
```

Default Parameters

C++ allows you to specify default parameters for methods in native types as well as global functions. To use default parameters, append =<value> to each parameter in the function declaration. Note that default parameters must start with the last parameter (moving from right to left), must be consecutive, and cannot be repeated in the function definition.

An example follows:

```
#include <iostream>
using namespace std;
int f(int i = 3)
{
    return i;
}
int main()
{
    cout << f() << endl;
}
```

Compiling and running, we get

```
C:\>cl /nologo /EHsc test.cpp
C\>test
3
```

The CLI still does not support default parameters, so if you try this with a method of a managed class, you get a compiler error. This might, nonetheless, change in the future. In the meantime, you can get away with a nifty but not very elegant workaround using paramarrays. Can you construct a managed method with default parameters?

C++ Runtime Library Functions

I'm not going to try and cover the entire C++ runtime library. There are dozens of books written on this subject, and the universe does not need another. Rather, I will try to introduce some of the major modules and outline some of their functions, with the goal here being exposure to the basics.

stdio.h

stdio is an acronym for "standard input/output." stdio.h is the include file that contains the prototypes for the major input/output functions, which include the following:

- printf: Formatted output to stdout, the console
- fprintf: Formatted output to a file
- sprintf: Formatted output to a string
- scanf: Formatted input from the console
- gets: Get a string from the console
- puts: Put a string to the console

The parameters of printf() are similar to the .NET method family for System::Console::Write() and String::Format(). All of these accept a format string, which determines the position of the parameters in a string, followed by the parameters themselves. Where the .NET versions draw information from the arguments themselves, the C++ versions require that you specify exactly what they are, and how they should be printed. The compiler does not check that the format specification is compatible with the arguments provided, so you have to be careful.

Here are some the function prototypes:

```
int printf(const char *format [,argument...] );
int wprintf(const wchar_t *format [,argument...] );
```

Some common format specifications follow:

- %d: integer
- %c: char
- %s: string
- %ld: long
- %f: float
- %x: hexadecimal integer

A complete list of format specifications is available on MSDN, along with the size and spacing parameters.

Here is a brief example:

```
#include <stdio.h>
int main()
{
    wchar_t s[20];
    printf("%d\n", 3);
    swprintf(s, sizeof(s), L"ABC \u00E9\n");
    for(int i=0; s[i] ; i++)
    {
        printf("0x%04x ", s[i]);
    }
    printf("\n");
    return 0;
}
```

Compiling and executing this, we get the following:

```
C:\>cl /nologo test.cpp
test.cpp

C:\>test
3
0x0041 0x0042 0x0043 0x0020 0x00e9 0x000a
```

stdlib.h

This include file contains the prototypes for the memory allocation and freeing functions, malloc() and free():

```
void *malloc(size_t size);
void free(void *ptr);
```

malloc() stands for "memory allocate", and size_t is a type standardized by ANSI C for defining sizes of strings and memory blocks. It is essentially an int on modern 32-bit architectures.

Every call to malloc() should be matched by a corresponding call to free(), or you risk a memory leak. The following local class version allocates and automatically frees a block of memory using C++'s deterministic destruction:

```
#include <stdio.h>
#include <stdlib.h>
void main()
{
    struct Memory
    {
        unsigned char *ptr;
        Memory(int n)
```

```
    {
        ptr = (unsigned char *)malloc(n);
        printf("Allocated %d bytes\n", n);
    }
    ~Memory()
    {
        if(ptr != NULL)
        {
            free(ptr);
            printf("Freed memory\n");
        }
    }
};
Memory m(10);
m.ptr[3] = 0;
}
```

After compiling and running this, we get

```
C:\>cl /nologo test.cpp
C:\>test
Allocated 10 bytes
Freed memory
```

Other Include Files

Here are some more include files that will be essential to your native C++ programming.

string.h

Functions:

- strcpy: Copy a string

- strlen: Get the length of a string

▓**Note** Strings in native C++ are zero-delimited arrays of 8-bit char. Wide strings are similar to C# strings, zero-delimited arrays of wchar_t, which in .NET is equivalent to System::Char.

memory.h

Functions:

- memcpy: Copy a chunk of memory

- memset: Set a chunk of memory to a value

time.h

Measurements:

- Date

- Time of day

- Time

math.h

Measurements:

- *Trigonometric funtions*: Secant, tangent, cosine, and sine

- *Pi*: 3.14159

STL

The Standard Template Library (STL) is a set of collection classes along with the methods that act on them. The genius of the library is that it is truly generic in that it decouples acting on a collection of data from acting on the data elements themselves.

Among other collection classes, it implements arrays called vectors, double-ended queues called deques, and doubly linked lists called lists. The STL has a string type and algorithms, such as sort, to rearrange elements.

Vectors build functionality on the concept of a basic array, so you can have the best of both worlds.

vector

The following example uses STL vectors:

```cpp
#include <vector>
#include <iostream>
#include <string>
#include <algorithm>
using namespace std;

int main()
{
    vector<string> VString;
    VString.push_back("String 1");
    VString.push_back("String 4");
    VString.push_back("String 3");
    VString.push_back("String 2");
    cout << endl << "In order:" << endl;
    for (unsigned int i=0; i < VString.size(); i++)
    {
        cout << VString[i] << endl;
    }
```

```
    cout << endl << "Sorted:" << endl;
    sort(VString.begin(),VString.end());
    vector<string>::iterator iter;
    for (iter = VString.begin(); iter != VString.end(); ++iter)
    {
        cout << *iter << endl;
    }
    cout << endl << "Reversed:" << endl;
    vector<string>::reverse_iterator revIter;
    for (revIter=VString.rbegin(); revIter!=VString.rend(); ++revIter)
    {
        cout << *revIter << endl;
    }
    return 0;
}
```

In this example, we take a vector of strings, add some values to it, display it, sort it, redisplay it, and display it reversed.

After compiling and executing, we get the following:

```
C:\>cl /nologo /EHsc test.cpp
C:\>test
In order:
String 1
String 4
String 3
String 2

Sorted:
String 1
String 2
String 3
String 4

Reversed:
String 4
String 3
String 2
String 1
```

deque

A deque is a double-ended queue. You can push and pop items from both ends of the queue, as well as iterate through the queue.

Here is a native C++ version of the Carwash using deque:

```
#include <deque>
#include <iostream>
```

```cpp
#include <string>
#include <algorithm>
#include <windows.h>
#include <process.h>
using namespace std;
namespace CarWashBusiness
{
    CRITICAL_SECTION IOcs;
    class Lock
    {
        CRITICAL_SECTION *pCS_;
    public:
        Lock(CRITICAL_SECTION *pCS) : pCS_(pCS)
        {
            EnterCriticalSection( pCS_ );
        }
        ~Lock()
        {
            LeaveCriticalSection( pCS_ );
        }
    };
    struct Car
    {
        string Name_;
        Car(string Name) : Name_(Name)
        {
        }
    };
    struct Process
    {
        bool open;
        CRITICAL_SECTION cs;
        deque<Car*> Queue;
        HANDLE hThread;
        unsigned int nThreadId;
        static unsigned int WINAPI Proc( void *param )
        {
            return((Process *)param) -> Run();
        }
        virtual unsigned int Run() = 0;
        Process() : open(false)
        {
            InitializeCriticalSection(&cs);
        }
        void Open()
        {
            open=true;
        }
```

```cpp
void Close()
{
    open=false;
}
size_t Count()
{
    Lock l(&cs);
    return Queue.size();
}
void AddQueue(Car *pCar)
{
    Lock l(&cs);
    Queue.push_back(pCar);
}
Car *GetNext()
{
    Lock l(&cs);
    if (Queue.empty())
    {
        return NULL;
    }
    Car *pCar = Queue.front();
    Queue.pop_front();
    return pCar;
}
void Done(Car *pCar)
{
    if (pNextProcess)
    {
        pNextProcess->AddQueue(pCar);
    }
}
Process *pNextProcess;
virtual void DoStage()
{
    while (!open)
    {
        ;
    }
    for (;open;)
    {
        Car *pCar = GetNext();
        if (!pCar)
        {
            Sleep(30);
            continue;
        }
```

```cpp
                Doit(pCar);
                Done(pCar);
            }
        }
        virtual void Doit(Car *pCar) = 0;
};
struct Vacuum : Process
{
    virtual unsigned int Run()
    {
        {
            Lock io(&IOcs);
            cout << "vacuum running" << endl;
        }
        DoStage();
        return 1;
    }
    virtual void Doit(Car *pCar)
    {
        Lock io(&IOcs);
        cout << "vacuuming " << pCar->Name_ << endl;
        Sleep(1000);
        cout << "vacuuming done " << pCar->Name_ << endl;
    }
};
struct Wash : Process
{
    virtual unsigned int Run()
    {
        {
            Lock io(&IOcs);
            cout << "wash running" << endl;
        }
        DoStage();
        return 1;
    }
    virtual void Doit(Car *pCar)
    {
        Lock io(&IOcs);
        cout << "washing: " << pCar->Name_ << endl;
        Sleep(1200);
        cout << "washing done: " << pCar->Name_ << endl;
    }
};
struct Done : Process
{
    virtual unsigned int Run()
```

```
    {
        return 1;
    }
    virtual void Doit(Car *pCar)
    {
    }
};
struct CarWash
{
    size_t Countin;
    bool open;
    string Name_;
    Vacuum v;
    Wash w;
    Done d;
    CarWash(string Name) : Name_(Name), open(false)
    {
        Countin = 0;
        {
            Lock io(&IOcs);
            cout << Name_ << " Car Wash" << endl;
        }
        v.pNextProcess = &w;
        w.pNextProcess = &d;
        d.pNextProcess = NULL;
    }
    void Open()
    {
        open = true;
        v.Open();
        w.Open();
        v.hThread=(HANDLE)_beginthreadex
            (NULL,0,Process::Proc,&v,0,&v.nThreadId);
        w.hThread=(HANDLE)_beginthreadex
            (NULL,0,Process::Proc,&w,0,&w.nThreadId);
    }
    void Close()
    {
        open = false;
        size_t Count;
        do
        {
            Sleep(30);
            Count = d.Count();
        }
        while (d.Count() != Countin);
        v.Close();
```

```
            w.Close();
            WaitForSingleObject(v.hThread, INFINITE);
            WaitForSingleObject(w.hThread, INFINITE);
        }
        ~CarWash()
        {
        }
        void Clean(Car *pCar)
        {
            {
                Lock io(&IOcs);
                cout << "Cleaning: " << pCar->Name_ << endl;
            }
            Countin++;
            v.AddQueue(pCar);
        }
    };
}
using namespace CarWashBusiness;
int main()
{
    InitializeCriticalSection(&IOcs);
    Car Volvo("Volvo");
    Car VW("VW");
    Car Audi("Audi");
    CarWash PicoAndSep("Pico and Sepulveda");
    PicoAndSep.Open();
    PicoAndSep.Clean(&Volvo);
    PicoAndSep.Clean(&VW);
    PicoAndSep.Clean(&Audi);
    PicoAndSep.Close();
    return 0;
}
```

After compiling and running, we get the following results:

```
C:\>cl /nologo /EHsc test.cpp
C:\>test
Pico and Sepulveda Car Wash
vacuum running
Cleaning: Volvo
wash running
Cleaning: VW
Cleaning: Audi
vacuuming Volvo
vacuuming done Volvo
vacuuming VW
vacuuming done VW
washing: Volvo
washing done: Volvo
vacuuming Audi
vacuuming done Audi
washing: VW
washing done: VW
washing: Audi
washing done: Audi
```

This example uses the deque<T> class to keep track of the cars at the washing and vacuuming stations, uses critical sections to control access to the queues and to the console, and uses threads to multitask and pipeline operations. In short, it does the same things as the example from Chapter 14, just in a native fashion.

list

list is a doubly linked list that supports bidirectional traversal.

auto_ptr

auto_pr is an intelligent pointer type that automatically frees memory when the pointer goes out of scope. It can help you when you forget your calls to the delete operator.

Summary

There are several great texts on native C++ that you should have a look at if you want to learn more about native programming. Some of my favorites include Stephen Prata's *C++ Primer Plus* (Sams, 2001), Stanley Lippman, Josée Lajoie, and Barbara Moo's *C++ Primer* (Addison-Wesley, 2005), any of Bjarne Stroustrup's C++ books, and Herb Sutter's *Exceptional C++* series (Addison-Wesley). I hope this chapter has given you a taste of native programming and inspired you to read on!

In the next chapter, we'll take a deeper look at multiple language integration and interoperability.

■ ■ ■

Multiple Language Support

The pursuit of truth and beauty is a sphere of activity in which we are permitted to remain children all our lives.

—Albert Einstein

In this chapter, I will cover the various ways to combine different .NET languages as well as interface with unmanaged code. I'll start by reviewing the standards that govern language integration and interoperability in .NET.

With the arrival of Microsoft Visual Studio 2005, it's easier than ever to develop applications using more than one programming language. Not only can you take advantage of full language integration between .NET languages, but you can also call native code with .NET interoperability.

Let's have a look at .NET language integration and then move on to .NET interoperability.

.NET Language Integration

The .NET platform is programming language agnostic. You can develop a class in Visual Basic, derive a class from it in C#, and then use both of these classes in C++/CLI. The keys to language integration lie in the Common Language Infrastructure (CLI), Common Type System (CTS), and Common Language Specification (CLS) standards.

The CLI standard describes the execution engine and file formats of .NET. All .NET implementations follow this standard, although they may implement the various elements in different ways on different platforms.

The Common Type System (CTS) is a subset of the CLI standard that describes the types available to a CLI compliant language.

The CLS is a subset of the CLI standard that describes language interoperability rules for items that are exported from an assembly. It does not apply to the internal implementation within an assembly. It affects a subset of the CTS types as well as methods that pertain to these types.

The practical import of all of this is that CLI-compliant languages can not only share data but also data types, and they can create polymorphic types based in one language and derived in another.

Gathering Metadata

The CLI defines metadata, the Common Intermediate Language (CIL) instruction set, modules, and assemblies. *Modules* are units of metadata that contain, among other things, type descriptions and managed code in CIL. *Assemblies* are units of deployment for one or more modules. Assemblies are packaged as a class library file (DLL) or an application file (EXE), and they can optionally load classes from other class libraries.

Language integration is typically accomplished by limiting modules to a single .NET language, optionally gathering these modules into assemblies, and binding the results together for deployment.

If a building block is a completed module, subsequent code will use this block by integrating it with other modules into a new module or an assembly. If a building block is an assembly, or class library, then subsequent code will use it by linking to it and loading it as a DLL file at runtime.

In the following example, we're taking the first choice—working with modules to create a single executable.

Tracking Students Example

Suppose we have developed a `Student` class in Visual Basic .NET. This class encapsulates everything administrative we need to know about students. It supports the `IComparable<T>` interface, which allows us to sort students by identification number using generic collection classes. On top of that, let's make a `Tree` in C#. `Tree` is a generic collection class of our own for organizing arbitrary types: it knows nothing particular about students, but it doesn't need to. Finally, let's finish with a C++/CLI class that overrides `Tree`'s tree-walking method, `VisitLeaf()`, to change the tree into a linked list. We'll display the list of students sorted by identification number.

Student in Visual Basic .NET

The VB `Student` class has a small `Main()` procedure for unit testing. The `Student` class has the following significant methods:

- `New()`: The constructor

- `CompareTo()`: Used for implementing `IComparable`

- `NewStudents()`: A static method for creating an array of `Student` objects

Here is the VB `Student` class:

```
Imports System
Namespace Sample
Public Class Student
    Implements IComparable(Of Student)
    ' Constructor
    Private Sub New(ByVal Id As Integer)
        Me.Id = Id
    End Sub
```

```vbnet
    ' IComparable
    Public Function CompareTo(ByVal other As Student) As Integer _
        Implements System.IComparable(Of Student).CompareTo
        Return Me.Id.CompareTo(other.Id)
    End Function
    Public Shared Function
        NewStudents(ByVal ParamArray Ids As Integer()) As Student()
        Dim students As Student() = New Student(Ids.Length  - 1) {}
        Dim index As Integer = 0
        For Each id As Integer In Ids
            students(index) = New Student(id)
            index += 1
        Next
        Return students
    End Function
    Public Overrides Function ToString() As String
        Return String.Format("ID:{0}", Me.Id)
    End Function
    ' Fields
    Private Id As Integer
End Class
Module Run
    Sub Main()
        Dim students As Student() = Nothing
        students = Student.NewStudents(5, 2, 6, 8, 10, 9, 7, 1, 3, 4)
        For Each student As Student In students
            Console.WriteLine(student)
        Next
    End Sub
End Module
End Namespace
```

Let's compile and run this:

```
C:\>vbc /nologo student.vb
C:\>student
ID:5
ID:2
ID:6
ID:8
ID:10
ID:9
ID:7
ID:1
ID:3
ID:4
```

The preceding Visual Basic command line compiles the sample into an assembly executable; later, we will compile the same sample into a module for use with C# and C++/CLI.

A Generic Tree Class in C#

Next, we examine the Tree<T> class in C#. It accepts types that implement the IComparable<T> interface. Let's examine the code a bit, as this program looks far worse than it really is. The Tree<T> class has a nested class named Leaf. Each Leaf not only contains a data element but also references to the left and right branches of the tree. Leaf contains the following methods:

- CompareTo(): Implements IComparable

- operator>= and operator<=: Shortcuts for the CompareTo() method

- Leaf(): The constructor

- ToString(): Displays the data element contained within the Leaf

The Tree<T> class is a generic collection of types that implement IComparable<T>. Tree<T> knows nothing about a Student class. It stores data items of generic type T in instances of the nested class Leaf. Tree<T> has the following public methods:

- Add(): There are two overloads of the Add() method: one adds a single data item to the tree; the other adds an array of data items. This method seems a little complicated, because it is long, but in reality, all it does is traverse the tree downward looking for a place to store the new Leaf.

- Inorder(): This method traverses the tree using the in-order algorithm; this algorithm visits the left child, the current leaf, and finally the right child. Based on the way we added the leaves to the tree, this algorithm will visit all of the leaves in the order defined by the results of IComparable<T> applied to two data instances.

- VisitLeaf(): This method is called by Inorder() each time a leaf is visited. It is currently implemented to write the leaf to the console using Leaf.ToString(). This method is important, because we will override it in the C++ class to save the leaf data rather than writing it to the console.

The code for Tree<T> follows:

```
using System;
using System.Collections.Generic;
namespace Sample
{
    public class Tree<T> where T : IComparable<T>
    {
        public class Leaf
        {
            public Leaf left = null;
            public Leaf right = null;
            public T data;
            public Leaf(T data)
```

```
        {
            this.data = data;
        }
        public static bool operator>=(Leaf lhs, Leaf rhs)
        {
            return lhs.data.CompareTo(rhs.data) >= 0;
        }
        public static bool operator<=(Leaf lhs, Leaf rhs)
        {
            return lhs.data.CompareTo(rhs.data) <= 0;
        }
        public override string ToString()
        {
            return data.ToString();
        }
    }
    public Leaf root = null;
    public void Add(T[] adata)
    {
        foreach(T data in adata)
        {
            Add(data);
        }
    }
    public void Add(T data)
    {
        Leaf leaf = new Leaf(data);
        if(root == null)
        {
            root = leaf;
        }
        else
        {
            Leaf current = root;
            for(;;)
            {
                if(current >= leaf)
                {
                    if(current.left == null)
                    {
                        current.left = leaf;
                        break;
                    }
                    else
                    {
                        current = current.left;
                    }
                }
```

```csharp
            else
            {
                if(current.right == null)
                {
                    current.right = leaf;
                    break;
                }
                else
                {
                    current = current.right;
                }
            }
        }
    }
}
    public virtual void VisitLeaf(Leaf leaf)
    {
        Console.WriteLine(leaf);
    }
    private void DoInorder(Leaf leaf)
    {
        if(leaf==null)
        {
            return;
        }
        DoInorder(leaf.left);
        VisitLeaf(leaf);
        DoInorder(leaf.right);
    }
    public virtual void Inorder()
    {
        DoInorder(root);
    }
}
class Test
{
    public static void Main()
    {
        Tree<int> tree = new Tree<int>();
        tree.Add(3);
        tree.Add(1);
        tree.Add(5);
        tree.Inorder();
    }
}
}
```

The final class Test is just for unit testing; it has a static public method Main(), so let's compile and run this as follows:

```
C:\>csc /nologo tree.cs
C:\>tree.exe
1
3
5
```

Again, the csc command line compiles the sample into an assembly executable; later, we will compile the same sample into a module for use with C# and C++/CLI.

Gathering the Pieces in C++/CLI

The goal of our C++ application is to create a linked list of students sorted by identification number. The Inorder() method in the Tree<T> class can traverse the tree in order, but it has the side effect of displaying the students on the console in the VisitLeaf() method. We can take advantage of this by deriving our linked list class from Tree<T> and overriding the VisitLeaf() method. Since VisitLeaf() is called for each element in sorted order when the tree is traversed, we can override VisitLeaf() in our derived class to add the element to a linked list. We use LinkedList<T> in System::Collections::Generic for our linked list.

This class is also a good example of working with nested classes using generics across languages because of the nested class Tree<T>::Leaf.

Here is the C++ code, which uses and combines the C# and VB:

```cpp
#using "System.dll"
using namespace System;
using namespace Collections::Generic;
using namespace Sample;
generic <typename T>
where T : IComparable<T>
ref struct LList : public Tree<T>
{
    LinkedList<T> list;
    virtual void VisitLeaf(Leaf^ leaf) override
    {
        list.AddLast(leaf->data);
    }
    virtual void Dump()
    {
        for each(T t in list)
        {
            Console::WriteLine(t);
        }
    }
};
void main()
```

```
{
    array<Student^>^ students = Student::NewStudents(25, 46, 34, 12, 1);
    LList<Student^>^ ll = gcnew LList<Student^>();
    ll->Add(students);
    ll->Inorder();
    ll->Dump();
}
```

This class is much simpler than the other two; LList<T> only has two significant methods:

- VisitLeaf(): Overrides Tree<T>::VisitLeaf() to add a data item to our linked list rather than displaying it as the base class method does

- Dump(): Displays the entire linked list on the console

This time, we want to create modules for both VB and C#. We'll compile the C++ code using these modules. We can compile and run the finished program:

```
C:\>vbc /nologo /target:module /out:student.netmodule student.vb
C:\>csc /nologo /target:module /out:tree.netmodule tree.cs
C:\>cl /nologo /clr:pure /FUstudent.netmodule /FUtree.netmodule test.cpp
C:\>test
ID:1
ID:12
ID:25
ID:34
ID:46
```

Note that we use /FU (force using) to add a reference to the C# and VB modules; using force using is equivalent to adding a #using statement within the source code itself.

Using the IDE

The core IDE project system only supports modules using custom build steps. In Visual C++, you can also do this with the /LN command-line option, which you can set in a project's properties. To take advantage of the power of the IDE, let's modify our application a tiny bit. We will create three projects: one in VB, one in C#, and one in C++.

We set the VB and C# targets as class libraries. Make sure the Root Namespace in the VB project's Property page (under Application) is blank, or else the entire VB application will be hidden inside of the root namespace.

Add references to the VB and C# projects in the C++ project. This automatically creates a dependency on the other two for the C++ project. In addition, make sure the C++ project is the startup project.

That should do it. This will create an executable that loads the VB and C# class library DLLs at runtime. The results will be the same as before, although your application will consist of three different assemblies, an EXE and two DLLs, rather than just the one EXE assembly in the previous example.

Summary

Well, gathering code together from three different languages wasn't that hard, was it? You do need a rudimentary knowledge of each language to pull it off, because you need to be able to map class declarations and method declarations across languages, but that isn't terribly difficult once you get the basic feel for each language. If you ever get stuck, there are several publically available language tools, including .NET Reflector, which can help you with the basic language differences.

Interoperability with native code is not as elementary, but it is straightforward for C++/CLI programs. Using language integration, we can also use C++/CLI as the bridge to native code and easily incorporate C++/CLI modules in C# or VB code.

.NET Interoperability

Interoperability, or *InterOp* for short, is the ability for a .NET application to connect with unmanaged, or native, code.

"Of course," you say, "this is important for legacy code development, but with so much development happening on the .NET side, does it really affect me?"

These days you might easily be misled into believing that native code doesn't matter anymore. Let me set the record straight right now—native development is vital.

When I spoke on C++ at TechEd 2006 in New Zealand, Jason McConnell, a Visual Studio product marketing manager, suggested I use the following slide:

```
Windows = Native + Managed
```

Much of the Windows API remains native, and that's not likely to change anytime soon, not even with Vista. The good news is that, when you use C++, it matters little whether an API is managed or native. InterOp is extremely easy to do with C++; it is built right into the language. Even developers who pass on C++ as a primary development platform for a particular project still rely on managed C++ modules or assemblies for calling native APIs. They also rely on .NET language integration to bind the managed C++ to their C# or VB assembly.

In C#, it's not so simple. You need to adhere to some mechanism, like platform invoke or COM InterOp, and take care to *marshal*, or translate, your data correctly between managed and native code. In addition, the C++ header files, which contain the definitions of the parameters that must be passed to native APIs, are not usable in C#, so you must define parallel constructs. If the API changes, your code breaks.

C++ has built-in interoperability, so you can access all of your native code and APIs directly. The native C++ header files are directly usable in C++/CLI, so that you don't go through an error-prone step to translate anything to a different language, and if the API changes, recompiling your code with the updated header file updates your code to the new API. What's just as important is that C++ knows about both native and managed types, so that marshaling is automatic. C++/CLI was designed so that native types would become a natural part of the language. For example, `int` can be considered either as a native type or an instance of `System::Int32`. Both paradigms are supported. C++ is also aware of the difference between a managed string and a byte or character array. It's built into the language.

Let's have a look at some examples of InterOp in C# and C++.

Wait for the Beep

Let's pick a very simple native Windows call, MessageBeep(). According to the MSDN definition MessageBeep() "plays a waveform sound. The waveform sound for each sound type is identified by an entry in the registry." The MessageBeep() code follows:

```
BOOL MessageBeep(
  UINT uType
);
```

Parameters

For a parameter, MessageBeep() takes the sound type, as identified by an entry in the registry:

uType

This input parameter can be one of the values shown in Table 19-1.

Table 19-1. *Possible uType Parameter Values*

Value	Meaning
−1	Simple beep. If a sound card is not available, the sound is generated using the speaker. Note that this value is resolved to 0xFFFFFFFF within the function.
MB_ICONASTERISK 0x00000040L	SystemAsterisk
MB_ICONEXCLAMATION 0x00000030L	SystemExclamation
MB_ICONHAND 0x00000010L	SystemHand
MB_ICONQUESTION 0x00000020L	SystemQuestion
MB_OK 0x00000000L	SystemDefault

Now let's see how to call MessageBeep(ICONEXCLAMATION) from C#.

C# Platform Invoke

Platform Invoke, or *P/Invoke* for short, is C#'s primary method for calling native code. We can use P/Invoke by declaring the MessageBeep() function within C# and defining the parameter definitions using C# language features. The very-useful, third-party web site called www.pinvoke.net can be used to get all the information you need to use P/Invoke on a Windows API call. If you are interfacing to other native code, you'll have to discover all of this on your own. While you're doing this, remember that methods for calling native code are all built-in and automatic in C++.

Here is the C# code for `MessageBeep()`:

```
using System.Runtime.InteropServices;
class Test
{
    public enum beepType
    {
        Beep        = -1,
        OK          = 0x00,
        Question    = 0x20,
        Exclamation = 0x30,
        Asterisk    = 0x40,
    }
    [DllImport("User32.dll", ExactSpelling=true)]
        static extern bool MessageBeep(uint type);
    public static void Main(string[] args)
    {
        MessageBeep((uint)beepType.Exclamation);
    }
}
```

Several things about this example are disturbing. First of all, we have to create an enum for the parameters passed to `MessageBeep()`. This is inherently error prone, as there are now two distinct definitions for the API: the original defined in `User32.dll` and declared in the C++ header files and our copy here.

We next have to marshal the data explicitly by casting our parameter to a uint for passing to `MessageBeep()`. Anytime you perform a cast, you run the risk of hiding things that should not be hidden, and this case is no exception.

A red flag that you pop out in this case is that there is a bug in the `MessageBeep()` API definition—we have an signed/unsigned mismatch for Beep in the API. The API expects an unsigned integer, as well as a -1, for a standard beep. There is a note on MSDN that 0xFFFFFFFF is used instead of -1 in this case, but it still points out the futility of trying to make something clean in C# that is not clean in reality.

A small improvement can be attempted by changing the enum definition to the following:

```
public enum beepType : uint
```

If we now compile this, we see

```
C:\>csc /nologo test.cs
test.cs(6,23): error CS0031: Constant value '-1' cannot be converted to a 'uint'
```

We could go about fixing our C# code to use 0xFFFFFFFF instead of -1, but this just causes us to deviate further from the published API, making our code less maintainable.

C++ Built-in Support

Here's the code in native C++:

```
#include "windows.h"
int main()
{
    MessageBeep(MB_ICONEXCLAMATION);
    return 0;
}
```

It's extremely clean, uses the Windows header file definition, and calls the API using the published API parameter definitions. No parameter cast or enum is required, and the code maintains itself.

In order to compile this, you'd enter the following:

```
cl /nologo test.cpp user32.lib
```

Note that user32.lib is added to the command line, since this is the location of MessageBeep() in Windows. There is a way to bring the library in using a DLL import style attribute in native C++ as well, but adding it to the command line or project is standard practice.

You probably find yourself unimpressed by how easy it is to call MessageBeep() from native C++. After all, it's a native API, so it's pretty intuitive that it would be supported seamlessly. Check out the following C++/CLI application though:

```
#include "windows.h"
using namespace System;
int main()
{
    MessageBeep(MB_ICONEXCLAMATION);
    Console::WriteLine("Did you hear the beep?");
    return 0;
}
```

We compile this with the /clr command line option:

```
C:\>cl /nologo /clr test.cpp user32.lib
C:\>test
Did you hear the beep?
```

Now, that is easy. All you have to do is add the /clr option, add your managed calls, and it just works. A hybrid of native and managed code is produced.

With Visual C++, you can keep your existing code and add managed functionality. Your migration to managed code occurs gradually and naturally as needed, and no one has a new paradigm forced down his throat. After all, the only thing more difficult to update than legacy code is a legacy programmer.

Let's review the compiler options for managed and native code again:

- `/clr:safe`: This produces an IL-only verifiable output file and can be used with managed types and managed code only.

- `/clr:pure`: This produces an IL-only output file (no native executable code) and can be used with managed and native types and managed code only.

- `/clr`: This produces a mix of native and IL output. Managed and native types and managed code and native code are allowed.

- `<default>`: No option is specified, so the program compiles for native execution.

For a visual representation, refer to Figure 19-1.

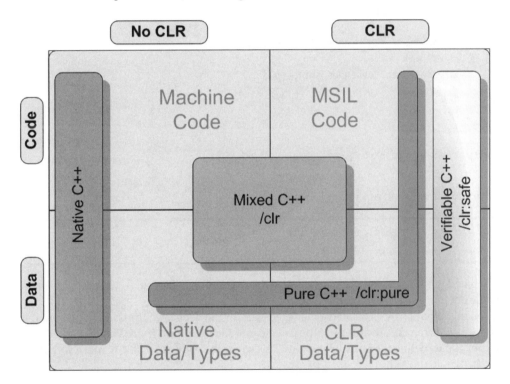

Figure 19-1. */clr command line options*

Using C++ for C# InterOp

In this section, I'll focus on how easy it is to use C++/CLI as a translation layer between C# and native C++.

Wrapping MessageBeep in a C++ class

Let's start by creating a C++ `/clr` application that wraps `MessageBeep()` in a reference type for use in C#:

```
#include "windows.h"
using namespace System;
using namespace System::Runtime::InteropServices;
public ref struct Beep
{
    enum struct BeepTypes : unsigned int
    {
        Beep        = (unsigned int) -1,
        Asterix     = MB_ICONASTERISK,
        Exclamation = MB_ICONEXCLAMATION,
        Hand        = MB_ICONHAND,
        Question    = MB_ICONQUESTION,
        OK          = MB_OK,
    };
    static void MessageBeep(enum class BeepTypes beep)
    {
        ::MessageBeep((unsigned int)beep);
    }
};
void main()
{
    Beep::MessageBeep(Beep::BeepTypes::Exclamation);
}
```

We can compile and run this as follows:

```
C:\>cl /nologo /clr beep.cpp user32.lib
C:\>beep
```

Too bad this book isn't written in "sound on" or something like that, so you'd be able to hear the beep.

You might notice that I created a managed enum for the beep as in the C# example, but this time, I was able to take advantage of the C++ header file definition from Windows and only had to explicitly define the basic beep as -1. This keeps the code more able to move with possible changes to the API.

Using the Wrapped Class in C#

Let's create a simple C# program that uses the wrapped C++/CLI class:

```
class Test
{
    public static void Main()
    {
        Beep.MessageBeep(Beep.BeepTypes.Exclamation);
    }
}
```

As you can see, this is extremely tight and clean. The difficulties of the managed native transitions and interface differences are hidden within the C++ portion.

Let's compile and run this final program. Again, listen for the sound of the beep, like the sound of one hand clapping.

```
C:\>cl /nologo /LD /clr beep.cpp user32.lib
C:\>csc /nologo /r:beep.dll test.cs
C:\>test
```

In this case, we create a mixed processor-specific assembly, beep.dll, and a processor-agnostic assembly, test.exe, and they work together to perform the managed/native calls.

Summary

Switching between C# and native C++ is not a trivial matter, but C++/CLI forms a natural bridge between the two. Also, since C++/CLI is on a par with C# as a managed language, developing applications completely in C++ is actually an extremely easy and convenient solution.

In addition, .NET language integration makes it simple to hook up modules and assemblies written in different languages. Gone are the days when code needed to be rewritten or to follow a restrictive API with marshalling hoops and hurdles in order to connect to other languages. The CTS and CLS standards ensure that .NET languages pass data in a compatible fashion.

All .NET programs target the same platform—the IL defined in the CLI standard. In other words, all .NET compilers share the same target language, and the runtime and JIT has no idea whether it is running IL generated from C#, C++/CLI, or even VB.NET. The VES reads and interprets the binary metadata produced by the compilers and executes the program.

Native C++ is a different story. It is composed of the actual machine code ready for execution by the processor. The intermediate layer that translates between native and managed code is supported by the runtime and is integrated transparently. It's all fairly well done, if you ask me.

In the next and final chapter, I will finish off the book by filling in some details and suggesting directions for further study.

CHAPTER 20

■■■

Final Thoughts

Pessimists, we're told, look at a glass containing 50 percent air and 50 percent water and see it as half empty. Optimists, in contrast, see it as half full. Engineers, of course, understand the glass is twice as big as it needs to be.

—Bob Lewis, InfoWorld

This chapter reminds me of Thanksgiving, which is said to be all about the stuffing—the goal of this chapter is to stuff in as much information as possible before this book ends.

Well, that seems rather backwards, don't you think? You'd think that a book is finished when an author has said everything that needs to be said. There are several reasons why this just is not true with a book on C++, to say nothing of what's true in the publishing industry. Before a book can be published, you need to dot every "i" and cross every "t" up to the end of the final chapter.

The problem here is that C++ is pretty much unbounded. The language features are finite, but the paradigms and practices are unlimited. C++ is a wonderful, general-purpose language. Since C++ is so versatile, general, and unlimited, there are points that don't quite fit elsewhere in this book but that are handy to know. In this chapter, I've picked some of the more important ones; these include the standard dispose pattern, function objects, pseudo-template special pointers, keywords for volatile, constant, and mutable data, and a few final thoughts on IntelliSense.

It's time to start stuffing.

Standard Dispose Pattern

To ensure that unmanaged resources are released when they are no longer used, in .NET programming, you need to follow the *standard dispose pattern*. This pattern, which uses the `System::IDisposable` interface, allows programmer-initiated destruction of objects while also working alongside the garbage collection thread to ensure that every object following this pattern is destroyed exactly once.

Although it is straightforward to implement the standard dispose pattern in C#, it is even easier to implement in C++ because of C++'s direct support for this pattern through deterministic destruction as well as the support of two special member functions related to the release of an object: the destructor and the finalizer.

Destructors and Finalizers

In both C# and C++, a *destructor* is a special member function that is called when an object is no longer needed. In C#, a destructor is an override of the System.Object.Finalize() method. This method is called nondeterministically by a garbage collector routine during garbage collection. Execution of this method is nondeterministic, because you have no control over when an object's resources are released. In C#, the standard dispose pattern provides a way for you to release an object's resources right after you are finished with it.

Having control over the release of objects is important in both native and managed code. If you rely on the garbage collector to release your managed resources, you get into trouble in native code, because not only do you have no control over when garbage collection is performed, but you have no guarantee that it will be performed at all. Your managed code could be cruising along doing what it needs to do while your native code grinds to a screeching halt as it becomes starved for resources.

In managed code, memory is managed for you, so that is not an issue. But what if you create an object that locks a file for exclusive use? If you put the release code in the object's destructor, you need to make sure that the destructor is called in a timely fashion or other processes that rely on that file will stall.

The standard dispose pattern handles this for you. It provides a method for you to call explicitly when you are finished with an object. This method can be called implicitly, if you create a using block, or explicitly, in a try finally block. In addition, it allows for the deterministic nature of garbage collection by handling the possibility that the garbage collection finalizing routine is called before your call to destroy the object and by suppressing the finalizing routine from being called afterwards.

In C++, the standard dispose pattern is also supported, but it is implemented directly within the language by the support of both a destructor and a finalizer, as well as deterministic destruction of objects. Deterministic destruction in C++ provides an implicit, nested C# using block for every allocated object.

In C++, a *destructor* is a special member function that is called either when an object allocated on the stack goes out of scope or when the delete keyword is called on an object's pointer or handle to release an object's resources. When a destructor is used on a managed class, it implements the Dispose() method of the IDisposable interface.

A *finalizer* is a special member function that overrides the System.Object.Finalize() method; it is equivalent to the C# destructor. Together, the C++/CLI definitions of the destructor and finalizer allow you to implement the standard dispose pattern implicitly.

Implementation in C#

In C#, the standard dispose pattern looks like the following code:

```
using System;
class R : IDisposable
{
    R()
    {
    }
    ~R()
    {
        Dispose(false);
```

```
    }
    public void Dispose()
    {
        GC.SuppressFinalize(this);
        Dispose(true);
    }
    protected virtual void Dispose(bool fDisposing)
    {
        if(disposed_)
        {
            return;
        }
        if(fDisposing)
        {
            Console.WriteLine("Free managed resources");
        }
        Console.WriteLine("Free unmanaged resources");
        disposed_ = true;
    }
    private bool disposed_ = false;
    public static void Main()
    {
        using(R r = new R())
        {
            ;
        }
    }
}
```

As you can see, it's not trivial to implement. You need to derive your class from System.IDisposable and implement this interface by defining the Dispose() method. The Dispose(bool) method is used to distinguish between direct calls to dispose the object, such as those generated by a using block, and indirect calls, such as those generated during garbage collection.

There are several keys to understanding this code:

- Use a local flag, such as disposed_ in the previous example, to ensure that resources are not released more than once by mistake.

- In the sample code, a distinction is made between code that is called via a direct call to Dispose from a using block and an indirect call from the garbage collector. The direct calls generate Dispose(true) calls, and the indirect calls generate Dispose(false) calls.

- If disposing of the object occurs during garbage collection, you should not free any managed resources associated with the object. Therefore Dispose(false) does not free managed resources.

- When Dispose() is called directly, such as at the end of a using block, the garbage collector must be notified that garbage collection is unnecessary and should be suppressed. This is accomplished via the call to GC.SuppressFinalize(this).

Implementation in C++/CLI

In C++/CLI, the IDisposable components are generated automatically by the compiler. The same example follows in C++/CLI:

```
using namespace System;
ref struct R
{
    R()
    {
        disposed_ = false;
    }
    !R()
    {
        Console::WriteLine("Free unmanaged resources");
    }
    ~R()
    {
        GC::SuppressFinalize(true);
        if(!disposed_)
        {
            disposed_ = true;
            Console::WriteLine("Free managed resources");
            this->!R();
        }
    }
    static void Main()
    {
        R r;
    }
private:
    bool disposed_;
};
void main()
{
    R::Main();
}
```

The C++/CLI sample is much easier to understand as well as to maintain. You do need to initialize the member variable disposed_ separately from the declaration and within the constructor, but you already saw this difference from C# in Chapter 6.

The C++ destructor houses the equivalent of Dispose(true), and the C++ finalizer houses Dispose(false). The code implements the IDisposable interface automatically, and allocating R on the stack in the method R::Main() ensures that it is destroyed when the method completes execution. This happens thanks to deterministic destruction in the C++ language.

Let's look at this C++ example decompiled using .NET Reflector:

```
private ref class R : public IDisposable
{
    // Methods
private:
    void !R() {}
public:
    R() {}
private:
    void ~R() {}
public:
    virtual void Dispose() sealed override {}
protected:
    virtual void Dispose(bool ) {}
protected:
    virtual void Finalize() override {}
public:
    static void Main() {}
    // Fields
private:
    bool disposed_;
};
```

As you can see, the compiler implements the IDisposable interface automatically. Let's compile and execute the C++ sample; the C# sample generates the same result:

```
C:\>cl /nologo /clr:pure test.cpp
C:\>test
Free managed resources
Free unmanaged resources
```

For Further Study

This introduction to IDisposable only shows the tip of the iceberg. Joe Duffy, a program manager at Microsoft, has written a somewhat exhaustive treatise on this topic. You can find at www.bluebytesoftware.com/blog by going to the Design Guideline category in the Browse By Category section of his blog and looking for "Dispose, Finalization, and Resource Management."

Function Objects

A *function object* allows an object to be called as if it were a function. This works well when you have a problem with a solution requiring a bit more than a function but less than a class.

Suppose, for instance, you have a function that reads data from a data store into a buffer. Ideally, you'd pass a pointer to the buffer to this function, the function would automatically update your pointer past the end of the data, and then the pointer would be ready for subsequent calls. The disadvantage of this approach is that you are always passing the same pointer variable to the function. It would be more efficient if the pointer variable were somehow internal to the function, like object would be.

Function objects solve this problem in C++ by granting function syntax to regular objects using operator().

A common example is a Fibonacci number generator that keeps track of the two integers needed to generate the next number in the sequence. An implementation follows:

```
using namespace System;
ref struct Fibonacci
{
    int f0;
    int f1;
    Fibonacci()
    {
        f0=0;
        f1=1;
    }
    int operator()()
    {
        int temp = f0+f1;
        f0 = f1;
        f1 = temp;
        return temp;
    }
};
void main()
{
    Fibonacci fib;
    for(int i=0; i<10; i++)
    {
        Console::Write("{0} ", fib());
    }
    Console::WriteLine();
}
```

Let's compile and run this:

```
C:\>cl /nologo /clr:pure test.cpp
test.cpp
C:\>test
1 2 3 5 8 13 21 34 55 89
```

In the preceding example, the fib object is called as a pseudo-function using the function syntax, fib(), and it is used to generate the next Fibonacci number in the sequence.

Special Pointers

C++/CLI supports two special types of pointers, other than tracking handles, for referencing data on the managed heap. Since the data on the managed heap is likely to move about without warning, you need to update the pointer when the data moves using a tracking pointer called an interior pointer or prevent the movement of the data on the managed heap using a process known as pinning.

Interior Pointers

Interior pointers are pointers that track the movement of data on the managed heap. They can also be used to point at native data, so they are an ideal choice for a single pointer object for referencing data on the stack, managed heap, and native heap.

In this example, we create a managed array on the managed heap as well as a native array on the stack and declare an interior pointer to reference each of them in turn:

```
using namespace System;
int native_array[] = {120, 24, 6, 2, 1};
void Show(interior_ptr<int> ptr, int length)
{
    for(int i=0; i<length; i++, ++ptr)
    {
        Console::Write("{0} ", *ptr);
    }
    Console::WriteLine();
}
void main()
{
    array<int> ^managed_array = {1,2,6,24,120};
    Show(&managed_array[0], managed_array->Length);
    Show(&native_array[0], sizeof(native_array)/sizeof(int));
}
```

Let's compile and run this:

```
C:\>cl /nologo /clr:pure test.cpp
C:\>test
1 2 6 24 120
120 24 6 2 1
```

In the preceding example, I also used `sizeof()` to calculate the number of elements in the native array, since a native array is not a descendent of `System::Object`, and thus does not have a member called `Length` that allows you to access the length of the array.

Note Interior pointers must be allocated on the stack. If you attempt to allocate one on the managed or native heap, you see a syntax error.

Pinning Pointers

Just as in C#, it is possible to temporarily fix the location of an item on the managed heap using a process known as *pinning*. This is generally a bad idea, as it potentially fragments the managed heap and negatively affects the performance of your application. Still, it is also necessary, so that the address of an object may be passed to native APIs.

Whenever possible, avoid pinning and use a temporary object to transfer data to native APIs. When this is not possible, the special pinning pointer and deterministic destruction make pinning easy in C++.

In C++, you create a pinned object by using the pin_ptr<T> special pointer. The supported paradigm in C++ is that the object is pinned when the pin_ptr is created and unpinned when the pin_ptr is destroyed. It is convenient to surround the usage of the pin_ptr with the curly bracket scope operators.

An example might be illustrative. This example mixes native and managed code in a single source file using the managed and unmanaged #pragma directives. The code creates an instance of a class, pins an element of the class, and modifies it using a native API. When the pin_ptr goes out of scope, the item is automatically unpinned. The changed class is then displayed using Console::WriteLine():

```
using namespace System;
#pragma unmanaged
void change(int *ptr)
{
    *ptr = 3;
}
#pragma managed
ref struct R
{
    R()
    {
        i = -1;
    }
    int i;
};
void main()
{
    R ^ r = gcnew R();
    {
        pin_ptr<int> p_int = &r->i;
        change(p_int);
    }
    Console::WriteLine(r->i);
}
```

Now let's give this a try:

```
C:\>cl /nologo /clr test.cpp
C:\>test
3
```

Notice that we need to use /clr rather than /clr:safe or /clr:pure because of the native code in this file. A common mistake using the pin_ptr pseudo-template is to pin the tracking handle to the object instead of the object itself. In the preceding code example, notice that we assigned the pinning pointer to data inside the object, R::i, rather than assigning the handle to the object, r.

The following code is incorrect; will it compile?

```
using namespace System;
ref struct R
{
    R()
    {
        i = -1;
    }
    int i;
};

void main()
{
    R ^ r = gcnew R();
    {
        pin_ptr<R^> p_r = &r;
        Console::WriteLine("R is not pinned");
    }
}
```

Remember, in C++, just because code compiles, that doesn't mean it is correct.

Templates Revisited

Templates are a rich and complex area of C++, and we really only scratched the surface of their applications in Chapter 15. I mentioned that you could not easily add functionality to built-in types using generics. The natural idea is to try to do something with a base class. With templates, you can use a template-type parameter as a base class as follows:

```
ref struct Base
{
};
template <typename T> ref struct Wrapper : T
{
};
```

```
public ref struct Test
{
    static void Main()
    {
        Wrapper<Base> ^b = gcnew Wrapper<Base>();
    }
};
void main()
{
    Test::Main();
}
```

Unfortunately, this trick won't help you add functionality to a built-in type, since built-in types are declared sealed and cannot be used as a base class. You have to be a little trickier to make a base class support a custom interface.

The following straightforward template code allows you to take a built-in or user-defined type, define an interface for it, and use this interface with a generic type to accomplish a mathematical squaring operation:

```
using namespace System;

generic <typename T>
interface class MyMath
{
    T Multiply(T lhs, T rhs);
};

generic <typename T>
where T : MyMath<T>, ref class
void square(T t, int N)
{
    while(--N > 0)
    {
        t = t->Multiply(t,t);
    }
    Console::WriteLine(t);
}

template <typename T>
ref struct Container : MyMath<Container<T>^ >
{
    T value;
    Container(T t)
    {
        value = t;
    }
```

```
    virtual Container<T> ^Multiply(Container<T> ^lhs, Container<T> ^rhs)
    {
        return gcnew Container<T>(lhs->value * rhs->value);
    }

    virtual String ^ToString() override
    {
        return value.ToString();
    }
};

void main()
{
    Container<int> ^r = gcnew Container<int>(2);
    square(r,4);
}
```

I suggest *C++ Templates: The Complete Guide* by David Vandevoorde and Nicolai M. Josuttis as the next stop in your template education (Boston: Addison-Wesley Professional, 2002).

Class Hierarchy Pitfalls

In the CLI, a class may implement multiple interfaces, yet it is limited to a single base class. That makes the C# syntax for accessing members of a base class quite logical and intuitive. You just use the base keyword:

```
using System;

public class B
{
    public void method()
    {
        Console.WriteLine("B method");
    }
}

public class A : B
{
    public new void method()
    {
        base.method();
    }

    public static void Main()
    {
        A a = new A();
        a.method();
    }
}
```

Let's compile and run this:

```
C:\>csc /nologo test.cs
C:\>test
B method
```

Here is the C++ equivalent:

```
using namespace System;

public ref struct B
{
    void method()
    {
        Console::WriteLine("B method");
    }
};

public ref struct A : B
{
    void method() new
    {
        B::method();
    }

    static void Main()
    {
        A ^a = gcnew A();
        a->method();
    }
};

void main()
{
    A::Main();
}
```

Now this seems quite natural, but what happens in C# if you add a new class D in the middle of the hierarchy?

```
using System;

public class B
{
    public void method()
    {
        Console.WriteLine("B method");
    }
}
```

```
public class D : B
{
    public new void method()
    {
        Console.WriteLine("D method");
    }
}

public class A : D
{
    public new void method()
    {
        base.method();
    }

    public static void Main()
    {
        A a = new A();
        a.method();
    }
}
```

If you now try to compile and run this, you get a different result:

```
csc /nologo test.cs
C:\>test
D method
```

In standard C++, there is no base keyword that refers to the base class. All references to base class explicitly name the base class, and this can produce different results. If we now insert a new class in the C++ hierarchy, the result is unchanged:

```
using namespace System;

public ref struct B
{
    void method()
    {
        Console::WriteLine("B method");
    }
};

public ref struct D : B
{
    void method() new
    {
        Console::WriteLine("D method");
    }
};
```

```
public ref struct A : D
{
    void method() new
    {
        B::method();
    }

    static void Main()
    {
        A ^a = gcnew A();
        a->method();
    }
};

void main()
{
    A::Main();
}
```

```
C:\>cl /nologo /clr:pure test.cpp
test.cpp
C:\>test
B method
```

As mentioned previously, the power of C++ lies in its flexibility and versatility. If the programmer wants to achieve the same results as the C# code snippet above, she can use the __super keyword, a Microsoft Visual C++ extension that behaves exactly as the C# base keyword. If we change the definition of A::method to the following:

```
void method() new
{
    __super::method();
}
```

and compile and execute, we observe exactly the same results:

```
C:\>cl /nologo /clr:pure test.cpp
test.cpp
C:\>test
D method
```

Type Aliases (typedef)

In C#, you can use the using statement to create a shortcut or alias for a type name. For example, consider the following lines:

```
using Hello = System.Console;
public class R
{
    public static void Main()
    {
        Hello.WriteLine("Hello, World");
    }
}
```

If we compile and run this example, we get

```
C:\>csc /nologo test.cs
C:\>test
Hello, World
```

In C++, a typedef is an alias for a type definition. typedefs play an extremely important role in native C++, because type declarations can become extremely complex. They play a smaller role in CLI programming because of the simplified type structure.

A typedef is created by prepending a declaration with the keyword typedef. The identifier in the declaration becomes the name of the alias for the type.

You might typically use a typedef when you are maintaining a list of objects of different types. Perhaps you need to keep track of all the assignments a student completed; you might have a CEssay, CArtwork, CMidterm, and so on.

In CLI programming, all objects are descended from System::Object, so it is natural to create a list of references to this base class, as described in Chapter 14. In native code, there may not be a common base class, and you might describe an object as a pointer to void or as a pointer to some definition header (e.g., the first integer in every object might determine the type) and use some other mechanism to cast back to the original data type at a later time.

If we were to use a pointer to a void, it would be nice to create a new data type, rather than always needing to refer to objects as void*.

An example follows:

```
typedef void * pvoid_t;
```

In this case, the identifier pvoid_t is used to refer to a pointer to void as a data type. Remember the nasty example at the end of Chapter 9? Look how much easier it is to deal with using a typedef:

```
using namespace System;
ref struct R;
typedef R ^ (**(*(*pDEF)(int, char))[])(int);
void main()
{
    pDEF p;
}
```

Friends

Native C++ and the CLI have different visibility and accessibility paradigms. The CLI defines a way that you can grant access to classes beyond a hierarchy tree by allowing access within an assembly.

In C++, you can also grant specific access of a class to another class or function using the `friend` keyword. As the name implies, a `friend` class is allowed access that would otherwise be denied outside of the class hierarchy or even the class itself. Here is a simple example:

```
using namespace System;

class CPlusPlusModule
{
    friend class CSharpModule;
    static int CSharpModuleCount;
};

int CPlusPlusModule:: CSharpModuleCount=1;

struct CSharpModule
{
    int MyCount;
    CSharpModule()
    {
        MyCount = CPlusPlusModule:: CSharpModuleCount++;
    }
};

void main()
{
    CPlusPlusModule cpp;
    CSharpModule cs0;
    CSharpModule cs1;
    Console::WriteLine(cs1.MyCount);
}
```

In this example, `CPlusPlusModule` has a private static member `CSharpModuleCount` that is used to keep track of instantiations of other classes, `CSharpModule` in particular. Without the `friend` declaration inside `CPlusPlusModule`, instances of `CSharpModule` would not be able to access its private data. This example shows how `friend` declarations work and how C# modules are friends with C++ modules in the neatly integrated and tightly interoperable .NET environment.

Volatile Data

The `volatile` keyword in C++ has similar meaning to its C# counterpart. It indicates that a field might be modified behind the scenes by another thread or process, so the compiler should not optimize the value of this variable. An example follows:

```
void main()
{
    volatile bool fWait = true;
    WaitFiveSeconds(&fWait);
    while(fRun)
    {
        Sleep(1);
    }
}
```

The preceding example calls a routine to spawn a timer thread for five seconds, and this thread resets the fWait variable to false. Without the volatile keyword, the compiler reads fWait's value once at the beginning of the loop and loops forever. The volatile keyword instructs the compiler to disable optimization of fWait and continue reading the value of fWait to see if it has changed.

Constant and Mutable Data

The special keywords const and mutable are used to make read-only objects. In C++, an entire instance of a class may be set to const by declaring it as such. If you have a const object, you can only call member functions that are also set to const. The keyword mutable allows you to make fields nonconstant within a const object, for example:

```
#include <iostream>

using namespace std;

struct N
{
    int ValueC;
    mutable int ValueM;

    void Show() const
    {
        cout << ValueC << " " << ValueM << endl;
    }

    N()
    {
        ValueC = ValueM = 0;
    }
};

void main()
{
    const N n;
    n.Show();
```

```
    n.ValueM = 3;
    n.Show();
}
```

We create an `const N` object `n`. We can call `n.Show()`, since it is a `const` function. Also, we are allowed to change `n.ValueM`, because it is declared `mutable`.

Let's compile and run this:

```
C:\ >cl /nologo /EHsc test.cpp
test.cpp
C:\ >test
0 0
0 3
```

Attributes

In C++, you can attach attributes just as in C#. For example, in Chapter 3, I mentioned that `out` parameters had special syntax in C++. Here is how you do it using C++:

```
using namespace System;
public ref struct R
{
    static void f( [System::Runtime::InteropServices::Out] int % i)
    {
        i = 20;
    }
};
void main()
{
    int Number = 0;
    Console::WriteLine("Before: {0}", Number);
    R::f(Number);
    Console::WriteLine("After: {0}", Number);
}
```

Let's compile and run this:

```
C:\>cl /nologo /clr:pure test.cpp
test.cpp
C:\>test
Before: 0
After: 20
```

There are attributes in native C++ as well. You can refer to the Visual C++ documentation for, say, ATL attributes.

More on IntelliSense and Source Browsing

IntelliSense and Source Browsing are the names Microsoft assigns to the array of features that help you resolve references as well as assist with coding within the editor. IntelliSense encompasses everything related to presenting to the programmer information about his code. Source Browsing, sometimes called Live Browsing in Visual Studio 2005, deals more with information about how the code is referenced and interacts with itself.

The major IntelliSense features are Quick Information, Auto Completion, and Parameter Help. Alvin Chardon of the Microsoft Visual C++ Team has written a wonderful article on MSDN that describes the features in greater detail as well as comments on their design and implementation. You can find it at

```
http://msdn.microsoft.com/library/default.asp
?url=/library/en-us/dnvs05/html/vcintellisense.asp
```

Some of the more helpful features of Source Browsing are Class View, Object Browser, Call Browser, Find All References, and Code Definition Window. Some of these features are available in Visual C# as well. Ameya Limaye and Boris Jabes, also of the Microsoft Visual C++ Team, wrote an article for the *MSDN Magazine* highlighting some of the Source Browsing features, as well as discussing its usage and limitations. You can find it at

```
 http://msdn.microsoft.com/msdnmag/issues/06/02/PureC
```

These are very powerful features that come to the aid of the programmer to help develop applications faster using Visual C++. Take advantage of them!

Summary

In this chapter, you learned about the dispose pattern, function objects, and a bit about constant, mutable, and volatile data, in addition to some other details.

If you've made it to this paragraph, you've certainly learned a lot of C++, and you should have built a very strong foundation in C++/CLI. C# maps to a subset of the C++ language, C++/CLI. This book's intention is to use your C# roots to get you to a place where you are comfortable with C++ programming, so you are able to build on your C# knowledge to learn all about C++ without compromising that knowledge. You are well prepared to tackle—undaunted—any of the dozens of excellent texts on native C++ that you'll find crowding the shelves of your favorite bookstore. Although C++ can be esoteric at times, it is a beautiful language with a rich history and is well worth the effort.

Index

You Need the Companion eBook

Your purchase of this book entitles you to buy the companion PDF-version eBook for only $10. Take the weightless companion with you anywhere.

We believe this Apress title will prove so indispensable that you'll want to carry it with you everywhere, which is why we are offering the companion eBook (in PDF format) for $10 to customers who purchase this book now. Convenient and fully searchable, the PDF version of any content-rich, page-heavy Apress book makes a valuable addition to your programming library. You can easily find and copy code—or perform examples by quickly toggling between instructions and the application. Even simultaneously tackling a donut, diet soda, and complex code becomes simplified with hands-free eBooks!

Once you purchase your book, getting the $10 companion eBook is simple:

❶ Visit **www.apress.com/promo/tendollars/**.

❷ Complete a basic registration form to receive a randomly generated question about this title.

❸ Answer the question correctly in 60 seconds, and you will receive a promotional code to redeem for the $10.00 eBook.

2560 Ninth Street • Suite 219 • Berkeley, CA 94710

eBookshop

THE EXPERT'S VOICE™

Offer valid through 5/27/07.